Find Strength In Your Struggle

Discover The Miracle In You

By

Dr. H. Jean Wright II

Exulon
ELITE

Find Strength In Your Struggle
Discover The Miracle In You
by Dr. H. Jean Wright II

Printed in the United States of America.

ISBN 9781498430685

1. Cover Copy – Jim Kochenburger
2. Book Cover Art Work – Isaac Lester, Jr.
   www.myfunnyside.com
3. Author Photo – Ra Hall ~Photographer
   ArtThruTheEyeOvRa.Com
   ArtThruTheEyeOvRa@gmail.com

www.xulonpress.com

Josh

A pleasure to worship with you and to discuss our love for service. Thank you for your support — God bless

Al. Jean

Table of Contents

Introduction

Why a Book on Overcoming Spiritual Depression?

———◇○◯◯◯○◇———

We are living in a time marked by great human achievement: wonderful discoveries, miraculous medical cures, and seemingly never-ending technological advances. Yet, have you watched the news on television lately? Read your local newspaper recently? Traveled through cyberspace to some far distant land to peek in on life in some other part of the world? Or, does it seem that news reports, near and far, are filled with too many negative, all too familiar stories that make you numb to life outside your immediate surroundings? Do you believe that being exposed to negative events—especially in your community, neighborhood, or home—increases stress and has a cumulative negative impact on your physical, mental, emotional, psychological, and spiritual health? On that of your family? On that of your community? If you answered yes to any of the questions above, this book may be helpful to you.

Because life happens; it is not always possible to avoid the stressors that naturally come our way. However, we can learn to become more proactive in understanding the impact of stress on our whole person and our families. We can also learn how to be at our best even when the inevitable, unintentional, and unforeseen seem to linger at our door.

This book will carefully identify the issues that lead to, increase, or exacerbate stress in our lives. It can serve as a guide to help you navigate your way through the deep oceans and raging seas of life circumstances that for many, far too often, dock them in the confines of spiritual depression.

"Not My Fault" Stressors

Most would agree that our society has been subjected to numerous negative events. Our recent history is marked by many natural disasters, such as tsunamis, horrific hurricanes, earthquakes, and a myriad of man-made disasters: terrorist acts, wars, rumors of wars, and greed/mismanagement so extreme that not long ago, national and international financial markets and institutions were nearly brought to collapse.

Not surprisingly, people are succumbing to devastating and preventable human conditions, such as disease, starvation, and homelessness (see epidemiological citations in Appendix D). Individuals suffer the greatest of adverse physical, psychological, emotional, and spiritual reactions to the chaos and confusion of trying to survive in a violent and troubled world, while facing the daily grind of a hectic life.

It bears repeating: This level of stress is not just a Western culture phenomenon. It is documented in the daily experiences of individuals the world over (see epidemiological citations for developing countries in Appendix D). Trying to cope with everyday human problems such as divorce, domestic violence, loneliness, physical or mental illness, addiction, unemployment, financial difficulties, death, and many other challenges, can become overwhelming at times.

It is also important to note that stress is not only associated with negative events or painful situations. On the contrary! The pressure of performance on a new job, relocating your family to a new house in a new neighborhood, raising children, or even traveling abroad on vacation can trigger stress, even though all are seemingly positive endeavors. During extended periods of trouble, disappointment, or even joyous anticipation, it is not unusual for individuals to eventually succumb to the travails of unrelenting stress and fall prey to suffocating degrees of disillusionment and discouragement. Individuals who endure prolonged periods of stress are not only susceptible to a myriad of physical problems, but if left unresolved or untreated, they also make us prime candidates for developing deficits in emotional, psychological, behavioral, and spiritual functioning. In short, just like prolonged stress sets us up for developing symptoms of anxiety and depression; unchecked and cumulative stress could lead to spiritual depression.

Most Common Mental Health Disorders

If unrelenting, unresolved stress is often the precursor for developing symptoms of anxiety and depression. It should come as no surprise that in the United States of America, anxiety and depression are the most prominent mental health diagnoses, followed by substance use disorder, and bipolar disorder. According to the National Alliance on Mental Illness (NAMI), major depression is a serious medical illness affecting fifteen million American adults, or approximately five to eight percent of the adult population in any given year.

Among all medical illnesses, major depression is the leading cause of disability in the U.S. and many other developed countries (NAMI, 2008).

Over the past two decades, I have treated thousands of individuals who showed marked deficits in functioning on the psychological and behavioral level. A high percentage of these individuals presented with symptoms that can be diagnosed as clinical depression.

As we will soon review, symptoms of depression can manifest themselves in a variety of ways and settings.

Interestingly enough, one unique observation I have consistently been able to make while treating individuals diagnosed with depression is that the vast majority seem to acknowledge and embrace a belief in God, or as commonly stated, a "higher power," whether or not they were affiliated with a particular religious organization. Those who did acknowledge preference for a specific organized religion or faith-based community often admitted their lack of consistent participation in religion outside of predictable holidays and "special occasions." However, many seemed to be comforted and encouraged while discussing their spiritual beliefs. A high percentage of these individuals indicated that their improvement (as measured by self-reported reduction in depressive symptoms, a successful return to their previous level of functioning, or an increase above and beyond their previous level of functioning) was enhanced when a spiritual component was added to their treatment plan.

Historically, traditional interventions or treatments for depression ignored or discounted the importance of the spiritual part of people, focusing instead on the physical, mental/psychological, and emotional parts. These observations increased my curiosity to further explore the connection between behavioral health and spirituality. It was at this intersection that it dawned on me that those individuals who sought treatment for clinical depression and expressed a spiritual void in their lives might also be experiencing what I have come to see as "spiritual depression."

Human beings are composed of physical, mental/psychological, emotional, and spiritual parts. In the case of "spiritual depression," the spiritual part of the individual is disturbed, leading to disruption in the other parts of the whole (physical, mental/psychological, emotional). Much of what makes depression so common, yet so overwhelming, is the fact that from a holistic point of view, a part of the whole is out of sync with the rest of the organism.

Fortunately, research in the areas of psychology, religion, and spirituality are much more prevalent these days, providing pertinent information vital to promoting "best practices" in treating and supporting interventions geared to address the whole person. As a result, psychology, in general, has acknowledged the relevance of addressing spirituality in individuals, and many clinicians who recognize the importance of this holistic approach are more open to including a spiritual component in the treatment plans of individuals.

Contrasting and Comparing Spiritual Depression to Clinical Depression

Before comparing the concepts of clinical and spiritual depression, it is important to define these terms, as they will be used throughout this book.

Clinical Depression

Webster's II New Riverside Dictionary, Revised Edition (1996) defines *depression* as "an emotional disorder characterized by an inability to concentrate, insomnia, and feelings of guilt and dejection." Webster also defines *depressed* as "low in spirits; dejected; suffering from psychological depression; suffering from social and economic hardship; hollow." Synonyms for the term, depressed, are: "backward, disadvantaged, impoverished, and underprivileged." Thus, a general meaning of lacking in what is essential for living a happy an productive life.

The Diagnostic and Statistical Manual of Mental Disorders, Fourth Edition-TR (DSM-IV-Text Revised (2000), which is a primary resource used by mental health professionals, defines depression in terms of categories (e.g. Major Depressive Episode, Major Depressive Disorder, etc.), and distinguishes between mild, moderate, or severe forms of depression.

The DSM-IV-TR lists a multitude of symptoms to describe depression, and you may recognize a few (or several) symptoms in relation to your own experience, or that of someone close to you.

> Essential features of depression are: feeling sad or empty, irritable mood (especially in children and adolescents), diminished interest or pleasure in most activities, significant weight loss or weight gain, decrease or increase in appetite, too much or too little sleep, or interrupted sleep throughout the normal sleep cycle, fatigue or loss of energy, feelings of worthlessness or excessive or inappropriate guilt, diminished ability to think or concentrate, or indecisiveness, and recurrent suicidal thoughts. In addition, "the symptoms cause clinically significant distress or impairment in social, occupational, or other important areas of functioning," and "are not better accounted for by the direct physiological effects of a drug or medication, a general medical condition, or Bereavement" (DSM-IV-TR, 2000, p. 356).

That is a lot of technical jargon to describe a condition that many of us may simply recognize as someone "having the blues," "feeling sad," or "constantly tired." As noted, the essential elements have to do with *feelings* of sadness, guilt, or shame. Quite often, individuals that are depressed experience disturbances in their normal sleep patterns, either sleeping too much or very little. They may lose interest in activities they once found exciting or pleasurable. Lack of energy and fatigue sometimes cause people who are depressed to miss school or work, or stay away from people, places, and things that were once important to them (isolation). People who are depressed may have difficulty concentrating or maintaining their focus, and they may experience deficits or impairments in memory, making it difficult to excel in school, work, or other activities that require consistent concentration.

Individuals' experiencing severe depression may have thoughts of suicide, or otherwise hurting themselves or others. That is a very quick look at clinical depression, along with common symptoms. Now let's break down "spiritual depression."

Spiritual Depression

Webster's II New Riverside Dictionary, Revised Edition (1996) defines the term *spiritual* as: "of, relating to, or having the nature of spirit; of, or relating to religion or religious matters." Webster also defines the term *spirit* as: "a vital or animating force; the part of a human being associated with the feelings and mind; The Holy Ghost."

We can use a combination of Webster's definition of *depression* and *spirit/ spiritual* to define *spiritual depression* as: a spiritual condition characterized by hollowness of spirit, spiritual dejection, suffering emotional and mental hardship, spiritual "backwardness," spiritual impoverishment, and low spiritual vitality or animating force. Said another way; spirituality is about hope. Depression is the loss or lack of hope and the concomitant physical, emotional, and social consequences that are associated with the loss.

Now that we have a definition for spiritual depression, we can draw a more thorough comparison between clinical and spiritual depression by looking at the essential features of each condition.

For the purpose of introducing the concept of spiritual depression in relation to the above definition and symptoms of clinical depression, we can focus on feelings of worthlessness, guilt and shame, discouragement and disillusionment, and an increasing belief that the negative aspects of life will not only continue but also grow worse over time. These thoughts and feelings are equally common in both clinical and spiritual depression. Both clinical and spiritual depression can be categorized by degrees of severity: mild, moderate, and severe.

In keeping with this phenomenon of spiritual, mental, and behavioral connectionism, the aim of this book is to take a very common, and oftentimes debilitating mental condition (clinical depression), and make comparisons to an equally common and debilitating spiritual condition (spiritual depression). The express purpose of this comparison is to facilitate a better understanding of how our core concept of God influences whether we have a positive or negative spiritual belief system. For example: if you think God is punishing and uncaring then you may believe your struggles in life are caused by a tyrant-God that bullies those that do not obey "his rules" and whatever good that happens is pure luck. On the other hand; if you see God as loving, caring, and patient; then you may believe that your trials and tribulations are allowed by a Father-God that is preparing you for greater, and when good things happen it is because of grace and mercy; and love from a father to his children. In essence then, it is the God you believe in, or do not believe in, that determines whether you "Find Strength in Your Struggle," or feel forever defeated when difficulties arise.

Research Supporting "Strength in Your Struggle"

Another aim of this book is to highlight published support for how spirituality and faith-based affiliations act as protective factors for individuals to find strength in their struggle. This association between utilizing spiritual and faith-based supports as coping mechanisms is especially pertinent as highlighted by a survey conducted by the Pew Research Council. It showed that the United States remains a country where most citizens claim adherence to some religious affiliation, with the vast majority (82 percent) of US adults that participated in the survey identifying their religious preference as Christian (March, 2002. See Appendix D for full report including a breakdown of the top five religious denominations in the USA). As noted earlier; recent research acknowledges a connection between spiritual beliefs and actions (i.e. prayer) and positive outcomes. In the *Handbook of Religion and Health, 2nd Edition* (Koenig, King, and Carson, 2012), Harold

Koenig (et al) provide several examples of how religious/spiritual connection correlates with positive outcomes: positive world view, hope and motivation, sense of control through prayer, social support, and many others. In *Faith and Mental Health: Religious Resources for Healing* (Koenig, 2005), Dr. Koenig shares his research on spirituality and mental health, showing spiritual involvement is related to:

* Greater well-being and happiness
* Less depression, faster recovery from depression
* Less anxiety, faster recovery from anxiety
* Less alcohol use/dependence
* Less drug use/dependence
* Less suicide and more negative attitudes toward suicide
* Significantly greater meaning and purpose in life
* Significantly greater hope
* Significantly greater forgiveness
* Significantly more altruism/volunteering
* Significantly more gratitude, compassion, kindness
* Significantly greater social support

It is this type of empirical support that confirms my belief that God in us provides the wherewithal to meet the challenges of everyday life. Through God's written Word, and by exercising a healthy prayer life, we have the tools to increase our faith, move past difficulties, and help others. This book seeks to highlight how a combination of biblical, empirical, and clinical information can be great resources and serve as protective factors for physical, mental, emotional, and spiritual health.

What This Book Can Do for You

My hope is that you will:
- receive enlightenment in terms of how the trials and tribulations of everyday life can impact your mental and spiritual health
- embrace how the miracle in you can become a powerful energy to offset the debilitating effects of spiritual depression

My prayer is that those experiencing spiritual depression will:
- have a renewed determination to seek the face of the "divine counselor," Jesus
- strengthen their faith and trust in establishing a covenant with God
- recognize that an increase in one's belief in an all-powerful, divine being simultaneously increases belief in oneself
- recognize that God empowers each of us to do more than just survive the challenges and difficulties of this world, but to thrive and achieve miraculous results in our lives.
- recognize that recovery is not only possible, but probable, when utilizing faith as a protective and healing factor in conjunction with the most appropriate interventions. Whether we are recovering from behavioral health challenges, divorce, financial failure, or loss due to a death of a family member or friend (or any manner of loss in our lives), we are all recovering from something.
- recognize that developing and/or maintaining our connection with God provides strength, hope, and healing above and beyond reliance on self or others.

How to Use This Book

This book will have the most impact if used as a resource by individuals:
- as a guide for recognizing the stressors in your life, and how your stress impacts your physical, mental/emotional, and spiritual health
- as a source of encouragement to increase one's knowledge of one's spiritual self
- as a challenge to search the depths of God's love for oneself

This book can be used as a resource by families:
- as a guide to identify problems/challenges/areas of need within their family system
- as a source of encouragement to seek out biblical examples that mirror their current experiences

- as a reference to specific referral sources that can help mitigate the impact of stress and trauma

This book can be used as a resource by groups:
- as a means of collective spiritual discovery and interpersonal support within faith-based organizations/communities, churches, and more
- as a focal point to initiate discussions of how we as individuals and families (biological and spiritual) can best uplift one another
- as a source of encouragement by showing how we, as individuals and families (biological and spiritual), can be part of the solution in our faith-based organizations/communities, churches, and more, and not part of the problem

Structure/Design of This Book

The remaining content of this book will be divided into three sections, focusing on the family, the church (in general), and the individual, sampling everyday common experiences and situations to demonstrate how unrelenting and unresolved stress negatively impacts and influences behavior in ourselves as individuals, our families, and our churches. I chose to highlight these three areas in reference to the impact of spiritual depression because I believe (and research bears this out) that for the vast majority of people, family and church/community (as made manifest in individual circumstances) provide significant social support and make up a common experience called "life"!

For example, family and church/community can be identified as long-standing, cherished institutions, not just in the United States but the world over, regardless of religious affiliation. The individual is the most vulnerable part of these two great institutions (i.e. it is often the individual who suffers silently in the midst of family and church/community). Often, the individual must compromise or take a more selfless role for either the family or church/community to run smoothly and be successful (success as measured by divine expectations).

From a biblical perspective, family is the most important part of church, community, and country. The church, as designed by God, reflects His values on family by making comparisons and references to the family structure in Scripture. In Matthew 22:2, 25:10, and Revelation 19:7, Jesus represents the groom. The church symbolizes the bride, and we, the individuals, make up the host of God's royal family (the "body of Christ")!

God created us, therefore, we are God's children. We acknowledge our heritage by praying to and giving praise to our Heavenly Father. As earthly children, our own biological parents are the only "God" we will know until they teach us of the divine God.

Moreover, family is addressed first because it is the foundation upon which God chose to build our knowledge and acceptance of Him. When family is in disrepair or destroyed altogether, it is reflected in our churches and our communities. Moreover, it is the individual who suffers mightily when family and church/community do not provide a safe haven or protection from the harsh realities of this world. The individual naturally seeks strength, love, and acceptance through family and church/community support. So when these things are nonexistent in the family and/or church/community, the result is confusion, chaos, disillusionment, and discouragement. The negative impact of these issues and feelings undermine and slowly erode a solid foundation, and spiritual depression is a predictable result.

Throughout this book, using family, church/community, and individual as the backdrop, we draw parallels between the concept of spiritual depression and clinical depression by highlighting examples of everyday life as a platform. However, the spiritual solutions sought and suggested will be anything but common as we hold up the Son of God—Lord and Savior of the universe, Jesus—as the predominating force to counteract the debilitating effects of spiritual depression. In doing so, we will rely heavily upon the Word of God, through biblical Scripture as our foundation, for it is my belief and bias that the Bible is truth inspired by God: "All Scripture *is* given by inspiration of God, and *is* profitable for doctrine, for reproof, for correction, for instruction in righteousness" (2 Timothy 3:16, NKJV).

It is through life's difficulties that we receive instruction and correction, which develop character. Through character we are able to rise above the trials and tribulations that are inevitable in this life.

It is through the development of (and reliance on) a strong and stable spiritual support system that we are able to develop a strong and prevailing faith, thereby preparing us to withstand all challenges and discover the true strength within each of us. I am pleased and thankful that you chose to join me on this journey to *Find Strength In Your Struggle: Discover the Miracle in You!*

*NOTE: If you, or someone close to you is experiencing symptoms of depression, please do not hesitate to visit (or encourage them to visit) a mental health professional and/or family physician as soon as possible for a full physical/ mental health checkup.

Dedication

⟡⟡⟡⟡⟡⟡⟡⟡

*T*his book is dedicated to my father, Dr. Walter L. Wright Sr., who I long to see, touch, and hold again; and for whom I live each day of my life, determined to replicate and provide to my own wife and children the love you have given me.

To my mother, Jacqueline Cook Wright, who is a constant reminder of just how good God is, and who is generous and consistent with her love, encouragement, support, and prayer.

To my uncle and namesake, Harold "Brother James" Wright, who I miss immensely, and who provided a model of courage, confidence, and comportment for me to emulate (in which I fail miserably in comparison).

To my wife, Poungpen Kumpua Cabral-Wright, who is the love of my life, my friend, my confidant, and my greatest supporter. I truly could not have completed this journey without you. Thank you!

To my son, Ethan Thanasak Kumpua Wright, who inspires me every day to give my best.

Acknowledgments

I want to thank Elder Isaac Lester, my uncle, and someone I have always looked up to as one of the most intelligent, articulate, and wise men I have ever known. Thank you, Elder Gary Burns, family and friend. Thank you, Stanley McDowell, brother, friend, and supporter. Thank you, Walter L. Wright Jr., brother, supporter, and advisor. Thank you, David C. Wright, brother, friend, and advisor. Thank you, Yvette Wright, sister, friend, supporter, advisor, challenger, and comforter. Sis, I love you with all my heart and everything you have meant to me from day one of our lives' intersecting. Thank you, Lisa Wright McDowell, sister, friend, supporter, advisor, and comforter. Sis, there are no words to convey my love and appreciation for all that you are in my life! Thank you, Lyn Wright, sister, friend, supporter, and advisor. To my children; Brooke, Marc, Dante, Candi, and Ethan, and grandchildren; Marcus and Langston, thank you. To Flonzie Brown Wright ("Aunt Flonzie"); your life as a servant-leader is an inspiration. Thank you for your early support for this project. To Kathy Cameron, friend, supporter, and advisor; thank you for believing in this project from day one. Thank you for your encouragement early in the process. Your energy and enthusiasm were needed and appreciated. Thank you, Rev. Nick Taliafero, friend, supporter, and advisor. Thank you, Clifton Davis, brother, friend, supporter, and advisor. Thank you, Eric "Big E" Kelly, for providing a model for me to emulate. Thank you, Maine Prince, brother, friend, supporter, and advisor. Thank you for your constant support, Dr. Frank Hale Jr., mentor and friend; I miss you. Thank you, Dr. James Dobbins, mentor and friend. Thank you, Uncle Vic and Aunt Snookie, for your encouragement early in the process. Thank you, Marci Wright, for all that you do. Thank you, Mary Harper, for your prayers, support, and resources. Thank you, Dan Rush, brother and friend. Jim Kochenburger, I am blessed that God placed you in my path. Your keen eye, attention to detail, and professionalism are a blessing beyond words. Thank you!

•

Endorsements

———————⟶∘⟜⟞⟞∘⟜———————

Your book, <u>Find Strength In Your Struggle: Discover The Miracle In You</u>, is a spiritually refreshing antidote for the inquiring and troubling victim of depression. What an expose' on the fact that it is impossible for man to exist by and for himself. You have provided a most searching, incisive and analytical approach to the problem of depression. It is a straightforward realistic set of recommendations that transcend the typical concepts, proposals, and actions so often proffered.

Keep on Soaring,

Frank W. Hale, Jr. Ph.D.

Vice Provost and Professor Emeritus

The Ohio State University

(Dr. Frank W. Hale, Jr. – 1927-2011, was a family friend, mentor, and all around wonderful man who challenged students, colleagues, and people in general to pursue their goals with energy and integrity. He is appreciated and greatly missed!)

Dr. H. Jean Wright has taken on the formidable task of bringing a psychological perspective to Biblical exegesis, and he succeeds! **Find Strength In Your Struggle** is an exploration into the Biblical narratives that reveal the varieties of human dilemmas that drag on the soul and heart, precipitating (potentially) depressed states of living. Wright takes an almost sermonic approach in unveiling the scenarios (he can't help it; the blood of a family full of preachers runs through this clinicians veins), and this gives life and verve to what might otherwise be a dry presentation on mental health.

Woven throughout the book is Dr. Wright's warm and resonant humanity; he cares about people and it comes through. The end result is a book that looks seriously at a debilitating mental illness through the lens of spiritual perception. It's a noble effort that helps to build a bridge over the unfortunate chasm that often exists between psychology and spiritual ministry.

Rev. W. Nick Taliaferro,
Former Executive Director of the Office of
Faith-Based Initiatives for the City of Philadelphia
Host, *The Nick Taliaferro Show,* on AM/900 WURD Radio

Most people have at least a fundamental awareness of the condition known as "depression"; many have spent more days than they'd care to admit suffering under its oppressive burden. In his new book, "Find Strength In Your Struggle: Discover The Miracle In You," Dr. Harold J. Wright not only defines depression in clinical terms, he expands the definition to include a "spiritual" dimension. Imagine trying to cope with symptoms of depression using ones spiritual resources, only to discover that your spirituality has succumbed to its symptoms as well. Thus, instead of finding relief, your self-examination reveals a previously undiscovered case of the spiritual doldrums!

With his well-developed skills as a Doctor of Psychology, who has spent decades in practice, and with his passion as a committed Christian, Dr. Wright makes a complicated subject accessible. His literary style breaks down the scientific into practical "down to earth" terms that the lay person can understand.

Dr. Harold J. Wright doesn't only expose an insightful perspective of a "problem", He also provides practical solutions. "Find Strength In Your Struggle: Discover The Miracle In You," will facilitate healing to the reader, both emotionally and spiritually. I highly recommend this book for the professional counselor, the pastor, the seeker and the individual. I guarantee it will help you to discover the miracle in you and equip you with strength for your journey.

Clifton Davis

H. Jean Wright provides invaluable insight and hope for those who are experiencing what he recognizes and defines as "Spiritual Depression." This book is well researched and helps to liberate individuals, faith communities and faith leaders from the stigma that often accompanies mental health issues.

This book continues to build the bridge and partnership between clinical care and spiritual health that provides realistic and holistic healing to the individuals, families and communities affected by mental health issues like "Spiritual Depression."

Find Strength in Your Struggle is a vital tool and guide for religious leaders and communities who are experiencing the negative effects of today's hyperactive, high-tech global society. It provides help, hope and healing for everyone. A must read for all concerned.

> Bishop Ernest McNear, Associate Professor , *Lancaster Bible College*
> *at the Center for Urban Theological Studies, General Secretary of the*
> *Church of God in Christ International (COGIC International)*

I've known Dr. Wright since childhood, and am a witness to the effectiveness of the personally tested and practical counsel that he offers in this book. He has recognized what many clinical psychologists ignore: we are spiritual beings. And he also recognizes that the source of depression for many has to do with our spirit. And that's where the miracle comes in. Don't miss this opportunity for sound bible-based spiritual support to help you successfully navigate through the stresses of life.

> Gary Burns, M.A. Religious Education
> Editor, *Lake Union Herald*
> Co-founder, Shae Foundation
> Director of International Teen Prayer Conferences
> Member of America's National Prayer Committee

Endorsement for *Find Strength in Your Struggle: Discover the Miracle in You,* by **Dr. H. Jean Wright II**: Through a combination of wide clinical experience, careful academic research, and thoughtful biblical reflection, Dr. Wright has assembled here a thoroughgoing assessment tool for social scientists, practicing psychologists and counselors, pastors, and, perhaps most importantly, individuals who have a sincere interest in unlocking the mysteries of spiritual depression in dysfunctional families and embattled congregations. Dr. Wright, an experienced clinical psychologist himself with a broad background in public health, juvenile justice, and behavioral health administration, has seen the beneficial results of a faith-based approach to mental health when it is combined with carefully monitored medical treatment. The age-old battle between religion and science dissolves in his thoughtful application of modern therapies in the context of Scriptural admonitions to trust in God's purposes (even through suffering) by applying the healing power of faith. Up-to-date with the latest scientific studies on the relationship of faith and health, Jean Wright's prescriptions here can be trusted to yield benefit to a reader from any denominational or faith tradition.

Linward A. Crowe: former Assistant Professor of history at Drexel University and Associate Minister at Tenth Presbyterian Church in Philadelphia, he is now a regional representative of The Navigators, an international Christian discipleship and mentoring organization with over 5,000 staff in more than 100 countries around the world.

Endorsement– Thoughtful and Provocative: In "Find Strength In Your Struggle: Discover The Miracle In You." Dr. Wright masterfully integrates psychological and spiritual principles of healing. He is resourceful, practical and expansive in the many internal resources he highlights.

R. Dandridge Collins, Ph. D.
Dr. Collins is the author of the nonfiction classic
"The Trauma Zone: Trusting God for Emotional Healing."

PART I

Spiritual Depression In the Family

---◇○⟪⟫○◇---

The first five chapters of this book focus primarily on issues that have high impact on families, and how specific situations/circumstances can cause stress, creating an atmosphere for developing spiritual depression. Because of the complex nature of the cited challenges within families and the necessary and desirable goal to provide pertinent and accurate information; chapters three, four, and five contain more technical terms and empirical information than the other sections of this book. However, the chapters on family also combines scientific outcomes, psychological theories, and psychosocial models with solid biblical principles and well-known Bible stories as references in order to produce a spiritual template that acknowledges the often stressful reality of daily life, and lifts up the name of Jesus in the midst of this reality.

Beginning with these first five chapters on family (and consistent throughout the rest of this book) is the message that regardless of the trials and tribulations that come our way, we serve a God who sees, knows, and understands the ups and downs of this life. In fact, we serve a God who took human form just to save us from ourselves (Hebrews 2:5-9). He experienced what we experience and demonstrated that reliance on divine will, not our own will, is the key to overcoming all that we encounter in a troubled and often depressing world.

The examples highlighted here are not exhaustive by any means. However, they are the issues most often shared by people who have come to me for help and, I believe, have the most impact on our families.

Chapter 1

We Are Not the First: Dysfunction in the Family Is Not New

———————————<>◦⌒⌒◦<>———————————

"What has been will be again, what has been done will be done again; there is nothing new under the sun" (Ecclesiastes 1:9, NIV).

Family Defined

What constitutes a family? Is it just the nuclear family: e.g. traditional two-parent head-of-household, consisting only of a father, mother, and their biological children? Dictionary.com (2011) defines *family* as: "A basic social unit consisting of parents and their children, considered as a group, whether dwelling together or not." Based on the definition above, and adding in the reality of life circumstances in the twenty-first century, we can conclude that, with or without children, just about every combination of human relationships, whether traditional or non-traditional, are indeed families.

With such a vast variety of family types in existence, as a result of many different and often difficult circumstances, it is no wonder the modern family is experiencing a myriad of stressors that, over time, have combined to create breakdowns in communication, compassion, and the very capacity to address basic physiological, psychological, emotional, and spiritual needs. However, I wonder if it has always been this way for the family institution, and if so, why? After all, family is the oldest institution ordained by God (Genesis 2:18, 21-24).

Debilitating Stress and Trauma in the Original "First Family"

Family continues to be the foundation of community the world over. From major metropolises, to suburban and rural communities, to remote villages, whether huddled in arctic icescapes, submerged in humid rain forests, spread across Midwestern plains, or in a valley surrounded by glorious mountains, family is the backbone of human existence. The establishment of the family as the hub of human relationships is no accident. For it was in the beginning, after God created the heavens and the earth and all the animals to inhabit the earth that He said, "It is not good for the man to be alone. I will make a helper suitable for him." . . . Then the Lord God made a woman from the rib he had taken out of the man. . . . That is why a man leaves his father and mother and is united to his wife, and they become one flesh. (Genesis 2:18, 22, 24, NIV)

All man needed to do was to obey God's command to "be fruitful and increase in number" (Genesis 1:28 NIV) to jump-start the world community of family. That is exactly what Adam and Eve did (Genesis 4:1, 2). Our first example of family was well on their way to fulfilling God's original design. Everything seemed to be going according to plan. Adam and Eve were increasing in number and the world of family was growing as God intended. "Adam lay with his wife again, and she gave birth to a son and named him Seth, saying, 'God has granted me another child in place of Abel, since Cain killed him'" (Genesis 4:25, NIV).

What? Wait a minute! Is that a misprint in the "good book?" What on earth is Eve talking about: Seth replacing Abel because Cain, his own brother, murdered him? Unfortunately, this is exactly what happened: "Now Cain said to his brother Abel, 'Let's go out to the field.' While they were in the field, Cain attacked his brother Abel and killed him" (Genesis 4:8, NIV).

Here we have the first recorded case of murder in the Bible. Most surprisingly, it came by way of family dysfunction! You can read the whole sordid incident in Genesis, Chapter 4. Cain's issue with his younger brother, Abel, was all about jealousy and misdirected anger. Where did that level of negativity and destruction come from so early in the development of our first family?

Unfortunately, the seeds of dysfunction had been planted between Adam and Eve and their offspring because of a most tragic decision by the world's first parents. When Eve and Adam disobeyed God and ate from the "tree of the knowledge of good and evil" (Genesis 2:17, NIV), they ignited an explosion of tragic and traumatic events that destroyed the love and harmony within their immediate family, and launched a ripple effect of crippling sin for all families throughout history (Genesis 3:15, 16). Adam and Eve's tragic mistake opened the door to pass down the ugliness of sin through intergenerational transference, that is, they passed down negative personality traits, thought processes (ways of viewing the world), and behaviors from their generation to the next.

The Impact of Intergenerational Transference

This intergenerational transference resulted in family dysfunction of epic proportion, and has been duplicated in families from Adam and Eve on down, a billion times over (and over and over again). As a result, there are several apt examples of family intergenerational transference in the Bible:

- Abraham ("father of all nations") lied about Sarah, his wife, being his sister (Genesis 20:2). Then he got impatient with God's promise for Sarah and him to have children, and had a child (Ishmael) with his wife's servant (Genesis 16).
- Isaac and Rebecca were blessed with twin boys, but then turned the blessing into dysfunctional disaster by choosing favorites: Isaac loved Esau; Rebecca loved Jacob (Genesis 27).
- Jacob and his twelve sons made up a blended family of disastrous proportions (Genesis 28-30).
- King David and his sons provided a portrait of lust, incest, betrayal, and murder (2 Samuel 11-13, 15-18).

Remember Isaac, son of Abraham (the "father of all nations")? He followed his father's instructions to go to Abraham's relatives and marry a woman living amongst his people (i.e. a good "church" girl), and raise a family in the fear and admonition of God (Genesis 24). There was nothing dysfunctional about that, right? Not with Isaac, but there was with Isaac's wife, Rebekah, who conspired with her youngest son, Jacob, to deceive Isaac when he became old and blind. Jacob lied to his father and deceived him with an elaborate impersonation (Genesis 27:19), thereby tricking Isaac into giving Jacob, his older brother Esau's rightful blessing (Genesis 27:30). This deception would come back to haunt Jacob in future years, as the tables were turned on him and he became the recipient of deception when he sought to start a family of his own.

Jacob, you may recall, also took his father's advice, and sought after a "church girl" from within his father's lineage (Genesis 28:1-7). Jacob found the daughter of his uncle, Laban—Rachel—to be to his liking. Jacob loved Rachel so much that he promised to work for his uncle for seven years to earn Rachel's hand in marriage. After seven years of labor, on the night Jacob was to receive his bride and consummate their union, Laban pulled a cruel trick on him: He sent his eldest daughter, Leah, in to Jacob, to be his wife instead of Rachel.

Naturally, Jacob was upset at being so cruelly deceived (Genesis 29:23-25), and had to work seven additional years after receiving his true love, Rachel, to be his wife. Until he was deceived himself, Jacob had no idea that "what goes around, comes back around."

There is unmistakable irony in the fact that the brother of his mother, Rebekah (Genesis 28:5), deceived Jacob. After all, it was his mother who initiated this heritage of lies with her own two sons. If you read the rest of Genesis 29 and Genesis 30, you can follow the family dysfunction within Jacob's household between his first wife (Leah), and the wife he loved (Rachel, Leah's younger sister), not to mention the handmaids that both Rachel and Leah used to bear children for Jacob during a mind-boggling competition of one-upmanship between the two sisters (using the birth of children).

To make matters worse, Jacob's earlier deception, and theft, of his brother Esau's birthright, was still an issue after all those years because Esau, seeking revenge, was in hot pursuit of his younger, deceitful twin brother (Genesis 32). God delivered Jacob from his brother Esau's intent on revenge (Genesis 33), and blessed him and his generations, keeping his covenant with Jacob's grandfather (Abraham).

Still, this intergenerational curse of deception continued to follow and plague Jacob. He was deceived again, this time by his own children, when ten of his sons lied to him concerning the health and whereabouts of their younger brother, Joseph, who they had conspired to kill, but eventually sold into slavery all because of *jealousy* and *anger* (Genesis 37)! Remember that it was Cain's *jealousy* of his brother Abel and his subsequent *anger* that influenced his act of hatred against his own flesh and blood. The sin of our original parents perpetuated itself down into Jacob's family. This intergenerational web of lies, deceit, and revenge eventually became the conduit for which the children of Israel were enslaved in Egypt for 430 years (Exodus 12:41). Intergenerational transference of sin has devastating consequences, to say the least!

David and His Sons

Contrast Jacob's family history of intergenerational transference of lies, deception, and theft, with that of King David's family history of intergenerational transference of lust, infidelity, and murder. David lusted after another man's wife, Bathsheba, took her to be his own, got her pregnant, and then tried to cover it up (2 Samuel 11:2-13)!

When the cover-up failed, David (being king of Judah), made sure that the husband of his partner in infidelity was sent to the front lines of a battle between Israel and the Ammonites, which was conveniently taking place all while this occurred (2 Samuel 11:14-16). This time David's plan was successful, and Bathsheba's husband, Uriah, was killed in battle (2 Samuel 11:24). David then had the dead man's wife brought to his palace to live as his own wife (2 Samuel 11:26, 27).

David's lust, deception, and treachery are a perfect example of how nothing we do "in secret" is kept secret from the Lord. Our "family secrets" are not only in full view of God Almighty; immoral and disgraceful behaviors might even be exposed to the public at some point, if God so chooses. For example, in 2 Samuel 12:1-6, the Lord sent Nathan to David to let him know that the Lord was very upset and disappointed in what David did to Uriah's family, and his brutal attempt to cover it up. If you read 2 Samuel 12:7-12, you get a detailed look at how David's cruel deception was exposed, and the ultimate price he paid, which included the death of more innocent people.

The words *sordid* and *sorry*, do not do justice in trying to describe the tangled mess King David brought upon his own head, and his future generations. If you read the rest of David's story you will find that it was his humility and remorse that made him beloved by God. Yet David's family still suffered the consequences of his disobedience and dysfunctional behavior.

The child David conceived with Uriah's wife died (2 Samuel 12:13-19). However, David had other sons, Amnon, Absalom, and Solomon, who had inherited their father's lusts, appetites, and treachery. In 2 Samuel 13, read about Amnon's inappropriate lust for his half-sister, Tamar (Absalom's sister). Amnon concocted a deceitful plan. He pretended to be ill so that his father, David, would send Tamar to tend to his illness. This allowed Amnon access to her in his bedchamber. Amnon raped his half-sister and sent her away in shame (2 Samuel 13:10-19).

When David found out about the disgraceful mess within his family, he was angry and distraught. I am not sure whether David's mind harkened back to the prophet Nathan's words, or whether the thought occurred to David that his very own sins were being made manifest in the lives of his children. However, when Absalom found out how Amnon had assaulted, abused, and disgraced his sister, he plotted revenge. In fact, Absalom waited two full years to exact his revenge on Amnon (2 Samuel 13:23-29). After Absalom arranged his own brother's death, he fled, as his father, David, mourned yet another tragedy.

David had no idea at that moment that Nathan's prophetic words, from the Lord Himself, were about to greatly increase his sorrow.

David eventually learned of his son Absalom's betrayal toward him: undermining the king's authority throughout Israel and Judah, and openly sleeping with his father's wives and concubines. (Remember Nathan's words from the Lord in 2 Samuel 12:11, 12, including how his son would seek the life of his own father (2 Samuel 15, 16, 17, 18), and predicting the eventual death of Absalom at the hands of King David's servants (2 Samuel 18:15). 2 Samuel 18:33 speaks to David's love for his son, Absalom, irrespective of Absalom's obvious lack of character, moral fiber, and decency. David knew that his sins (the sins of the father) were being made manifest in his sons. (You can read about the exploits of another son of David, Solomon, in 1 Kings, chapters 1-12, and in Song of Solomon/ Song of Songs.)

Solomon was the brother of Absalom, and was conceived during the period David comforted his grieving wife, Bathsheba (former wife of Uriah), after the death of their son, as prophesied by Nathan (2 Samuel 12:24). How bad was this intergenerational transference of lust, lies, deception, and disobedience? Solomon had seven hundred wives of royal birth and three hundred concubines—not exactly a successful formula for a happy home!

David's story of intergenerational transference of dysfunction and treachery are similar to Jacob's in that, too often, the exact nature of the flaws of the parents were passed down through generations. Yet through God's mercy and grace, forgiveness was not only promised but delivered to those who confessed their sin and sought forgiveness. However, though God forgave the sinner, the byproduct of sin continued to manifest through natural consequences. Disobedience to God always has too high a price. One of the highest prices of our sin and disobedience are the negative impact on our families.

Other Biblical Examples of Stress and Trauma in Families

Abigail and Esther

Moving away from specific intergenerational transference, the Bible also contains powerful examples of how the variety of family types of that time are comparable to our family types today. The stories of Esther and Abigail are fascinating because of the wide divide in contrast, yet with notable similarities. Both Abigail and Esther were gracious, attractive, and intelligent (Esther 2; 1 Samuel 25). Both carried themselves with dignity and respect. Both were married to powerful men: Esther, to King Ahasuerus; and Abigail to Nabal, whose "possessions were in Carmel; and the man was very great" (1 Samuel 25:2, KJV). That is where the similarities end and the contrast begin.

Esther was orphaned after the death of her parents and taken in by her uncle, Mordecai (Esther 2:7). Mordecai took great care in how he raised Esther, and made sure she was of great character, obedient to God, and upheld the teachings and traditions of Jewish faith.

When Esther was presented to King Ahasuerus, he was "attracted to Esther more than to any of the other women. . . . So he set a royal crown on her head and made her queen" (Esther 2:17, NIV).

There is no mention of Abigail's parents or upbringing, but the Bible does say, "she was an intelligent and beautiful woman" (1 Samuel 25:3, NIV). And, where Esther's husband was powerful and honorable (for he loved Esther), Abigail's husband was just the opposite: He "was surly and mean in his dealings" (1 Samuel 25:3, NIV). Abigail's full story is shared in Chapter 2, and is mentioned here only as an example of the different types of stress and issues that develop within the family system—even from way back in "ancient" times.

Family Dysfunction: Nothing New

The point for reviewing the lives of these people in the Bible is to better understand that family dysfunction and/or difficulties (i.e. being orphaned, domestic violence) are not something new or mysterious. Family dysfunction and/or misfortune are as tragic and debilitating today as they were for our original family: Adam and Eve. However, even with the debilitating effects of sin, God continued to bless Adam and Eve (as he did Abraham, Isaac, Jacob, David, and all who have called on His name since) to heal their families and allow them to prosper. There are lessons to be gleaned from reviewing the mistakes made by those who came before us:

1) No one is perfect—not one of us.
2) Disobedience will cause us to behave in ways that dishonor God; potentially destroying family harmony for generations to come.
3) None of us need remain disobedient to God's plan for our families.
4) Recovery from life's challenges is assured when we reach out to God.

Although the consequences of our mistakes may ultimately bring sorrow and pain; healing is available. God does not leave us to our own devices when we ask for His healing power for our families. "Nevertheless, I will bring health and healing to it; I will heal my people and will let them enjoy abundant peace and security. I will bring Judah and Israel [families] back from captivity and will rebuild them as they were before." (Jeremiah 33:6-7, NIV, brackets added)

It is never too late to present our families before God, the great healer. All it takes is a willing and contrite heart, acknowledging that we have made mistakes that have been harmful. Asking forgiveness is but the first step. We must also be willing to change our behavior. Jesus said, *"Humanly speaking, it is impossible. But with God everything is possible"* (Matthew 19:26, NLT, see also Mark 10:27).

Please review the Further Reading and Educational Information sections in Appendix B and D for available support for individuals and families.

Chapter 2

Families Under Stress:
We Need The Divine Counselor

——◇◦❧◦◇——

"For a child is born to us, a son is given to us. The government will rest on his shoulders. And he will be called: Wonderful Counselor, Mighty God, Everlasting Father, Prince of Peace" (Isaiah 9:6, NLT).

Modern Realities of Stress and Trauma in Families

With the sordid history of sin, failure, and dysfunction of our original parents, Adam and Eve, it should come as no surprise that via inter-generational transference, negative traits and characteristics have been passed down to us as an inheritance from our immediate family just as surely as eye color, height, and body type. In looking back to what Cain did to Abel, it is no wonder our families in modern times have continued down a similar spiral of destruction and despair, which regrettably, we witness on a daily basis through multimedia reports, word of mouth, and sadly for some, personal experience.

Everywhere we turn we hear about how the family is falling apart or being destroyed from within. Examples are all around us. Daily news reports often chronicle yet another disastrous happening or event within a family or community of families. Far too often we are inundated with news reports of horrific occurrences, like a father fatally wounding his wife and three children, and then turning the gun on himself, completing an unspeakable tragedy of five dead. We cringe when we hear reports of police finding some number of bodies, adults and children, with no motive given for the brutal display. As a nation, we held our collective breath when it was reported that a mother, later discovered to be overwhelmed with stress, intentionally drowned her five children in the family bathtub. We gasped in shock all over the country when we learned of the mother who placed her three children in the family car, pushed it into a lake to drown them, and then filed a false report that a stranger was responsible for their deaths. Alas, stories with this same brutal theme are reported almost daily all over the United States.

However, the breakdown of families is not a condition reserved strictly for the U.S. and other western culture nations. A few years ago, *60 Minutes,* the national TV news program reported a story that, unfortunately, still exists today: In some countries around the world where families experience great poverty, parents allow their children to be bought and sold as sex slaves just to bring money to the family to survive. They do so with no regard to the damage being done to these young lives—their own flesh and blood! All the world over, the innocence of children is being stripped from them by parents, guardians, and/or other adult authority figures who are sick with a distorted definition of love, a perverse desire for sexual gratification, and unchecked impulses of power, coercion, and intimidation.

Where Is the Love?

Most of us assume that all families love each other and try to do what is right by their most vulnerable members: children, the elderly, and the uniquely gifted. Considered against the backdrop of Adam and Eve's family dysfunction, and based on the turmoil reported within families these days, "love" is apparently defined quite differently, depending on the culture and/or family in which one happens to reside. The apostle Paul provides a wonderful definition of love:

> "Love is patient, love is kind. It does not envy, it does not boast, it is not proud. It does not dishonor others, it is not self-seeking, it is not easily angered, it keeps no record of wrongs. Love does not delight in evil but rejoices with the truth. It always protects, always trusts, always hopes, always perseveres. Love never fails ..."
> (1 Corinthians 13:4-8, NIV)

I believe that the world over, the majority of families attempt to invoke most aspects of Paul's definition of love. However, something else is also going on within many families that would sicken most people to their stomachs. Things which may seem extreme and foreign to the minds of most people—sexual abuse, physical and emotional abuse, and even murder—are occurring in such exponentially increasing numbers within families that separate legal courts had to be created just to process these domestic (family) court cases.

The criminal justice system, juvenile justice system, and family court dockets are overflowing with cases directly connected to the crime and violence that occurs within the walls we affectionately call "home." However, even the "average family" in which members do not display such heinous behavior toward one another are experiencing potentially debilitating issues from within. If left unchecked, these issues will eventually lead to the breakdown of the family unit.

Too often, parents are too busy trying to resolve marital issues to put significant energy into raising their children and showing them how to love others. Constant parental disagreements begin to wear on the family unit as a whole. Parents who are not on the same page in terms of household boundaries, or who have diverging philosophies on important issues such as financial responsibility, discipline strategies for their children, or on priorities for how the family system will work together, are heading for predictable stressors with negative impact. As a result, too often we focus an inordinate amount of attention on the day-to-day struggles, allowing our children to see and feel our worries, sorrows, and anger. Part of showing love and modeling a healthy, proactive response to life's challenges is demonstrating patience in the face of difficulties.

For example, when our children make mistakes (as they inevitably will), it is important that we use the situation as a "teaching moment" to point out not only what is right, but to emphasize our love for them. Just as Christ is disappointed with our mistakes, but still loves us, we model Christ-like behavior when we express disappointment with our child's mistakes, but remind them of our love for them just the same. And, since God is love (1 John 4:8), our loving behavior toward our children is a model for them of how God loves them too. Showing love and patience during difficult times translates well with our children, as they observe the relationship between fathers and mothers as well. After all, it is in the home that children learn behaviors they will take outside the home and into all their relationships. Our children learn more from what we do than from what we say to do. Showing love first and foremost within the family unit becomes a catalyst for all other positive learning experiences.

Conflict Resolution: Our Children's Reactions to Stress Come from Us

More often than not, for many families that experience the overwhelming stress of day-to-day survival in the twenty-first century, the result is unresolved stress, and soon after, unbridled conflict. The way in which adults handle conflict within the family becomes a model for the way children will approach conflict resolution in their own life experiences.

In today's world, what can families do during periods of high stress to mitigate the negative impact of all these outside pressures? What can be done to keep them from destroying the family system from within? Politicians use the mantra of "getting back to family values" as if there is some secular, universal "how to" manual to right the wrongs of familial dysfunction. The very foundation of the world, its population, and its people was built upon the premise of family being most important. We find this throughout the history of mankind, in any country, and any culture, represented by all races, ethnicities, and national origins.

If family is so important to so many people, from every walk of life, what is wrong with *the world* of family? The fact that sin and tragedy originated within our first family is pertinent from a historical perspective, but having that knowledge does not provide any comfort in dealing with current circumstances within our immediate families. So, we should first take a realistic look at the many challenges families face on a regular basis.

We are living in stressful times, to say the least. We are living under overwhelming conditions. We are living amongst individuals who are at the very end of their rope and see no way out of nightmarish situations that have become cruel reality. We are living right next door to families who are on the brink of destruction. We are sitting in the church pew next to individuals and families whose level of hurt, pain, and discouragement seem so insurmountable to them that they dare not speak a word about it to anyone in the church/community, lest they be exposed, humiliated, and accused of being failures as parents, as people, and as Christians.

We are allowing the agonizing secrets of family dysfunction to manifest themselves to such an extent that they begin to fester like infected sores as they ooze puss-like, smelly innuendo, slowly breaking down the very foundation and core of families. Our families are under attack. Families are experiencing intense, unrelenting stress. The trauma that results from the pain of too many losses rarely gets addressed appropriately in many families, if ever addressed at all. We need some help for our families.

Stress and Trauma Defined

We often hear the words *stress*, and *trauma*, and how these words are fast becoming the culprit for all things negative in our human existence. Let's take a closer look at stress first then return to how stress connects to trauma. So, what exactly is *stress*? *The American Heritage Dictionary, 3rd Edition* (1994) describes *stress* in this way: "an applied force or system of forces that tends to strain or deform a body; a state of extreme difficulty, pressure, or strain." In view of that definition, we can conclude that stress has the effect of applying a level of force to our families to such a degree that it "tends to strain and deform" the whole family system. That seems pretty intense to me.

However, there is more than one type of stress. For our purposes, we will focus on two types of stress that affect the whole of our being:

1. Distress—This is the type of stress most of us are familiar with because it involves negative events or situations. You promised to take your child to an amusement park or event very important to them, and you're stuck in traffic, late again, and you have to make that phone call to your spouse (or custodial parent) with the news that has become all too familiar. You have to break the news to your family that you have been laid off from work. Or, you have the misfortune of having to explain to your children why their parents are getting a divorce. These are not happy times, and all are very stressful.

2. Eustress—This type of stress is less familiar because generally it involves positive events or situations that can also be stressful. It's Thanksgiving and you're hosting twenty-five of your favorite relatives and a few of your in-laws. You love to cook and love to host, but you also worry because you want everything to go well. Maybe it's your graduation weekend, and a host of friends and relatives are in town to help you celebrate. That is wonderful, right? Well, you are also getting married that same weekend. Still wonderful, right? Oh, and you and your new spouse are moving to another state, where he/she has accepted a brand new job. All these are great things, right? Of course! But all are very, very stressful.

These examples are called stressors. A stressor is an agent or condition that causes stress (think: people, places, and things). Most people see stress as a reaction to some nagging worry, or pressure to perform. But stress can also be much more serious and debilitating. The areas where stress is most damaging? Our whole being! For example:

1. Physical, resulting in illness or injury (sickness, headaches, backaches, domestic violence, sexual/physical abuse, and more).
2. Emotional, resulting in extreme mental fatigue, forgetfulness, anger, sadness, verbal abuse, lowered self-esteem, and more.
3. Psychological, resulting in mental disorders, behavioral dysfunction, emotional breakdown, and more.
4. Spiritual, resulting in discouragement, collapse of faith, rejection of doctrine, apathy toward things religious or spiritual, and more.

The examples above come across as somewhat sterile and academic. However, when the trials and tribulations of real life beat down heavily upon us, the pressure and stress we feel can become all too real and quite devastating! This devastation, for many, may also cause trauma.

Trauma and Loss

Trauma is most often defined *physically*: "a body wound or shock produced by sudden physical injury, as from violence or accident" and *psychiatrically*: "an experience that produces psychological injury or pain." Think of the times in your life when you or someone you love was diagnosed with some terminal illness or impacted by a debilitating condition or injury. Perhaps a loved one is taken from you due to an automobile accident, or meets with some other unimaginable fate. Your body, mind, and spirit—as a whole—are challenged to continue functioning in the way they were designed.

At the time you receive this news, it seems like the air is sucked out of the room—even breathing suddenly becomes a chore. You look around the room for some evidence that this is all a hoax: a terrible, cruel, misguided joke. You pinch yourself, attempting to wake from a horrible nightmare. The very core of your soul grows cold and feels hollow. You may ask yourself, "Is this real?" Denial and disbelief converge, and then collide with fear and anger. Confusion and chaos flood an otherwise stable and organized mind.

You may even find yourself pleading and trying to make "deals" with God: If He would just remove the problem, take away the pain, heal the disease, or grant just a few more months . . . or years.

For some, they may receive the answer to prayer they wanted. Hallelujah! Praise the Lord! For others, God may have another plan in mind that does not include their healing, the healing of their loved one, or the removal of their tragedy. It is especially during this time that individual differences and the family style of coping and resilience manifest themselves in a myriad of ways. For at such times we are exposed to the Creator of the universe, completely naked—stripped of personal pride and begging for answers (which, if provided, still could not be understood by our feeble human brains). Anger and self-pity may play a cruel game of keep-away with the growing knot deep in the pit of your stomach. You may not be able to resist the urge to turn toward God and shake a fist in the air—part of an anger-filled tirade—clothed in helplessness. During times like these, it becomes increasingly difficult, if not almost completely impossible (even for Christians), to shout hallelujah and sing praises to the Lord. This feeling often gets worse over time as we ask the question, "Why me?"

The "Why me?" Syndrome

In Dr. James Dobson's book, *When God Doesn't Make Sense*, he addresses the "Why me?" question by pointing out that God is not obligated to explain Himself to His creation. Even if He did, Dobson contends: "We lack the capacity to grasp God's infinite mind or the way he intervenes in our lives" (p. 8). To believe otherwise, or insist on God explaining himself in the midst of our trials sets us up to develop spiritual depression, which can potentially reverberate throughout our whole family unit.

Taking Dr. Dobson's spiritual wisdom to heart; instead of questioning God, we should become more familiar with His Word and use it as a spiritual blueprint to help us build a solid spiritual foundation, thereby increasing our faith and acceptance of God's will in our lives, whether it meets with our "approval" or not. Before spiritual depression creeps into your soul or takes over your whole family, it helps to be able to look at your circumstances from a different perspective.

I vividly remember my father's words when I used to fall into the "Why me?" trap. He would ask, "Why not you?" My father's question went deeper than that because he would remind me that I rarely (if ever) asked "Why me?" when things were going well, or when all my dreams were coming true. His insinuation was clear: We are all God's children, and "He causes his sun to rise on the evil and the good, and sends rain on the righteous and the unrighteous" (Matthew 5:45, NIV).

Stress-Producing Challenges for Families

For those who may be fortunate enough to have not yet lost a loved one, or suffered a debilitating illness or accident, there are still so many other stress-producing challenges that can have a negative impact on our lives or adversely affect the future outcome of our families.

Families today are suffering under financial burdens, due to a slow economy, unemployment, or wages that have not kept pace with inflation. They struggle to fulfill the needs of children, grandchildren, and extended family. Families living in poverty often cannot provide for basic physiological needs (e.g. food, clothing, shelter, etc.).

Working class families suffer without proper health care for children, adults, and seniors. Families are being devastated and destroyed by the pervasiveness of mental illness, drugs and alcohol, and domestic violence. Families are often forever fractured by incarceration, divorce, and mean-spirited child custody battles. The rolls of children's services organizations keep adding the names of abused and neglected precious little souls.

We have children giving birth to children, with very little means or appropriate support systems to nurture them and provide a secure, stable environment and future. We have siblings being separated from one another as they are placed in foster homes, and far too often being placed in residential treatment facilities and detention centers. Our families are in trouble and crying out for help!

Self-Help Misguided

Now more than ever we must ask ourselves some important questions: What type of role models are we providing for our children and youth? What is missing from the formula that used to keep families together and functioning as a strong and vibrant unit? With each and every cruel blow life has to offer, in the midst of our dark clouds, we are forced to seek a silver lining. Most of the time we are able to do just that. After all, we have faith and trust in a supreme being. We have evidence that He is alive and all-powerful. Yet, when we are challenged again and again with turmoil, we sometimes forget about the blessings in our lives. We forget about the victories God has orchestrated over and over again. We develop "selective memory," forgetting about the good in our lives, while focusing only on the bad. When faced with yet another day of what seems like swimming upstream, it is not unusual for the fatigue of discouragement and doubt to creep in and disrupt or dislodge our confidence in all we know to be true.

For many people, life's disappointments and discouragement lead to attempts to "heal" themselves through any means necessary. Families inside and outside of church are negatively impacted by the influence of drugs and alcohol. Decisions to self-medicate are not always a result of faulty thinking that things will get better, but rather (more often), motivated simply by a desire to escape the reality of one's current existence and past experience, even if only for a few hours or fractured minutes at a time. It is this level of intense pain and anguish that provokes so many to abuse this chemical and/or that alcoholic beverage. For many, if escape is not possible, then temporarily forgetting—or more accurately, temporarily not feeling or caring—will have to do.

There are so many physically, psychologically, emotionally, and spiritually damaged souls, who comprise many physically, psychologically, emotionally, and spiritually damaged families, with a need and desire to forget so much. Physical, psychological, emotional, and spiritual trauma are the main sources of damage to our families. As an example; psychological trauma can be defined as experiences that are emotionally painful and distressing and that overwhelm an individual's capacity to cope (Corbin, Bloom, Wilson, and Rich, 2010). Corbin (et al) state that the primary trait of trauma is the feeling of powerlessness. Psychological trauma frequently triggers mental health and substance abuse problems.

In his book, *The Trauma Zone*, Dr. R. Dandridge Collins takes a creative and spiritually sensitive look at those who remain perpetually entangled in the snare of their feelings due to trauma, and how their inability to cope with emotions becomes the catalyst for continued emotional pain and heartache. He states, "The very nature of trauma is to become overwhelmed with your emotions . . . you are inundated by your feelings. Sometimes you feel your emotions so intensely that it hurts to feel. It's easier at times to feel nothing at all" (p. 14).

Trauma has an especially devastating impact on children. In their Adverse Childhood Experiences (ACE) study, the Center for Disease Control and Prevention and Kaiser Permanente (1998) found almost two-thirds of study participants reported at least one adverse childhood experience of physical or sexual abuse, neglect, or family dysfunction. More than one of five reported at least three or more such experiences. Experiencing adverse childhood experiences (ACE) is associated with increased risk for negative health and behavioral health in adulthood (i.e. depression, suicide, drug use). Not surprisingly, the study revealed that the estimated cost of untreated trauma-related alcohol and drug abuse alone was $161 billion in 2000.

Counselor Above All Others

With so many burdens and obstacles creating so much stress and trauma, our families are prime candidates to develop spiritual depression.

Clearly, we need someone or something that can address all these areas of individual stress that result in stress for entire families, and eventually entire communities. We need Jesus, the Divine Counselor! Jesus is a specialist in the human condition! He has the cure for all the behavioral and spiritual dysfunction that individuals and families display. By definition, all humans suffer from spiritual dysfunction, manifested by disobedience to God, which is exacerbated by the pain and distress we endure on a daily basis. Romans 3:23 states: "For all have sinned and fall short of the glory of God" (NIV). We need a family therapist who knows our every weakness.

God knows the families we come from. He knows the difficulties and stress we have endured and is aware of the challenges before us. God knows how we got to be the way we are. He sees how we suffer from trauma because of all manner of issues and concerns that act as obstacles to our healing and barriers to our recovery from life's challenges.

Jesus sees the roadblocks to our salvation and offers us hope. Psalm 71:5 states: "For you have been my hope, Sovereign Lord, my confidence since my youth" (NIV). God, in His great and infinite wisdom, has created the ultimate treatment plan: Keep his commandments (Exodus 20:1-17; Deuteronomy 5:22). If we follow the treatment plan we can recover from family dysfunction. We can be cured of our spiritual insanity. You know the popular and oft quoted definition of insanity: "To continue the same behavior, expecting different results." Well, it is spiritual madness for us to continue to ignore the spiritual dysfunction of families. Contrary to misguided belief, problems do not disappear if we ignore them long enough. Things do not get better by denying a problem exists. This is spiritual madness! Individuals who suffer with mental illness and/or substance dependence desperately search for relief and long for the happiness of a clear and stable mind. Similarly, the wayward soul whose spiritual insanity is suffocating the joy out of his or her relationships, home, and life longs for the relief and happiness of a clean heart and a renewed spirit. Psalm 146:5-6 says: "Blessed are those whose help is the God of Jacob, whose hope is in the Lord their God. He is the Maker of heaven and earth, the sea, and everything in them—he remains faithful forever" (NIV). We can trust the Divine Counselor with our family issues.

Troubled Families in the Church and Outside the Church: Jesus Died for All

It is naïve to think that only families *outside the church community* are in trouble. Our families within the church are also in crisis. They are experiencing similar levels of dysfunction, trauma, disillusionment and depression as families that do not belong to an organized religious community (1 Peter 4:3; Titus 3:3). However, God has provided to every man, woman, and child the same opportunity: the ultimate treatment plan of obeying His commandments. Jesus Himself is our intervention specialist for sin. He intervened by taking our place and dying on the cross.

As with any successful treatment plan, the person in recovery must willingly participate with the therapist. We must be consistent with our interaction and stay in constant contact with our intervention specialist. It is as simple as accepting a free gift, the gift of salvation. As with any treatment plan, there will be times when we fail to live up to our side of responsibility, and we will relapse. God has designed the ultimate relapse recovery plan: Prayer!

Prayer changes things. We must seek the face of the supreme family therapist—our intervention specialist. Jesus has promised He will be there for us. He will never leave us, even when things look to us to be too devastating and too difficult. He will not leave us!

He says in John 14:18, "I will not leave you comfortless: I will come to you" (KJV). Jesus will come through on His promises. And, just to make sure we are never alone, Jesus sent the Holy Spirit as Counselor (John 14:16, 26; 15:26; 16:7) to provide comfort and keep constant watch over us. Oh, what a marvelous intervention and treatment plan God has provided each and every one of us. Isaiah tells us that Jesus is a "Wonderful, Counsellor, the mighty God" (Isaiah 9:6, KJV). How fortunate we are to have unlimited access to the Divine Counselor. If we follow His treatment plan, our families can be healed from the spiritual dysfunction that leads to spiritual insanity.

Embracing a Spiritual Support System

Spiritual depression also tends to worsen in those afflicted by cutting themselves off from their spiritual support system. Isolation from friends and loved ones is a common by-product of discouragement, disillusionment, and depression. Staying away from the "power source" of like believers, and isolating oneself from spiritual support is paramount to "spiritual suicide." Do not allow the stress of guilt, shame, and perceived failure convince you to isolate yourself from the power source.

Instead of isolating ourselves from Jesus, we must run to Him and embrace Him by any means necessary. For some, that will mean connecting with an organized religious community. For others, it may mean simply reaching out to others whose actions and behaviors indicate they have been with Jesus. After all, Jesus Himself tells us how we can become members of His royal family: "For whoever does the will of My Father in heaven is My brother and sister and mother" (Matthew 12:50, NKJV). Obedience to God makes us children of the Father in heaven: "See what great love the Father has lavished on us, that we should be called children of God! And that is what we are! The reason the world does not know us is that it did not know him" (1 John 3:1, NIV). Obedience to God may cause the world not to recognize you—even to reject you. However, be not dismayed because accepting Jesus Christ brings the most important recognition one can have: acknowledgment before God the father. "Whoever acknowledges me before others, I will also acknowledge him before my Father in heaven. But whoever disowns me before others, I will disown before my Father in heaven" (Matthew 10:32-33, NIV). Followers of Jesus Christ know of God's power to heal and save our families. We are grateful for His love, His mercy, and His grace. Jesus wants to save us from the stress and dysfunction that has become so common in our families. He wants to make us spiritually, emotionally, psychologically, and physically whole. When was the last time you talked to Jesus and told Him your troubles? How long has it been since you prayed to the Lord just to praise His name and thank Him for your life, even when things were difficult?

I ask myself these questions often. And when I do, I think of one of my favorite songs, written by Mosie Lister and recorded by the Brooklyn Tabernacle Choir, "How Long Has it Been." Take a moment and allow the lyrics of this song to pour over you:

How long has it been
Since you talked with the Lord
And told Him your heart's hidden secrets
How long since you prayed
How long since you stayed
On your knees 'til the light shown through
How long has it been
Since your mind felt at ease
How long since your heart knew no burden
Can you call Him your Friend
How long has it been since you knew
That He cares for you

How long has it been
Since you knelt by your bed
And prayed to the Lord up in heaven
How long since you knew
That He'd answer you and would
Keep you the long night through
How long has it been
Since you woke with the dawn
And felt that the day's worth the living
Can you call Him your Friend
How long has it been since you knew
That he cared for you?

Composition/Song Title: How Long Has It Been
Writer Credits: Mosie Lister

51

How long has it been since you scheduled some time with the Divine Counselor? You do not have to wait. There is no waiting list or appointment log. You have access to Jesus in an instant. Schedule some time with Jesus, today. The spiritual health and salvation of your family depend on it!

Note: Along with all suggestions in this book, please take advantage of the group of mental health, family therapy, and behavioral health services available to you (including substance abuse/dependence), provided by professionals in your community. God provides these services through men and women trained specifically in these areas to be most helpful for you. (Review the Educational Information in Appendix D.)

Chapter 3

Love Gone Bad:
The Horror of Intimate/Domestic Violence

"Husbands, love your wives and do not be harsh with them"
(Colossians 3:19, NIV).

I heard it! I heard everything! The screaming, crying, yelling! Glass breaking and Momma saying: "Why are you doing this? Leave her alone!" I would shudder in my bed with only a sheet over my body to keep me from the cold air. I listened to the rats as they ran in and around the holes in my bedroom walls as though in some kind of laboratory maze. I was scared and felt alone, but the sound of the rats provided a strange comfort, a sense of stability, because they were there but didn't hurt me. There were seven of us girls and no boys (as if that would have made some kind of a difference if they had a son). Though terrified, I would never acknowledge what was going on around me because my love for my father kept me in denial. I knew my father had issues, but my mother was of a different caliber. She was loving, compassionate, intact, and a disciplinarian. I loved both my parents. Ironically, I was angry with my mother for not being selfish enough to take us away from him and his madness. The nights in my house were filled with fear, pain, sadness, and bewilderment. The next day, things would go on in the house as if nothing had happened the night before. This was the beginning of my distortion of what love is supposed to be like and how I'm supposed to be treated. I would not discover the strength to seek a different kind of love until after I had allowed that same sickness of sadistic power and control to come into my adult life in the form of my own husband, the father of my children. They saw what I saw as a child. They must have felt what I felt, yet it took me a long time to gather the courage I so desperately wanted my mother to have, displayed so many painful years ago.

(Shared with permission from a dear friend who experienced the horror of intimate violence in her home growing up, and in her own marriage as an adult.)

Domestic Violence Defined

Domestic violence is a major occurrence in our families today. Unfortunately, domestic violence is anything but new. There is a long and sordid history of abuse in our families, and for some, it is a reprehensible tradition that stretches across several generations. Crime scenes marked off with yellow tape after police are summoned to break up a domestic dispute, are far too common a sight in our communities. Responding to family disturbances is one of the most dangerous activities police perform (Greene and Heilbrun, 2014). The level of danger involved when intervening in a domestic dispute is not surprising, considering that strangers (not known to the victim) perpetrated 39 percent of the violent crime in 2010. The remaining 61 percent of violent offenses were perpetrated by family members, neighbors, and others known to the victim (Bureau of Justice Statistics, 2010).

Unfortunately, and unbelievably, domestic violence has become an accepted reality in many cultures. Domestic violence has invaded the sanctity of families representing a variety of races, ethnicities, social economic status and cultures within and outside the United States of America.

The title of this chapter is "Love Gone Bad," but domestic violence is not love at all. Domestic violence is a skewed and deformed expression of inadequacies, insecurities, and control; wrapped in distorted feelings of inferiority, fear of abandonment, and rage. Families living with the debilitating effects of domestic violence are surely experiencing spiritual depression at a very high level.

The abuse of a spouse, child, parent, or senior constitutes the lowest of acts within the family system. It totally goes against everything God designed when He created the institution of marriage and the union of family. We cannot possibly be obedient to God and live in accordance with His will while abusing our families. So, it is imperative for us to develop a clear understanding of what constitutes abuse and seek out exactly what God expects from each and every one of us.

> **Definition**—Domestic Violence is a pattern of coercive behavior that may include physical, sexual, economic, emotional, and/or psychological abuse by an intimate or family member. It is often referred to these days as *Intimate Violence* or *Intimate Partner Violence* (IPV). ("Understanding Intimate Violence", Barbara Couden, Editor, 1999).

This is what we know about domestic violence: Domestic violence crosses all racial, ethnic, socioeconomic, and sexual orientation boundaries and disproportionately impacts women five to eight times more often than men (Couden, 1999; Flitcraft & Stark, 1996).

Domestic abuse is most often child abuse, abuse of a spouse or domestic intimate partner, and a growing (and disturbing) trend of abuse toward seniors (Kunzman, 1990; Couden, 1999). Some of the key elements of domestic violence and/or abuse are intimidation, humiliation, physical injury, and neglect. Neglect occurs more often with children, seniors, and disabled persons because they are most vulnerable.

It is important to note that domestic violence is not the result of losing control, as some perpetrators would have us believe. Domestic violence in action is intentionally trying to control another person. The abuser is purposefully using verbal, nonverbal, physical, and even financial means to gain control over another human being.

Inside the Heart and Mind of Perpetrators

During my time as a staff psychologist in a State prison system, part of my daily responsibilities included conducting therapeutic groups and individual sessions with convicted sex offenders and individual's convicted of violent crimes. I never entered the prison gates, nor walked into a cell or group, without first praying to the Divine Counselor to guide my steps and make me a useful vessel. God always answers prayer. To a man, they all expressed their love for their families. Of those incarcerated specifically for violence against family, many voiced sorrow or some level of remorse for their grotesque expression of emotion, vulnerability, need, and desire masquerading as love.

Certainly I cannot read minds, nor do I have the capacity or authority to judge a man's heart. Therefore, taking each at his word, and using what little predictive ability one can have in such matters (and throwing in a pinch of common sense), I concluded that though warped and misguided, this deformed remnant of love, need, and rage was the only thing that could be identified in these men as "feeling" or "emotion."

Knowing what we know about heredity, environment, and the propensity to repeat behaviors demonstrated by one's own adult caregivers, it is more than possible (actually quite probable), that many of those men were victims of emotional, physical, and sexual abuse themselves. Clinical interviews with each man confirmed this fact in better than eight-five percent of my caseload. And so, as each man opened a grieving heart, swallowed huge lumps of pride, and reluctantly reached for courage inexplicably nonexistent in their past; they began to trace the evolution of their childhood development and the origin of their abusive shield. What they could not protect for themselves as children, many allowed to morph into a disturbing tendency toward rage, violence, and vicious immorality exacted upon innocent others.

This is a good place to review the specific types of domestic violence and the unfortunate results of such abuse on the intimate partner, children, and anyone else who may reside with the abuser. It is also a good place to identify particular symptoms and acts of behavior of those who would perpetrate such a heinous crime.

Types of Abuse

1. Verbal Abuse (psychological/mental abuse and emotional abuse by way of screaming at a person, calling a person terrible names, cursing, belittling a

person with comments about their physical appearance, demeaning another's intellectual capacity, and more)

2. Nonverbal Abuse (staring or looking at an individual in a mean or intimidating way, cleaning a gun in the presence of someone one wishes to frighten or intimidate, placing a gun on a table in view of someone, pointing a loaded or unloaded gun at someone, making intimidating gestures toward someone, ignoring someone for long periods of time, and more)

3. Physical Abuse (physically laying hands on someone in a violent manner with the intent to intimidate, harm, maim, or kill)

4. Sexual Abuse (exploiting someone sexually with the intent to coerce, intimidate, and control)

5. Stalking (physically tracking) or Cyber Stalking (using a personal computer or other technology to invade someone's personal space and/or privacy)

6. Economic or Financial Abuse (controlling someone's freedom of movement and/or ability to realize some level of independence, neglecting access to medical services, withholding medical treatment, and more)

7. Spiritual Abuse (disturbing someone's core center and belief in self in such a way that it has a negative impact on their self-esteem, disturbing someone's ability to adhere to and seek out spiritual and/or religious beliefs and/or practices, and more)

You may be able to think of other examples of abuse, but the list above is a representative sample of abuses I have encountered on a regular basis as a professional psychologist. Taken at face value, you would be right to wonder how a human being could exact this type of abuse on anyone, let alone someone close to them—someone whom they claim to love.

Therein lies one of the most confusing and unexplainable things about living in a troubled world: How is it that the expression of human love has become distorted, twisted, and perverted to the point that genuine intimacy and real love are unrecognizable to some and unimaginable to others? I submit to you that domestic violence and abuse can only take place in a world that has allowed its focus on God to slip dramatically below morally acceptable standards. Circumstance and pressure have combined to exact overwhelming stress on families, where individuals wilt under the weight of the physical, psychological, and emotional strain of spiritual depression.

Causes of Domestic Violence

It is important to review some causes of domestic violence, and to identify the type of individuals who are most vulnerable to become victims or act as perpetrators. Before that, it's important to review some causes:

A strong predictor of domestic violence in adulthood is domestic violence in a household in which the person was reared (Couden, 1999). For example: a child's exposure to their father's abuse of their mother is the strongest risk factor for transmitting domestic violence from one generation to the next. This is called *intergenerational violence*, and this cycle of domestic violence is difficult to break because the parents have presented violence as a norm (Couden, 1999). Moreover, individuals living with domestic violence in their households have learned that violence and mistreatment are acceptable ways to vent anger.

This "learned behavior" for conflict resolution has taught children, adolescents, and adults alike that violence is an effective means of control over others.

Another identifiable cause of domestic violence and abuse is that as the child, adolescent, or adult learn this distorted way of managing conflict resolution, no one in the past has stepped in to address, interrupt, or stop their violent tendencies as this behavior develops. And stress, as previously established, is a major precursor for acting out behaviors in individuals who have experienced physical violence and/or emotional intimidation during their early development.

More often than not, these individuals have not learned proactive, more constructive ways to express negative feelings or learned more appropriate alternatives in dealing with relationship issues. They have not developed the proper problem-solving skills or social skills to build competence or confidence in their ability to navigate an ever changing and challenging social environment. It is difficult to get any more "changing" and "challenging" than in intimate relationships!

According to Couden (1999); a less frequently cited cause or initiation of domestic violence is provocation by the intimate partner. This is not to say that the intimate partner, child, or elderly member of the household is responsible for the perpetrators' verbal outburst or violent actions. It is to say that almost anything can set perpetrators off when they are on the verge of an emotional or physical explosion. However, an intimate partner does not always sit around and wait for the outburst to occur. It is not unusual for the intimate partner being abused to sense that the perpetrator is slowly moving toward an argument, and to then say or do something that will expedite the argument to the point of turning it into a fight, just to get it over with!

Some intimate partners may intentionally cause a fight to get to the "honey-moon" phase of the domestic violence cycle (a period during which the abuser is apologetic for his or her behavior, becomes very nice, is extra attentive, gives gifts, wants to have sexual intercourse, and more) simply to bring on some sort of "positive" feelings—a brief time period when the perpetrator is not raging. During the honeymoon phase, it is not uncommon for the abuser to actually exude some level of remorse and apologize for his or her behavior. However, this is part of the overall cycle of domestic violence and should not be confused with genuine feelings of remorse, or a higher probability that the abuse will not occur again.

Other common reasons for domestic violence and abuse to occur are: economic hardship, (such as prolonged unemployment and/or mismanagement of finances), depression, desperation, jealousy, insecurity, emotional immaturity, fear of aban-donment, and poor anger management skills. Any one of these issues can place an intimate relationship or family unit under a tremendous amount of stress, but when experienced in multiple combinations, a serious level of familial dysfunc-tion is bound to exist. Spiritual depression often manifests under these conditions.

When individuals live under conditions of domestic violence and abuse, there is often a higher level of acceptance of this way of life. Sometimes this is due to the victim(s) feeling helpless and unable to escape the perpetrator. Sometimes it is just a matter of the perpetrator having so much control over the victim(s) that the victim(s) convince themselves that trying to leave is futile, or would create much more serious problems. The growing statistics on fatalities for women who attempt to escape their abuser tell us that this, unfortunately, is often the case.

The Negative Effects of Domestic Violence on Victims

The results of domestic violence and abuse are far-reaching and negatively impact a wide range of human functioning:

- Sleeping problems
- Depression
- Anxiety/Panic attacks
- Low self-esteem
- Lack of trust in others
- Feelings of abandonment
- Anger
- Sensitivity to rejection
- Diminished mental and physical health
- Inability to work
- Poor relationships with children and other loved ones
- Substance abuse as a means of coping

Physical abuse may result in death if the victim does not leave the relationship. And, as mentioned before, victims who do attempt to leave are also in grave danger from perpetrators who resort to stalking as a way of keeping the victim from moving on with his or her life. This form of intimidation and control usually has a tragic conclusion, ending in injury and even loss of life.

That is the chief reason victims of domestic violence must establish a well thought-out plan of escape for themselves and their children.

Consideration of children's safety becomes even more paramount when reviewing outcome data which indicates that between 1993 and 1998, 45 percent of all victims lived in households with children under the age of twelve. And, for three out of four women who have experienced domestic violence, the incident(s) occurred in or near their homes. Sixty percent reported it occurred between the hours of 6 p.m. and 6 a.m. (Freidman and Creeden, 2005. Children Who Witness Violence. *Children Who Witness Violence Project:* Cleveland Ohio).

Problems Associated with Domestic Violence on Children Specifically

- Behavioral, social, emotional problems
- Higher levels of aggression, anger, hostility, oppositional behavior, disobedience
- Poor peer, sibling, and social relationships
- Fear, anxiety, withdrawal, and depression

As children and teens develop and grow up in abusive households, they are more likely to display:

- Poor school performance
- Lack of conflict resolution skills
- Limited problem-solving skills
- Pro violence attitude
- Adoption of rigid stereotypes and male privilege

Exposure to domestic violence puts children at increased risk for:

- Exposure to additional traumatic events
- Neglect
- Losing one or both parents (incarceration, death, or abandonment)
- Depression and trauma symptoms in adulthood
- Tolerating and using violence in future adult relationships

(Freidman and Creeden, 2005. Children Who Witness Violence. *Children Who Witness Violence Project*: Cleveland Ohio).

Who Are The Abusers?

Domestic abuse knows no age or ethnic/racial boundaries. Perpetrators of domestic violence come from a wide range of cultures and customs. They can be men or women from some of the most respected career fields and community leadership positions. We read about religious leaders, physicians, social service employees, law enforcement personnel, educators, judges, lawyers, pro athletes, entertainers (and more) being accused and/or arrested for domestic violence.

Most psychological, medical, and legal experts agree that the vast majority of physical abusers are men. Women can also be perpetrators of domestic violence. However, due to the likelihood of physical size and strength differences between men and women, women are seven times more likely to require medical or emergency attention as a result of domestic violence (Stark and Flitcraft, 1996; Couden, 1999). The vast majority of stalkers are men stalking women. However, stalkers can also be women stalking men, men stalking men, or women stalking women.

Negative Impact of Domestic Violence on Families

It is easy to see why domestic violence has such a pervasive negative impact on our families. Yet there are no easy answers to counteract the magnitude of such immoral behaviors. Remember, our children will ultimately carry the heaviest burden of domestic violence and abuse because it does—and will—affect the rest of their lives, on into adulthood. This is where the intergenerational transfer of domestic violence takes root, spiraling out of control, generation after generation, leaving a family legacy that, at the least, is shameful and disobedient to God. Domestic violence distorts and disrupts normal childhood development, creating a society of painfully angry and disillusioned offspring who will eventually attempt to raise children of their own!

If we do not take serious steps to remedy this ugly pattern of abuse of spouses and children, we will continue setting ourselves up for a future of trying to provide healing for a generation of people who are physically, psychologically, emotionally, and spiritually damaged, placing more and more pressure on social services organizations that are already overwhelmed and undermanned. Seeking the face of the Divine Counselor certainly must be a part of any solution that has any reasonable chance of success!

As with all topics in this book, domestic violence is highlighted because it is of grave concern within our families, our churches, and our communities. We cannot continue abusing our families and expect to avoid dire consequences for the future of these United States, in particular, and the rest of the world, as a whole.

God's Instructions to Develop Healthy Families

A few Bible texts referenced earlier in this chapter bear reading in their entirety as we summarize God's instructions for how we should treat our spouses, our children, our elderly, and any human being within our home, our church, and our community. I hope you take the time to read them in their entirety and make note where they can have a positive impact in your life.

As mentioned earlier, the vast majority of domestic abusers are men. Therefore, it is imperative that we provide these men with clear instruction from the Most High God. Ephesians 5:25 tells us, "Husbands, love your wives, just as Christ loved the church and gave himself up for her" (NIV). Several references in the Bible compare God's people to a "bride" and God as the "groom" (Old Testament: Isaiah 62:5; Jeremiah 2:2; Jeremiah 2:32), Christ as a "groom," and the church as a "bride" (New Testament: Matthew 9:15; 25:1-10; Mark 2:19, 20; Luke 5:34, 35; John 3:29; Revelation 19:7-9; 21:2, 9; 22:17). Apparently, God takes the institution of marriage quite seriously, and expects his creation to do likewise. Ephesians 5:28-29 goes on to say: In this same way, husbands ought to love their wives as their own bodies. He who loves his wife loves himself. After all, no one ever hated their own body, but they feed and care for their body, just as Christ does the church. (NIV).

Imagine if every husband loved his wife as much as he loved himself. Or, imagine if every man treated women, children, and our most vulnerable citizens in the same way he would like to be treated. Certainly domestic violence and abuse would decrease dramatically. However, to assume that people love themselves assumes too much! It is a lack of "self-love" that allows individuals to abuse others.

Ephesians 5:30 says, "for we are members of his body" (NIV). We are all members of the body of Christ. It makes no sense for parts of the body to mistreat or attack other parts of the body. That is tantamount to a body attacking itself. Mental health professionals know all too well that an individual who attacks himself (i.e. self-mutilation, suicide ideation, and more), is crying out for help in the worst possible way. It is the same as with spouses and domestic partners who seek to hurt one another, their children, elderly relatives, or others who are most vulnerable. Proverbs 11:29, tells us: "Those who bring trouble on their families inherit the wind. The fool will be servant to the wise" (NLT). It is a foolish thing to abuse one's family. Domestic violence and abuse sap the energy of all involved and remove any semblance of real love as God intended.

I have never met an individual who abuses and hurts others who could honestly say they loved themselves. When the Bible talks about "loving others as you love yourself," it assumes that each individual person has a natural affinity and love for himself or herself, as originally designed through God's creation of human beings. This still makes sense for a vast majority of people. However, for far too many unfortunate souls, sin has created a platform for evil thoughts and actions which have totally distorted the concept of love for God, love for self, and love for our fellow man.

God's Instructions for Healthy Marriages

It is this distortion of God's original plan for loving relationships that has instead created a love gone bad. I do not believe it is possible to love oneself and then abuse one's spouse, children, or the elderly. A person who does not love and respect himself or herself cannot participate successfully in a committed, loving relationship with another human being as God intended.

God designed marriage to be a positive institution of love, respect, and support for His creation that would stand as a model symbolizing the intended relationship between Jesus and the body of Christ (the church). Ephesians 5:31 declares, "For this reason a man will leave his father and mother and be united to his wife, and the two will become one flesh" (NIV). This indicates to me that as we mature into responsible adults, we are expected to seek more mature relationships with one another and with our Creator.

Ephesians 5:32-33 goes on to say: This is a profound mystery—but I am talking about Christ and the church. However, each one of you must love his wife as he loves himself, and the wife must respect her husband (NIV).

Clearly, Paul is addressing the pressing issue of marriage and giving instruction to the early church of Ephesus. However, the advice is still sound today, and the comparison of Jesus Christ's relationship to His church with that of the union between a husband and wife also remains particularly poignant. The issue for us today is to recognize that there are too many people who do not love themselves, and therefore, find it almost impossible to demonstrate genuine love towards others.

Now, this is not to say that everyone who has low self-esteem, or finds it difficult to love themselves is predisposed to become an abuser of spouse and children—absolutely not. I am specifically singling out that group of people who have a combination of intense anger and self-loathing which manifests in negative interactions with others and produces predictably poor outcomes through poor communication skills, poor social skills, poor conflict resolution skills, and poor impulse control (an inability to self-regulate, moving quickly from anger to rage).

There are many already involved in relationships, so it is too late to seek Paul's advice beforehand. I strongly suggest that women who are currently trapped in an abusive relationship review the family resources section in Further Reading (Appendix B) and Educational Information section contained (Appendix D), contact their local family assistance agency, and/or, speak to a medical/mental health professional who can direct them to social service assistance in their local area.

Your life, and the lives of your children may depend upon you finding the courage to develop a plan to ensure the safety of your family. At the bare minimum, everyone should have safety and survival. However, you also need to consider both the poor quality of life for you and your family under abusive conditions, and how seeking professional help can potentially increase the quality of life for you and your children.

Biblical Examples of Domestic Violence

The Bible provides real life examples of every physical, emotional, social, psychological, and spiritual trial that confronts us in our daily lives. Domestic violence is no exception. In 1 Samuel 25, we are shown the life of Abigail, who is described as "an intelligent and beautiful woman," and her husband, Nabal, who is described as "a Calebite," who "was surly and mean in his dealings" (1 Samuel 25:3, NIV).

The story goes on to tell of how Nabal intentionally insulted King David and his men, who had been kind to Nabal's servants during a previous encounter. It tells of how Abigail's wisdom and kindness pacified David's anger, turning him away from his intentions to kill Nabal and everyone in his house (1 Samuel 25:4-35).

When Abigail came home to tell Nabal what had happened and what she had saved him from, she found him drunk (per usual), so she told him nothing until the next morning, once he was sober. When Abigail told Nabal about King David's intent, "his heart failed him and he became like a stone. About ten days later, the Lord struck Nabal and he died" (1 Samuel 25:36-38, NIV).

This is a significant point, especially for victims of domestic violence who contemplate revenge against those who have harmed them. There is nothing you can do to an abuser that is worse than what God will do to them. Hebrews 10:30-31, tells us: For we know him who said, "It is mine to avenge; I will repay," and again, "The Lord will judge his people." It is a dreadful thing to fall into the hands of the living God (NIV).

Not only will God reprimand those who have abused wife, mother, and child in their home, and the most vulnerable in society; He will also take care of those who have been abused. When King David learned that Nabal was dead, he sent for Abigail and made her his wife (1 Samuel 25:39-44).

The Lord rewarded Abigail for her integrity and her faith in his ability to resolve her issues with an abusive husband. Abigail is remembered because she demonstrated a firm belief in God and the courage to do the right thing by her family.

When Seeking Help Trust in God

As you seek the courage to make bold decisions for the safety of you and your family, remember to watch and pray. If you have one person in whom you can trust, enlist their help to initiate your decision to empower yourself and your children. If you do not have such a person in whom you can trust, seek assistance from your local church, faith-based, or community program.

As you pray and seek direction, take time to read the story in Luke 13:11-13, about a woman "who had been crippled by a spirit for eighteen years. She was bent over and could not straighten up at all" (NIV). The story relates that the woman had a disability, was unable to lift herself up, and had difficulty moving around. I submit to you that being trapped in an abusive relationship, with a dangerous person , is as disabling (perhaps more so) as being trapped in a physical body which does not allow you the freedom to move about as you desire. Luke 13:12-13 says: "When Jesus saw her, he called her forward and said to her, 'Woman you are set free from your infirmity.' Then he put his hands on her, and immediately she straightened up and praised God" (NIV).

Living within an abusive relationship is not really living at all! In Psalm 31:12-17, David's description of his feelings during one of his lowest moments seems apropos for how one must feel in an abusive relationship:

> I am forgotten as though I were dead; I have become like broken pottery. For I hear the many whispering, "Terror on every side!" They conspire against me and plot to take my life. But I trust in you, Lord; I say, "You are my God." My times are in your hands; deliver me from my enemies; from those who pursue me. Let your face shine on your servant; save me in your unfailing love. Let me not be put to shame, Lord, for I have cried out to you; but let the wicked be put to shame ... (NIV)

Expressed Emotions Do Not Have to Be Negative

David is one of my favorite poets and songwriters of all time because he seemed to know exactly how to convey in words and in song what both the brokenhearted and the joyful experience and feel. Sorrow and joy are two of the most difficult emotions to understand and describe. And, because they are also two of the most primitive and naturally occurring emotions in human beings, I think we take them for granted far too often.

Anger is at the top of that list as well. However, it is important to remember that anger, in and of itself, is not a bad thing. On the contrary! Anger is one of the most naturally occurring emotions for any of us. Anger can be a great catalyst for narrowing one's focus, confronting issues directly in the here and now, and increasing motivation to be proactive.

The problem occurs when an individual does not possess an inner censure or the requisite skill level to process anger properly, thereby allowing it to boil over into rage, which usually results in negative consequences for the person feeling rage (feeling overwhelmed/out of control), and for those closest to them (being abused/ violated). Abuse and violence are *not* signs of love or respect for self or others. Abuse and violence are signs of fear, self-loathing, and a need to control others.

Dr. Angel M. Rodriguez, director of the Bible Research Institute, Silver Spring, Maryland, makes the case: "Violence designates an antisocial behavior that violates God's established order. It is motivated by hate [not love] or egotism and could lead to physical and social attacks. In some cases it results in murder or exploitation of others for personal benefit" (Atonement and the Cross of Christ, 2008, *Adult Sabbath School Study Guide*, p. 26). I agree wholeheartedly with Dr. Rodriguez, and find it particularly despicable when people attempt to use religion or God to excuse or hide behind abusive and/or violent behavior toward those they claim to love.

I also take issue with those who try to rationalize abusive and/or violent behavior by claiming, "I just have a bad temper and cannot control myself when I get angry," or "When my spouse and I argue, he/she just knows how to push my buttons," and more. Look, anyone who has ever been married for any length of time, or has children/parents living in the home, can relate to the frustration of not seeing eye to eye with a spouse or loved one. However, disagreements should never escalate into disrespectful verbal exchanges or full-fledged physical fights.

Some people are able to avoid name-calling and physical confrontations, but practice an equally destructive model of abuse by being passive-aggressive (giving others the "silent treatment" or "playing nice" while actively undermining the targeted individual), ignoring someone's physical/psychological/emotional needs, and/or withholding financial or medical assistance, all for the sake of "winning" an argument or controlling others.

Ephesians 4:26-27 tells us, "'In your anger do not sin': Do not let the sun go down while you are still angry, and do not give the devil a foothold" (NIV). Paul is telling us to not go to bed angry with one another. Trying to sleep while angry only causes negative thoughts and feelings toward one another to build up and fester. When you wake up (if you get any sleep at all) you are often more angry than the day before. Some couples that do this end up not speaking to each other for several days, or worse, have physical confrontations.

Another piece of good advice Paul offers to the church as a whole, but is certainly appropriate for married couples, in particular. It is found in Ephesians 4:29-32:

> Do not let any unwholesome talk come out of your mouths, but only what is helpful for building others up according to their needs, that it may benefit those who listen. And do not grieve the Holy Spirit of God, with whom you were sealed for the day of redemption. Get rid of all bitterness, rage and anger, brawling and slander, along with every form of malice. Be kind and compassionate to one another, forgiving each other, just as in Christ God forgave you. (NIV)

These passages tell us to be careful how we speak to our spouses, to our children, and to other family members (including members of the body of Christ). We should speak words of encouragement and not words that belittle, embarrass, or humiliate.

Encouragement for Couples

Even when our anger toward a loved one is for legitimate reasons, we must still be thoughtful in our expression of angry feelings so the focus remains on the incident in question or the behavior of the person in question, and not toward the individual. This is difficult for some, and it does take practice, patience, and prayer. Also, while praying about your inability to process your anger properly, you should seek professional intervention. Remember, God has provided professionals in all areas to help us *while* we continue to pray. The area of couples and family therapy is no exception.

Many of today's youth are being raised in families where a healthy example of how to process conflicts within the home is nonexistent. So, these children cannot be expected to develop appropriate conflict resolution skills for their encounters outside the home. Far too many parents are coming from abusive households themselves, and have not learned or acquired the necessary skills for healthy interactions.

A surprising number of parents are uncomfortable with basic confrontational situations within and outside the home, and either avoid them at all costs or plow into them, head down, like a bull in a china shop. Children raised in these households are either witnesses or victims of emotional, physical, and sexual abuse and/or violence. Unfortunately, too many of these child victims grow up to be perpetrators themselves and/or are re-victimized, thus continuing the vicious cycle of abuse and violence through multiple generations of families.

Words of Wisdom from the Wisest Man on Earth

If you are not yet married, or not currently in a serious romantic relationship, I implore you to take your time and make it a matter of prayer *before* choosing a mate. I am especially concerned about young people today who find themselves under all sorts of pressure, in general, who may find themselves being drawn into a romantic relationship too early, or coerced to do things against their will. This can be a major aspect of pressure for young people, leading to stress which, if left unchecked, can certainly lead to spiritual depression.

Solomon was considered a wise man, perhaps the wisest. He provides some very simple and concrete suggestions on things (and certain people) to avoid when seeking a mate, or even just seeking companionship. Here are a few of my favorites:

- Proverbs 22:24, 25 (NIV): "Do not make friends with a hot-tempered person, do not associate with one easily angered, or you may learn their ways and get yourself ensnared."
- Proverbs 29:22 (NIV): "An angry man stirs up conflict, and a hot-tempered person commits many sins."
- Proverbs 30:33 (NIV): "For as churning cream produces butter, and as twisting the nose produces blood, so stirring up anger produces strife."

You've got to love Solomon's simple and direct advice. No mincing of words for this wise man. He makes it clear that you should do your "homework" before choosing a boyfriend or girlfriend.

Solomon seems to be suggesting that we pay close attention to the behavior of our friends and acquaintances for whom we have a romantic attraction, or even those we just want to keep as friends. We should watch and see how they handle conflict and disagreements in their own lives, and pay attention to how we feel in our "gut" when witnessing their confrontations.

Females should especially take note of how their male friends and acquaintances treat the women in their own family, particularly their mother and sisters. They should note whether he treats his elderly relatives with honor and respect and his younger relatives with helpful care and concern. In short, the oldest and youngest in our families are most vulnerable. Women need to know how their potential life partner treats these precious souls, especially when he has had a "bad day" or some level of disappointment or conflict arises in his life.

Encouragement for Families

Certainly it is always possible that even if we follow Solomon's advice to the letter, and appreciate Paul's admonitions, we will still make mistakes in judgment. This is why it is so important to *not* lean upon our own understanding. We must pray sincerely for God's guidance in helping us choose a life partner and those we should keep close to us as friends.

Sound impossible to sort out people who are potentially troublesome for our lives? Luke 1:37 states, "For nothing will be impossible with God" (NRSV). Still believe that you are unable to discern who is good for your life and who is not? Jesus replied, "What is impossible with man is possible with God" (Luke 18:27, NIV). Present all your needs, desires, and choices before the Lord first and you cannot go wrong.

Finally, I would be remiss if I did not reiterate the fact that even when you do your best to protect yourself and your children, you still may not be able to prevent all the actions of evil people who perpetrate abuse.

We do not always understand why we encounter particular trials and others do not. This is why it is so important to rely upon Jesus, who loves you, and especially loves your children. Jesus stated how He feels about children:

> Then he said: "I tell you the truth, you must change and become like little children. Otherwise, you will never enter the kingdom of heaven. The greatest person in the kingdom of heaven is the one who makes himself like this child." (Matthew 18:3-4, NCV)

Those who choose to abuse others will be made to answer on God's terms (Proverbs 11:17; 12:21; 22:8). This may include having to face the laws of the land here on earth and under the justice system in their local area. Research from a collection of projects known as the Spouse Assault Replication Program has shown that arresting the violent partner significantly reduced future victimization, independent of other criminal justice sanctions or individual factors (Maxwell, Garner, and Fagan, 2002). That would be the hope of all who seek justice and want healing. However, it is also a realistic possibility that justice is not meted out in the way victims and victim's families would desire. In such cases, it is especially important to seek the comfort of divine power, mercy, and grace in one's life. This also helps us to keep our disappointment from morphing into revenge, and to resist the temptation to act out in ways that will further damage our children, our life, and our future.

I cannot think of a more difficult circumstance in which to maintain one's faith than when dealing with the perversion that is domestic violence and abuse. How does one explain to innocent minds, reassure confused eyes, and comfort anguished hearts in the midst of domestic violence?

It takes the inner strength and determination of one's spirit to hang on to God in the midst of one's trial — to maintain a belief that this too shall pass and *a better day* will come. During times like these, music and song can combine to supply a salve of psychological and emotional love that helps heal the spiritually depressed soul.

One of my favorite songs seems especially appropriate when I think of the damage domestic violence and abuse does to those most vulnerable, and to all of us who have grown increasingly weary of the evil perpetrated on our troubled world. Regardless of what each of us must endure from day to day, every day we need to remind ourselves that each morning when we awake from sleep, it is a significant sign from God that He has a plan for our lives.

Each day has the potential to be *a better day* than the one before, especially as we hold on to Jesus, remain faithful, and continue to trust in His Word despite what appears to be overwhelming odds against us. When I feel that I have reached the end of my endurance, and I try to convince myself I cannot take another step, I focus on the lyrics of this song, written by Eleanor Wright, then genuinely hope for — and pray for — *a better day*!

A Better Day
A better day after while
There will be a better day, a better day
Ooh, child
There'll be a better day after while.

A better day after while
There will be a better day, a better day
Ooh, child
There'll be a better day after while.

I'm gonna trade all my troubles in
For a lifetime of smiles
I'll forget how hard it's been
To run these last few miles.

And when Jesus says to me,
"Welcome home, my child"
All the bitter heartache here
Will surely be worthwhile.

A better day after while
There'll be a better day, a better day
Ooh, child
There'll be a better day after while.

I'm gonna trade all my troubles in
For a lifetime of smiles
I'll forget how hard it's been
To run these last few miles

And when Jesus says to me,
"Welcome home, my child"
All the bitter heartache here
Will surely be worthwhile

A better day after while
There'll be a better day, a better day
Ooh, child
There'll be a better day after while.

I'm gonna ride on a rainbow road
Travel on the Milky Way
I'm gonna live in a home
Where I'll have no more rent to pay
No more snow and no more rain
One long, clear summer day
Lord, I pray for the coming of the day
When I can fly away. It's gonna to be a

Better day after while
There'll be a better day, a better day
Ooh, child
There'll be a better day after while.

NOTE: A myriad of agencies and/or organizations can help women and children experiencing abuse to find safety, create realistic plans to leave their abuser, and move toward lives of self-respect and higher functioning. Please review the Further Reading section in Appendix B for information specific to Domestic/Intimate Violence/Abuse.

Chapter 4

Relationship in Crisis (Part I): The Parent/Child Disconnect (The Early Years)

———————◇◦⟨⟩◦◇———————

"Fathers, do not make your children angry, but raise them with the training and teaching of the Lord" (Ephesians 6:4, NCV).

The Most Important Relationship of All

We have talked about the family relationship as a whole, and we have discussed the intimacies between father and mother. Now is a good time to focus on the relationship between parents and children. It may all begin with mom and dad, but once "little Johnny" or "little Suzy" come on the scene, things quickly change, as will the focus of the parents, and soon, the focus of the child.

Outside of the relationship between God and man, and husband and wife, the relationship between parent and child is utmost supreme. God Himself uses the parent/child metaphor as an example for us to gain some understanding of how He sees His relationship to His creation (Proverbs 3:11, 12). God has provided instruction to parents on how to raise their children to His glory: "Start children off on the way they should go, and even when they are old they will not turn from it" (Proverbs 22:6, NIV). We will come back for more of Solomon's wisdom offered to parents before this chapter ends, because parents prepare their offspring for the world ahead and the kingdom beyond.

In that sense, I cannot think of a more awesome responsibility than that of a parent! And today, the relationship between parents and children is under more strain and pressure than in years past.

Relationships between parents and children in the United States, and around the world, are complicated and show evidence of more stress and strain than years gone by. Evidence for this can be found in the news reports of dysfunction and trauma that pervade seemingly every media outlet.

The Impact of Trauma

In chapter two, we cited scientific research that identifies how childhood trauma impacts childhood development. Recall The Adverse Childhood Experiences (ACE) study conducted by the Center for Disease Control and Prevention and Kaiser Permanente (1998). It found almost two-thirds of study participants reported at least one adverse childhood experience of:

- Physical or sexual abuse
- Neglect
- Family dysfunction

More than one of five reported three or more of such experiences. You might recall from chapter three that an individual's experience of trauma impacts every area of human functioning:

- Physical
- Mental
- Behavioral
- Social
- Spiritual

Psychological trauma frequently triggers mental health and substance abuse problems. Experiencing adverse childhood experiences (ACE) (e.g. emotional/

physical neglect, one or no parents) is associated with increased risk for negative health and behavioral health outcomes in adulthood (e.g. depression, suicide, drug use).

Stress and Trauma at Home Impact Children's Behavior in the Community

Parental divorce is a major source of stress, especially for children. Rates of divorce have risen dramatically over the past half century in the United States, Canada, and northern Europe. Currently, close to half of children in many of these countries experience their parents' divorce by the time they reach middle childhood. In contrast, divorce remains rare in southern Europe and in non-Western countries (Arnett, 2012). Overall, children respond negatively to parents' divorce in a variety of ways, especially boys and especially in the first two years following divorce.

Children display increases in both *externalizing* problems (such as unruly behavior and conflict with mothers, siblings, peers, and teachers) and *internalizing* problems (such as depressed mood, anxieties, phobias, and sleep disturbances) (Amato, 2000; Clarke-Stewart & Brentano, 2006). If the divorce takes place during early childhood (ages 3-6), children often blame themselves, but by middle childhood most children are less *egocentric* (cognitive inability to distinguish between one's own perspective and another person's perspective) and more capable of understanding that their parents may have reasons for divorcing that have nothing to do with them (Hetherington and Kelly, 2002).

In one renowned longitudinal study of divorces that took place when children were in middle childhood (ages 6-12), the researches classified 25 percent of the children in divorced families as having severe emotional or behavioral problems, compared to 10 percent of children in two-parent nondivorced families (Hetherington & Kelly, 2002). The low point for most children came one year after divorce. After that point, most children gradually improved in functioning. By two years post-divorce, girls were mostly back to normal. However, boy's problems were still evident, even five years after divorce. Problems for some children continue into adolescence (Arnett, 2012).

Not all children react negatively to divorce. Even if 25 percent have severe problems, that leaves 75 percent who do not. Of the factors researchers have identified that influence how a divorce will affect children, *family process* (the quality of relationships between family members before, during, and after the divorce) has received increased focus. In all families, whether divorced or not, parental conflict is linked to children's emotional and behavioral problems (Kelly and Emery, 2003). When parents divorce with minimal conflict, or when parents are able to keep their conflicts private, children show far fewer problems (Amato, 2006). Clearly, regardless of the state of the parental union, parents need to focus on establishing and maintaining a healthy relationship with their children.

Unhealthy parent/child relationships have also had a negative impact on school systems, as demonstrated by the types of misbehavior children present in school. Check any local school system—urban, suburban, or rural—and you will find children, parents, and a system that do not always work in harmony. However, the level of trauma many children experience (and bring to school) goes far beyond the lack of harmony.

Schools were once a safe haven for children to acquire an education and learn how to socialize with peers and show respect for authority figures. Yet far too many schools today are battlegrounds for gangs, drug traffickers, and bullies. More and more, we read about children bringing weapons to school for protection because of fear for self, while others conspire to carry out some misguided plan of revenge against teachers and/or classmates they perceive to have wronged them in some way. It seems that our children have not acquired the skills of successful conflict resolution. Where do our children learn such maladaptive behaviors?

This is likely a direct result of what they have witnessed and experienced in their own homes. Not surprisingly, the things that go on inside the family home are what children bring to school. Look at it this way: The quality of parent's relationships with their children is being broadcast every time they leave your home and wander about in public!

Taking a closer look at the word, *relationship*, we see it has a much deeper meaning than merely describing interaction between two or more individuals. In trying to describe the ultimate positive relationship between parent and child, these phrases come to mind: "life source," "physical provider," "emotional glue," "self-esteem adjuster," and finally (my personal favorite), "continuous and consistent source of unconditional positive regard."

Heredity: Nature versus Nurture

Now we have a working definition for *relationship* to refer to as we go forward in our attempt to emphasize just how serious, powerful, and life-changing the parent/child relationship can be for them. How important? Well, to start, everything they are and are not, parents pass down to their children through the sometimes cruel (and not so comical) process of heredity.

What can be passed down? We have all heard people say: "She has her mother's eyes," or "He's a chip off the old block." These are common phrases that denote a child having physical and personality characteristics very similar to their biological parents. Most of us are just familiar enough with genetics to understand that features such as hair and eye color, height, certain personality traits, and more can be passed down from generation to generation. However, what about something as nebulous as *spirituality*?

Is it possible to pass on to our offspring a belief in God? Is it possible to inherit from our parents godly traits, spiritual convictions, and/or religious beliefs? Well, just as sure as parents can pass down many negative traits such as substance abuse, violence, racism, promiscuity (and others), they can also pass along to their children belief in a higher power, trust in a divine being, faith above and beyond the limitations of humanity, and other characteristics that help to form a strong spiritual foundation. This is especially true for children in the adolescent stage of development (see chapter 5, "Parent/Child Disconnect Part II: Adolescence").

A discussion that includes genetics and heredity automatically pulls in the age-old social science debate of *nature* versus *nurture* in which nature represents what is passed down from parent to child, and nurture representing how children are influenced by their environment (Plomin, 1990). Psychologists specializing in childhood development suggest that there is a critical period between birth and six years of age when children are most susceptible to learning and developing their personalities. Call this the *hardwiring phase*, if you will.

During this early development period, children are like sponges, absorbing anything and everything around them, both good and bad. This is the most crucial time for parent and child because the parent is seen by the child as all-knowing and all-powerful. Parents are the only "God" children know until the real God of the universe is introduced to them. Another way to look at this is that parents have more influence over the nurture part of the equation than they do the nature part. After all, we are what we are, and parents themselves are a product of their parents and so forth, and so on.

From the very time a child is received into this world, the learning for both parent and child begins in earnest. For some parents, the learning curve is steep. For others, access to parenting experience is all around them through older (sometimes wiser) relatives and/or friends who have raised children of their own. This lightens the load slightly. However, parenting remains a major challenge and mistakes and misunderstandings seem to grow as the child grows. However, for most, the joys of parenting far outweigh the negatives.

Parental joy often takes the form of pride, thankfulness for good health, an expectation of achievement for the child, and more, but mostly, the thrill and excitement of having created (with divine help) a miniature version of self.

As parents, we do not always think about or focus on the intricacies of childhood development and how our parental style and the environment around us (nurture) impact the biological, physiological, psychological, and emotional development (nature) of our little ones, as well as their behavior and spiritual outcomes. To be sure, the important *nature* versus *nurture* debate will continue for many more years because the human organism is such a complex system of creation. David realized this even back in his day and praised the Lord accordingly when he said that we are "fearfully and wonderfully made" (Psalm 139:14).

The "Joy" and "Pain" of Parenting

To better understand the complex relationship between parent and child, it is important to look first at our developmental foundation, review in more detail the relationship between childhood development and parental style, and explore how this interaction positively or negatively impacts the quality of the relationship (which develops with our children). Developmental psychologists divide childhood development into three domains: biosocial, cognitive, and psychosocial.

Biosocial development entails biological growth (i.e. brain, sense organs, bones, muscles, and more), motor skills (i.e. sexual development, how we use our bodies to move around, and more), and the effects of aging, such as changes in eyesight, muscular strength, agility, and more, but does not include physical changes that result from illness or accidents. As is the case with other forms of development, physical growth or maturation often spans across very long periods (Seifert and Hoffnung, 1997).

Cognitive development involves changes in reasoning and thinking, language acquisition, and the ways individuals receive, store, and recall knowledge of their environment. It includes what we commonly call "learning," but more than just the comparatively permanent changes in thinking, feeling, and behavior that result from relatively specific experiences or events. Often, learned changes occur over a short period of time, whereas many important cognitive developments take much longer to occur.

Psychosocial development concerns changes in feelings or emotions as well as changes in how individuals relate to other people. It includes relationships with family, peers, and teachers as well as an individual's personal identity or sense of self. Identity and social relationships tend to evolve simultaneously. This is important to keep in mind when exploring relationships between parent and child, child and peers, and child and significant others, including teachers and other authority figures. Each form of development appears to influence all the others. You can easily see how the three developmental domains interconnect in many ways throughout the life span.

With this surface understanding of childhood development, we can now bring into the mix the temperament of the child and parenting styles. These augment our exploration of how important and complex the relationship is between parent and child. Here is just a brief look at what researchers have discovered about temperamental styles of infants and young children.

Child Temperament versus Parenting Style

Child Temperament

Did you know that very young infants are sensitive to the positive and negative emotions of their caregivers, and quite capable of responding to adult fears and anxieties (Seifert and Hoffnung, 1997)?

These responses are likely based on cues similar to those adults use, such as slight variations in voice quality, smell, touch, and variations in facial expression and body language. As they get older, infants display these feelings with increasing frequency and predictability. In other words, your infant is capable of recognizing your positive and negative moods. As they get older they are more likely to respond in kind, based on what they have observed in you. Social scientists go on to tell us that infants have particular temperaments that are inherent at birth (nature), which are developed as they grow and mature (nurture). Temperament includes qualities such as activity level, irritability, soothability, emotional reactivity, and sociability. You can think of temperament as the biologically based raw material of personality (Goldsmith 2009; Rothbart et al, 2000). Researchers on temperament believe that all infants are born with certain tendencies toward behavior and personality development, and the environment then shapes those tendencies in the course of development (Arnett, 2012).

In most cases, the degree to which an infant's early temperament style contributes to personality development is likely influenced by the reactions the child evokes from parents and other caregivers. Also significant is how well the child's temperament style fit with the attitudes, expectations, and responses of the parents. For example, the fit between an infant who is very active and demanding with parents who expect this of their child is likely to be much better than that between a similar baby and parents who expect their child to be more passive and less demanding (Rickman and Davidson, 1995; Thomas and Chess, 1977, 1984).

Infant-family fit can also influence the degree to which infant temperament remains constant or changes. Thomas and Chess (1977) proposed the concept of *goodness-of-fit*, meaning that children develop best if there is a food fit between the temperament of the child and environmental demands. In their view, difficult and slow-to-warm-up babies need parents who are aware of their temperaments and willing to be especially patient and nurturing. Subsequent studies provided support for the idea of goodness-of-fit, finding that babies with negative temperamental qualities were able to learn to control their emotional reactions better by age three if their parents were understanding and tolerant (Warren & Simmens, 2005). Other research has shown that babies who are low in emotional reactivity respond more favorably to face-to-face interaction with a parent than babies who are high in emotional reactivity (Jahromi et al., 2004). Conversely, parents who respond to an infant's difficult temperament with anger and frustration are likely to find that the infant becomes a child who is defiant and disobedient, leading to further conflict and frustration for both parents and children (Calkins, 2002).

Another factor that influences the various temperamental styles of children is the particular culture in which they are raised. Various temperamental styles can be assigned different meanings and be responded to differently, depending on the culture of parent and child. However, regardless of culture, researchers found that temperamental differences may be as much a product of the mother's behavior as the infant's (Prior et al., 1987).

So, what can we conclude from the research on childhood development and temperament of infants? Infant temperament is certainly an important influence on early social and emotional development. In most cases, however, a child's temperament is best understood as a product of the ongoing interactions among an infant's inherited temperament predispositions, the responses of his or her parents and other caregivers, and the overall developmental environment. In other words, the connection between parent and child is the most important ingredient to determine the quality of the parent/child relationship.

Remember, we are talking about the *parent/child disconnect*. For many families the disconnect between parent and child occurs early in the life of the child. This is a good place to quickly review what researchers have observed about parenting styles and just how early it influences the relationship between parent and child.

Parenting Style

Have you heard the joke about the man who, before he had children, had five theories about how they should be raised? Ten years later he had five children and no theories. Jokes, aside, most parents do have ideas about how best to raise children, even after they have had children for a while (Tamis-Lamonda et al, 2008). In research the investigation of this topic has involved the study of *parenting* styles, that is, the practices that parents exhibit in relation to their children and their beliefs about those practices. Virtually all of the prominent scholars who have studied parenting have described it in terms of two dimensions: demandingness and responsiveness (also known by other terms such as *control* and *warmth*). Parental *demandingness* is the degree to which parents set down rules and expectations for behavior and require their children to comply with them. Parental *responsiveness* is the degree to which parents are sensitive to their children's needs and express love, warmth, and concern for them. Building on research by Diana Baumrind, 1971; researchers have identified four distinct parenting styles:

Authoritative, Authoritarian, Permissive, and Disengaged parenting styles (Collins & Laursen, 2004; Maccoby and Martin, 1983; Steinberg, 2001).

Authoritative parents are high in demandingness and responsiveness. They exert a high degree of control over their children and demand a lot from them, but they are also responsive, child-centered, and respectful of their children's thoughts, feelings, and participation in decision making. For example, instead of making it easier by responding to a child's request to help them get dressed by doing it for them, an authoritative parent is likely to provide just enough help to enable the child to successfully accomplish the task for himself. Such parents tend to be more democratic and rational in their decision making and respond to their children with warmth, empathy, and support.

When their children misbehave, authoritative parents attempt to understand why and to explain the reasons for the discipline that follows. Preschoolers of authoritative parents tend to be self-reliant, self-controlled, and able to get along well with other children. Authoritative parenting is also associated with high self-esteem, internalized moral standards, psychosocial maturity, autonomy, and academic success.

In addition, authoritative parenting appears to promote relationships with peers and family that show the same qualities of warmth and respect for others during middle childhood, adolescence, and beyond. Children can be taught to be warm and engaging. They can be taught to be honest and respectful. They can be taught to be positive influences in their schools, churches, and communities.

Authoritarian parents are also demanding of their children and exert high control over them. However, they tend to be less warm and responsive than authoritative parents. Authoritarian parents also tend to be arbitrary and not so democratic in decision-making. They tend to impose their rules or views on their children based on their own greater power and authority, with little sensitivity to their children's thoughts and feelings. Parent-child relationships that depend on arbitrary, "power-assertive" control and ignore children's thoughts, emotions, and need for independence often have a negative effect on children. Children of authoritarian parents tend to be relatively distrustful of others and unhappy with themselves. They tend to have poorer peer relations, inferior school adjustment, and lower school achievement than children with authoritative parents.

It is important to note that in the extreme, the combination of rigid and arbitrary power assertion and insensitivity to a child's thoughts and feelings can increase the likelihood of child maltreatment. And, by modeling disrespectful and insensitive behavior, such parenting can draw out and reinforce similar behavior in children and lead to escalating cycles of negative reinforcement and coercion. In other words; children can be taught to be bullies. They can be taught to be violent. They can also be taught to be victims by learning to allow others to trample on their dignity and self-respect!

Permissive parents are low in demandingness and high in responsiveness. They are warm, sensitive, caring, and generally responsive to their children's thoughts and feelings. However, they exert low levels of control and make relatively few demands, permitting their children to make almost all of their own decisions. While they clearly communicate their warmth, love, and caring, their communication tends to be less clear in situations requiring that they set limits on their children's behavior.

These are the parents who find it difficult to be "the bad guy" or "the most uncool person alive" when the time comes to discipline their child, trying instead to be their child's "best friend." What is needed in such cases is responsible parenting. Children with permissive parents tend to lack self-reliance and self-control and to have lower self-esteem as they enter adolescence. Children can be taught how to be spoiled. They can be taught to feel entitled in response to the rest of the world. They can be taught to be lazy and avoid responsibility for their actions.

Finally, *disengaged* parents are low in both demandingness and responsiveness. They are detached and emotionally uninvolved. They are inconsistent in setting and maintaining age-appropriate standards and expectations with their children and in fulfilling their parental responsibilities. Disengaged parents seem to be emotionally detached and to not care what their children do. These parents send a message to their children that what they do, where they go, and with whom they keep company are not important to the parent.

Children with this type of parent also tend to lack self-reliance and self-control, and have lower self-esteem. These children tend to have varying degrees of developmental difficulties, including a low ability to tolerate frustration and to control their impulsive and aggressive behavior. They also tend to have difficulty in making life choices and setting long-term goals. At the extreme, disengaged parents neglect their children's physical and emotional needs, leaving them with more serious developmental and emotional problems associated with child abuse and neglect.

Children can be taught that they are not important. They can be taught that love, kindness, and emotional safety do not exist for them. They can be taught that their feelings do not matter.

Impact Above and Beyond "Style"

Not surprisingly, most parents do not fit neatly into any one category. Most show mixtures of all four parenting styles. Even the best parents ignore their child's misbehavior at one time or another. Parents can sometimes become numb and blind to the chaos or noise a child creates in the grocery store or while sitting in the back seat of a car. And even the most patient, loving, and compassionate parents justify themselves on the basis of absolute power from time to time; like when they hear their little one ask the question "Why?" for the hundredth time. Such parents may simply respond, "Because I said so!"

In addition, the situation in which families live may influence the effectiveness of a particular parenting style. For example, the clear-cut expectations and no-nonsense standards of behavior associated with authoritarian parenting may offer certain advantages to families living in drug infested, high crime, violent neighborhoods, where even the smallest error can lead to tragedy.

Parenting styles also tend to change over time. For example, authoritarian parents often relax a bit and shift to a more permissive or authoritative style as their children grow older. Changes in family dynamics, such as the birth of another child, can also make a difference. Because of the experience gained from raising their first child, parents frequently are more comfortable and flexible in raising the children who follow. On the other hand, more children usually means more economic responsibility, so more relaxed parenting is not always the outcome.

Other changes in the family situation, such as employment, standard of living, and health may also influence child rearing. Families that are under stress tend to be more rigid, arbitrary, and authoritarian in raising their children than families under not as much stress. In addition, because they lack confidence and competence in clearly setting or negotiating limits, permissive parents may find it more difficult to shift to being authoritative and democratic than authoritarian parents who must, in turn, ease up on their one-sided limit setting and learn to be more democratic.

Moreover, the parenting style and disciplinary method practiced by a parent may be influenced by the particular actions of the child. For example, one study on how mothers responded to their children's misbehavior found that the type of discipline the parents chose was determined more by what the child did than by a general child rearing style (Grusec and Kucynski, 1980). Threats of punishment were widely used for most misdeeds, but reasoning and discussion were frequently used when the child's actions caused psychological harm to others. Ultimately, it is the parents' responsibility to establish the sort of parent-child relationship that fosters the developmental goals they value for their children.

Maintain Your Sense of Humor

The key thing for parents to remember is that their child is totally and completely dependent upon them for all things in life. Of course, God handles the essential things that we don't even have to think about, such as making sure the intricacies of involuntary movement are on schedule (i.e. waking up each day, breathing, heartbeat, and more), and He provides the means to make it from sunrise to sunset.

However, it is the parents whom God allows to partner with Him to provide the basic necessities (i.e. food, clothing, and shelter). He expects them to provide teaching, care, nurture, and most importantly, a godly example of love in the home.

Even when parents adhere to Solomon's admonition to "train a child in the way he should go," it does not mean that children from Christian homes (or children raised in any religious background, for that matter) will be perfect and not find ways to get into trouble throughout their development. Children will present challenges to even the most prepared parents, often bringing disappointment, sometimes sorrow, and far too often these days—pain! However, this is half the fun of parenting, right? Seriously, I believe that the vast majority of parents want what is best for their children. Most parents do the very best they know to do at any given moment. And still, children seem to have an uncanny ability to render parents frustrated, sometimes angry, and oftentimes talking to themselves during fits of self-questioning heard through moans of, "Where did we go wrong?"

In the end, what's most important is that children feel loved. Regardless of the child's personality, and/or the personality of the parent, it is the parents' responsibility to recognize the strengths and unique gifts of their offspring. After all, it is the adult that is most mature (usually) and has the greatest ability (cognitively, emotionally, and spiritually) to identify challenges and make adjustments. It sounds simple enough, but anyone who has ever been a parent knows it's anything but. That's where utilizing God's gifts to parents, through his Word, can really make the difference. We owe it to our children to pass on the absolute best we possibly can! God will take our best and add what is needed for our children. Parenting is hard work! Trust and obey. Maintain your sense of humor!

Chapter 5

Relationship in Crisis (Part II): Parent/ Child Disconnect Part II (Adolescence)

———◇◦⟨⟨⟩⟩◦◇———

"Start children off on the way they should go, and even when they are old they will not turn from it" (Proverbs 22:6, NIV).

Adolescence: A Time of Growth and Challenge

*T*eenagers seem to provide the most complex challenges for parents from any culture, race, ethnicity, or religious background. Besides the obvious physical and emotional changes brought on by the onslaught of hormones and puberty, adolescence is a developmental phase of striving for self-identity, self-expression, and increasing independence. Not surprisingly, the agenda of the adolescent is often in direct conflict with that of the parent. The sweet little boy or girl you remember at age six through ten may be slightly unrecognizable by age twelve through eighteen.

Parents may find themselves involved in more and more heated discussions with their teenagers than they ever bargained for, while simultaneously discovering just how "uncool" they have become in a very short period of time! This is not a coincidence. However, just as every single toddler does not necessarily go through the "terrible twos", neither does every adolescent automatically change into an unappreciative financial liability, dressed as an argument waiting to happen.

Numerous studies have shown that adolescents and their parents agree on many of their beliefs and values, and typically they have a great deal of love and respect for one another (Moore et al., 2002; Smetana, 2005). Nevertheless, studies in Western countries also indicate that conflict with parents increases sharply in early adolescence, compared with middle childhood, and remains high for several years before declining in late adolescence (Dworkin & Larson, 2001; Laursen et al., 1998; Shanahan et al., 2007). Conflict in adolescence is especially frequent and intense between mothers and daughters (Collins & Laursen, 2004). Both parents and adolescents report more frequent conflict in early adolescence than prior to adolescence. By mid-adolescence, conflict with parents tends to become somewhat less frequent but more intense before declining substantially in late adolescence (Laursen et al., 1998). When we look at social and cultural contexts for adolescence, what we see are natural developmental patterns that are relatively predictable. However, individual differences make the interaction with your own teenager a unique learning experience. (Who said God had no sense of humor?) Watching parents raise teenagers is proof that God enjoys a good laugh from time to time!

So, getting back to the sweet little boy or girl we might remember from the elementary school years, we might ask ourselves: What happened? Well, lifespan psychologists tell us that as children grow older and become more independent (i.e. spend more and more time outside of the home, and out of sight/supervision of parents), they are less and less influenced by parents, while becoming more and more influenced by peers. Somewhere between sixth and seventh grade (middle school age) teenagers begin to care more about what peers think and feel than what parents think and feel (Arnett, 2012). This is not to say that parents lose all control of their teens at a particular age or school grade.

Parental influence is still very strong in some of the most crucial areas: morality, religious affiliation, familial mores, and more. However, peer influence seems to become stronger in areas such as choices of clothing/hair style, music (i.e. self-identity/self-expression), and pleasure/leisure activities. Recognizing this (and remembering it at key times) should help keep parents from pushing the panic button every time their teenager comes home with a new (hideous) haircut or outfit, while listening to music the parent cannot identify as such. Parents, if hairstyle, clothing, music, and the fact that your teenager does not want to be seen with you in public are your biggest concerns—yet they are still attending school regularly, doing well, and do not come home smelling of alcohol, spaced out from drugs, or pregnant—relax! It is likely that they are simply expressing their identity and striving for independence.

On the other hand, it is important for parents to be well aware of those whom your child calls "friends," and what they do when they are away from your supervision. I believe the two biggest mistakes parents make are: not maintaining consistent communication with their children, and not providing reasonable supervision of them. As a parent, we have every right to know where our child is going, who they are with, and the activities in which they are involved. Parents need to be aware of what their children are doing inside the home as well.

No room is off limits where you are paying the bills! No personal effects are so private that they must be hidden from parent's eyes when parent and child are on the same page. This does not mean that parents should assume the role of law enforcement or private investigator. What it does mean is that the parent is not a peer, and hence, has a higher calling than being their child's friend or buddy. This means parents must be the "bad guy" more often than many care to be, or as previously mentioned, parents must listen to the repeated mantra of just how "uncool" they are.

Being totally uncool or the bad guy is a small price to pay to ensure that your teenager is supervised appropriately. Being a parent often means being unpopular with the teenager you love. This too shall pass.

Disconnection Often Results in Negative Outcomes

Making sure the home is safe from outside influences (i.e. people and things, and more) is another major part of providing parental supervision. Often there are younger children in the home along with teenagers, so it is imperative that parents see the big picture and not just relent to a pleading adolescent to relax their household standards, or allow children to be "in charge" when they are not developmentally prepared to do so. Parents must provide a safe and secure atmosphere in their home so that children are encouraged to come to them for any reason without fear of verbal or physical abuse. Naturally, this requires that open communication, along with a clear understanding, be established long before children reach the age of adolescence or even elementary school age.

When parents relax loving, well-thought-out discipline at the whim of a child, or never establish consistent communication and reasonable boundaries and expectations for children during early development, it becomes very difficult to try and pull the reigns in during the adolescent phase. In fact, it is unrealistic and predictably results in negative outcomes for parent and child. Teenagers without proper, consistent supervision and guidance are prone to make several mishaps in judgment. Unfortunately, many times these poor choices end up changing a young person's life forever, and rarely in a positive direction. Some of the most glaring examples of this today are the ever-growing problems of drug and alcohol abuse, truancy, and teenage pregnancy.

Regarding teenage pregnancy specifically; when children are allowed to take on adult roles or participate in adult behavior before being developmentally prepared to do so, it places both the child and parent in a confused state of role reversal. This is not healthy for parent or child. When children are not provided with consistent supervision, discipline mixed with an abundance of love, and encouragement to take their time and develop according to God's plan, the results can be quite undesirable. It can put children in danger of losing out on a wonderful childhood, and leave them ill-suited for the awesome and unrelenting responsibilities of adulthood. "Children raising children" (as the familiar phrase goes) is dreadful for everyone involved. When we see what is at stake, the relationship between parent and child becomes even more crucial.

Child development experts (i.e. Piaget, Erickson, Kohlberg, and others) theorized that a new "critical period" occurs during adolescent growth; one that is not only physical and emotional, but also moral and spiritual. It is during this phase of development that the young person has one foot still in childhood while the other foot is rushing to get to young adulthood (i.e. visualize one leg firmly on a dock and the other leg tentatively on a raft heading out to sea; the result is instability—a "split" in feelings, self-concept, competence, and more).

It is during this new critical period that teenagers become overwhelmed by a myriad of strong feelings and emotions, seemingly pushing and pulling them in all sorts of directions. This sense of confusion and instability from within acts as a catalyst, driving the behaviors witnessed without. Besides feeling split due to hormonal changes and peer pressure, teens also feel pressure from within their own homes. It is sometimes difficult to find "one's own voice" while simultaneously trying to live up to all that mom and dad expect and/or demand. So, not surprisingly, teens often scream to the mountaintops: "No one understands me!" There may actually be some truth to this belief; at least in the sense of *how* the teen would like to be understood.

From a parental point of view, it is probably more accurate to say that parents do not always understand the choices their teens make, or the mind-set that went into making those choices. Whether looking at life's situations through the eyes of a teen or parent, the truth, like most things, lies somewhere in between. Hence the importance of developing a mutually comfortable communication style between parent and child that begins in early childhood and lasts throughout adolescence, into young adulthood and beyond.

Following God's Plan of "Connection" with Your Children

Parents have an enormous and often daunting responsibility. They must enhance their children's critical thinking skills and provide them reliable "survival" tools to successfully work through life's many obstacles and temptations. Parents must help their children develop a sense of spirituality that can act as a buffer (protective factor) against peer pressures in the world and encourage maintenance of respect for self and others.

Repeating our questions from chapter 4 ("Parent/Child Disconnect Part I: The Early Years"); "Is it possible to pass on to our offspring a belief in God? Is it possible to inherit from our parents godly traits, spiritual convictions, and/or religious beliefs?" Research on adolescents and religious beliefs suggests the answer is a resounding "Yes!"

Like moral development (see Kohlberg, 1958; 1976; 1986), the development of religious beliefs reaches a critical point in adolescence, because adolescence is a time when abstract ideas involved in religious beliefs can first be fully grasped (Arnett, 2012). In general, adolescents and emerging adults in developed countries (the most affluent countries in the world) are less religious than their counterparts in developing countries (have less wealth than developed countries but are experiencing rapid economic growth as they join the globalized economy) (Arnett, 2012). Developed countries tend to be highly *secular* (based on nonreligious beliefs and values). In every developed country, religion has gradually faded in its influence over the past two centuries (Bellah et al, 1985). Religious beliefs and practices are especially low among adolescents in Europe. For example, in Belgium only 8 percent of eighteen-year-olds attend religious services at least once a month (Goosens & Luyckx, 2007). In Spain, only 18 percent of adolescents attend church regularly (Gibbons & Stiles, 2004). Americans are more religious than people in virtually any other developed country, and this is reflected in the lives of American adolescents (Smith & Denton, 2005). For example:

Religious Beliefs of American Adolescents (Smith & Denton, 2005)

Belief in God or a universal spirit	84%
Pray at least once a week	65%
Religion important in daily life	51%
Believe in the existence of angels	63%
Attend religious services at least twice a month	52%
Involved in church youth group	38%

However, religion has a lower priority for most American teenagers than many other parts of their lives, including school, friendships, media, and work. Furthermore, the religious beliefs of American adolescents tend not to follow traditional doctrines, and they often know little about the doctrine of the religion they claim to follow. Instead, they tend to believe that religious faith is about how to be a good person and feel happy (Arnett, 2012).

Many American adolescents are religious, but many others are not. So, what explains differences among adolescents and their religiosity? According to Smith & Denton (2005), family characteristics are one important influence. Adolescents are likely to embrace the importance of religion when their parents talk about religious issues and participate in religious activities (King et al., 2002; Layton et al., 2011). Adolescents are less likely to be religious when their parents disagree with each other about religious beliefs, and when their parents are divorced (Smith & Denton, 2005). Ethnicity is another factor. In American society ,religious faith and religious practices tend to be stronger among African-Americans than among Whites (Chatters et al., 2008).

The relatively high rate of religiosity among African-American adolescents helps explain why they have such low rates of alcohol and drug use (Stevens-Watkins et al., 2010). However, it is not only among minority adolescent groups that religiosity is associated with favorable outcomes. Across American cultural groups, adolescents who are more religious report less depression and lower rates of premarital sex, drug use, and delinquent behavior (Kerestes et al., 2004; Smith and Denton, 2005). The protective value of religious involvement is especially strong for adolescents living in the worst neighborhoods (Bridges and Moore, 2002). Religious adolescents tend to have better relationships with their parents (Smith and Denton, 2005; Wilcox, 2008). Also, adolescents who value religion are more likely than other adolescents to perform volunteer services to their community (Hart and Atkins, 2004). In other cultures too, religious involvement has been found to be related to a variety of positive outcomes, for example, among Indonesian Muslim adolescents (French et al., 2008).

It is essential then, that parents introduce to their children a belief system that embraces the true fact that there is a divine being that created not only them but also the world as they know it, as well as the entire universe. In addition, this God of the universe sees them as very special individuals, uniquely gifted, with a talent bestowed upon them by Him for the express purpose of being an example to draw others to Christ.

I believe that when children are taught that they are extra special to God, they want to live up to godly expectations. Again, this does not mean that our children will not make mistakes or take painful detours from the spiritual road we envisioned for them. It means that our children are given a goal and a guide from their earliest memory, and the natural phenomenon of reciprocity will motivate them to return to God the love they receive from Him. However, children must first feel that love from their parents before believing there is a God who loves them even more.

As with everything God designs, He does not leave parents hanging out there without a sure means to carry out His will. In the Bible, God has provided parents with instructions on how to pass spirituality down to their offspring. Deuteronomy 4:9 and 6:5-7, and Ephesians 6:4 talk about what is expected of a good parent. The underlining theme in these texts is that parents should teach their children and nurture them by providing what is good for them. This suggests more than just providing children their basic physiological needs, such as food, clothing, and shelter. The key element is to teach children Christian beliefs so that as they develop through the critical periods of life, they come to know Jesus as a personal friend and Savior.

Parents create the spiritual foundation for their children to use as a springboard in developing a more sound and sophisticated spiritual connection with the divine Creator. Just as the children of Israel repeated to their children the wonderful miracles of God, we are to pass down to our children the stories of God's blessings, His mercy, and His grace. By never forgetting how the Lord has blessed you and your family (even in the midst of trial and struggle), parents keep alive for their children the reality of the true and Living God. This becomes especially important as children grow into adolescents and mature into young adults.

This chapter comes down to three messages:

Children

My message to children is this: Jesus wants to comfort you and keep you! He wants you to know, understand, and believe that you are His child! In Matthew 18:2-5 (GW), it is clear how the Savior of the world feels about children:

He called a little child and had him stand among them.
Then he said to them, "I can guarantee this truth: Unless you change and
become like little children, you will never enter the kingdom
of heaven. Whoever becomes like this child
is the greatest in the kingdom of heaven. And whoever welcomes
a child like this in my name welcomes me." (GW)

Jesus was speaking to a group of adults (disciples) who were arguing over which one of them would be the greatest in heaven. Jesus made it plain that adults must adopt the attitude (humility) and mind-set (complete trust in God) of children, or they would not make it into heaven. You are that important to Jesus!

Teenagers

My message to teenagers is this: Parents have the responsibility to love you and raise you to love and respect God, as well as love your neighbor as you love yourself. They do this in part by teaching you to honor and respect authority figures, beginning at home with your parents. Your parents also want you to be kind to siblings and others outside the home. They want you to work hard in school and prepare for a life independent of them. Parents want you to be presentable to the outside world. They want you to make wise decisions so that your future remains bright. Proverbs 10:1 says, "A wise son brings joy to his father, but a foolish son brings grief to his mother" (NIV). Solomon says this in a different way in Proverbs 15:20: "A wise son brings joy to his father, but a foolish man despises his mother (NIV).

No child sets out to be foolish or to be an emotional burden to his/her parents. Bringing joy to your parents is one way to demonstrate your love and respect for them. It is not unusual for teenagers and parents to disagree or have differing points of view. However, disrespecting your parents is not only a poor solution to whatever conflicts you may have, but it also goes directly against God's instructions. Consider the fifth commandment: "Honor your father and your mother" (Exodus 20:12, NIV). The apostle Paul tells us this commandment is: "the first commandment with a promise—'so that it may go well with you and that you may enjoy long life on the earth'" (Ephesians 6:2-3, NIV). God is saying that when you pay proper respect to your parents He will extend your life and you will prosper.

Remember that your parents were once teenagers as well. They know and understand more about life than you give them credit. Godly parents want what is best for you. If your parents are not godly, it is still not okay to disrespect them, dishonor them, or abuse them. "Listen to your father, who gave you life, and do not despise your mother when she is old" (Proverbs 23:22, NIV). "The father of a righteous man has great joy; he who has a wise son delights in him." May your father and mother rejoice; may she who gave you birth be joyful" (Proverbs 23:25, NIV).

It is never okay to hate your parents and/or do evil against them. If parents do evil to their children, God will repay . This is way worse than anything you can do to them. Matthew 18:6 says: "If anyone causes one of these little ones—who believe in me—to stumble, it would be better for them to have a large millstone hung around their neck and to be drowned in the depths of the sea" (NIV). God is very serious about the consequences of hurting one of His children. So leave vengeance to the Lord, maintain your self-respect, and God promises to extend your life.

Young people, adults do understand that what you are going through is often complicated—not at all easy. Some may even acknowledge that your path is cluttered with many more obstacles and potential negative outcomes than they faced in their youth. Regardless of what is going on around you, never give up on your dreams or lose sight of your goals. Focusing on getting a good education should be your main priority. Acquiring a good education can open up the doors to your dreams.

Also, do not fall into the trap of blaming all things wrong in your life on your parents and/or authority figures. Some things are obvious, of course, but you must also take responsibility for your own behavior and your own decisions. Being responsible and accountable is just one aspect of truly being a mature adult. Unfortunately, you may need to find a way to rise above your home environment. It is possible. You must be stronger than your situation. You can do it! You must believe that God has got your back. Trust in His Word! Never give up!

Parents

Finally, I want parents to realize that their responsibility is much more than providing food, clothing, and shelter. You are to be a steady and consistent guide for your children to ensure they learn how to make appropriate decisions and common sense choices. Parents are to be a ready example of God's character toward those He loves. Parents should be a constant source of encouragement to their children. Colossians 3:21 states, "Fathers, do not embitter your children, or they will become discouraged" (NIV). Ephesians 6:4, says it a little differently: "And, ye fathers, provoke not your children to wrath [anger]: but bring them up in the nurture and admonition [instruction] of the Lord" (KJV). (brackets added)

Notice how the word *nurture* is being used in the text. Unlike *nature*, which is at the mercy of genetic predispositions, it is well within the control of a parent to *nurture* their children, leading them toward Jesus Christ. Taken together, these two texts say a lot about what God expects of parents. Children must be obedient to parents, for sure, but parents are not to be physical or psychological bullies toward their children either! So, when your beautifully created children are on the verge of driving you completely over the edge, hold on and do not give up! Even if you feel like you are losing the battle in your own home, never give up on a troubled child. God can (and has) worked miracles with troubled youth!

Parents, you are well aware of the many challenges for children that impact their concept of spirituality. During times of doubt and discouragement you need to remind yourself that Solomon was considered the wisest man on earth for a reason. It is evident that he had problems with his own children, or he would not have known to write such good advice for us to use today. Notice Solomon did not write of children: "and when he is old he will have lived a perfect life." Nor did he write, "She will not make bad decisions." What Solomon is telling parents is that if you do what God instructed you to do (follow the biblical blueprint) and teach your children about Him, He will make sure that they never forget it. This is the assurance God provides for parents who want to pass down positive spirituality and Christian beliefs to their offspring.

Parents, I encourage you to stay connected with your children by putting forth the maximum effort to develop strong, honest, and respectful relationships with them. You do your part and God will keep His promise.

"A luta continua, Vitoria e certa" ("The Struggle continues, victory is certain")

Part II

Spiritual Depression in the Church

———————⊹∘⟨≈⟩∘⊹———————

he question begs: What are faith-based institutions doing for spiritually depressed families and individuals in our communities? How are faith-based organizations dealing with our youth and the myriad of challenges that go along with being a teenager in today's society? Also, what can you say to church members who are doing all they can to survive while experiencing spiritual depression, even though they are serving the Lord to the best of their ability? These are the questions we will explore and hope to answer in the next two chapters.

It is important to note that our focus in these chapters refers to Western culture religious organizations in general, and is not specific to any particular doctrine or church dogma. As you no doubt have gathered from the first five chapters, I am a Christian psychologist, so naturally my perspectives will lean heavily toward that belief system, which includes a wide range of religious organizations and a vast variety of worship styles and customs. Any references or examples that sound exactly like your church family or come too close to home are purely coincidental and not intended to offend, belittle, or point the finger. We are all part of the body of Christ, therefore, it behooves us to take an honest look at ourselves as we strive to live Christ-like lives and spread the "good news" of Jesus, our Lord and Savior.

Chapter 6

Spiritual Depression in the Church (Part I)

—◦⟨⟨◦⟩⟩◦—

". . . so that there should be no division in the body, but that its parts should have equal concern for each other" (1 Corinthians 12:25, NIV).

What Do You Want/Need From Your Church?

The family forms the foundation of our religious institutions, providing the key to spreading a message of the two great commandments: "love the Lord your God" and "love your neighbor as yourself" (Matthew 22:37-40, NIV). I have been fortunate over my life span to have had the opportunity to visit a variety of church denominations and worship with godly men and women from many diverse backgrounds. I have discovered over the years that people are essentially the same when it comes to what they want and need from their church and spiritual leaders. People want to be loved and respected, supported in good times as well as difficult ones, treated like valuable members of the church family, and fed spiritually while being encouraged to contribute their gifts and talents to the church. These are just the basics people want and what a faith-based organization should offer and provide to their membership.

If a church organization and its leaders can provide opportunities and encourage spiritual growth, people will feel spiritually *nurtured* and will love that church.

They will support the spiritual leader and his or her programs and demonstrate loyalty to that church for as long as they live in or close to the neighborhood where the church is located. Some will even travel long distances and maintain their connection with a specific church family where they are most comfortable, to continue their spiritual growth. Also, because people are living with a myriad of challenges and concerns (many of which can be directly attributed to a history of trauma) a church must be sensitive to the overall needs of its membership (and the surrounding community) beyond just what happens on the day set aside for worship. In psychology and other health-oriented professions, we often focus on *trauma-informed care* and *continuity of care* to support individuals in recovery. Today's faith-based communities need to adopt a similar approach by embracing education/training on how to become a "trauma-informed congregation" and develop strategies on how to provide "continuity of spiritual care" for community members. At the minimum, faith-based organizations need to recognize the impact of trauma in their members and for people in their surrounding communities. Too often, well-intentioned (though uninformed) faith leaders and/or faith community members say or do things that have a negative impact on individuals recovering from trauma histories. For example: attributing an individual's behavioral health challenges to a "lack of faith." They question the "prayer life" or "connection with God" of traumatized individuals, which is tantamount to blaming them for their struggles. Not surprisingly, this unintentional "blaming" of the person in recovery often results in their feeling guilt and shame. Faith communities that embrace instruction/training on becoming trauma-informed can substantially reduce or entirely eliminate words and actions that too often hurt instead of heal. For more extensive information on becoming a trauma-informed congregation, please review the resource section in Appendix D.

The church should also develop strategies to provide *continuous spiritual care* to meet the complex needs of its congregation. If a church cannot or does not provide the very basics for people, they will either go elsewhere looking for spiritual connection and satisfaction, wither and die on the "spiritual vine" and leave the church altogether, or they will remain at that church and complain, become bitter, and make life at that church miserable for all who dare cross their unhappy path.

The Church as a "Spiritual Hospital"

Needless to say, very few churches can keep all the people happy all the time. Just as in individual families, there is conflict, confrontation, and sometimes a little in-fighting in church organizations, regardless of how much effort leaders, officers, or administrators expend trying to create a "stress-free," spiritually healthy and vibrant environment. Also, as shown in previous chapters on family, the church is made up of all types and varieties of individuals and families, each with their own idiosyncratic natures, needs, and yes, their own number of personal and spiritual issues! The fact is, the church provides the perfect soil for "the evil one" to plant seeds of discontentment and discouragement, resulting in an outgrowth of spiritual depression throughout the congregation, and on all levels of church leadership.

You might think that ministers, church administrators, and church members are immune from developing symptoms of spiritual depression. After all, churches were originally set up expressly for like believers to come together and worship God in a supportive environment where the Lord of the universe might dwell: "For where two or three gather in my name, there am I with them" (Matthew 18:20, NIV). On the contrary! Churches are the perfect breeding ground for spiritual depression precisely because of the variety of people who gather there, carrying a diversity of individual and family baggage into these melting pots of human nature.

Just as hospitals, clinics, and community mental health centers are set up to serve people and treat both physical ailments and mental/behavioral health challenges, God's church was designed to serve all those who enter. The church is set up to treat spiritual challenges and provide a comforting, supportive, and safe environment to soothe and heal the emotional and spiritual wounds caused by pain and suffering that infect the heart and soul.

How Does Spiritual Depression "Enter" the Church Body?

How does spiritual depression manifest itself within churches?

It is important to remember that church members of any faith are a unique lot. They come together, usually weekly (sometimes a couple times a week), to offer praise to a higher (divine) power for providing blessings like food, clothing, shelter, jobs, good health, and more. They make prayer requests concerning problems, unmet needs, and desires perceived to be most necessary. With this shared agenda that appears to be simple, cohesive, and godly, how is it that so many churches leave parishioners wanting more—needing more? Why do so many create environments that are not spiritually healthy?

The answer should be obvious on one level: Churches are made up of many "spiritually ill" people and families that have been traumatized by life's trials and tribulations. Moreover, parishioners have achieved different levels on their spiritual climb to be Christ-like. Because the church is made up of a variety of people with a wide range of personal issues, it should surprise no one that all manner of physical, emotional, psychological, and spiritual challenges accompany God's people as well: "For you have spent enough time in the past doing what pagans choose to do—living in debauchery, lust, drunkenness, orgies, carousing and detestable idolatry" (1 Peter 4:3, NIV).

Peter rightly points out that everything folks are doing "out in the world," God's people have also done, or continue to do, even as they walk on their Christian journey.

Those in the church who have managed, through God's grace, to put those old, unhealthy habits aside and allow God to turn them around must still deal with the friends and family they may have had to "cut loose" as they determined to serve the Lord: "They are surprised that you do not join them in their reckless, wild living, and they heap abuse on you" (1 Peter 4:4, NIV).

We have those in the church who are still struggling with all manner of challenges. These challenges followed them into the church. We have those church members who have been able to "conquer" a lot of the more "visible" (obvious) challenges, and likely feel pretty good about themselves and their walk with God. Then, of course, we have those in the middle of the road, not blatantly "sinning" all over the place in ways others can easily see (and report to the pastor), but at the same time, they are not doing so well in their Christian walk that they are ready to sprout wings and fly off to glory.

Oil and Water

We have identified an average collection of church members who are at three different levels of spiritual growth experience within the church: beginners, intermediates, and advanced. (Remember, it takes highs and lows added together to create an "average.") Think about how this combination of "saints" might end up mixing—like, well, oil and water.

In terms of how individual church members help to create unhealthy spiritual environments for themselves and others, one does not have to search very far or look too deeply to observe examples of misplaced pride, ego, selfishness, power struggles, envy, jealousy, and more. Negative energy provides fertile ground for enough group sabotage and personal infighting to develop into full-blown aggression and passive-aggressive behaviors (i.e. pretending to be loving, kind, and cooperative, but in actuality, sabotaging and undermining everything in sight).

Some congregations have so much negative energy floating around that it might be helpful to provide individual and group therapy sessions before allowing anyone to enter the sanctuary! To make matters worse, many churches and church leaders ignore the "pink elephant" in the room and go on with business as usual as long as the tithes and offerings are up to par, the choir sounds good, the preaching can still whip people into an emotional frenzy, and no one is physically beating others in the aisles. This is obviously an exaggeration for some congregations, but oh, so true for far too many others.

However, when one sees strife and ill will in the church, it is easy to become cynical and altogether unimpressed with the spirituality and "righteousness" that emanates from one church congregation to the next. What's worse, our children can recognize the myriad of social and relational problems that plague adults, even those that are "good churchgoing folk." Even children recognize people acting out with behavior that is not "godlike," and must wonder how people who call themselves "Christians" can demonstrate such behavior toward one another.

Looking for "Perfect" People?

Trying to mix people with different personalities, styles, preferences, agendas, and personal issues—on top of differences in spiritual maturity—is a major challenge. If you are looking for a perfect church, with perfect people, you will forever be disappointed, regardless of how many churches you "shop," visit, or compare. God's church really is a "spiritual hospital" for wounded souls and broken spirits. For some, church is a "spiritual hospice": the last chance to treat their terminal spiritual illness!

However, unlike "traditional" hospitals or hospices, in church, our healing is not dependent upon human hands or knowledge, nor is it measured by the physical, but by the spiritual. Jesus is the Great Physician. He can and will heal all that ails you, spiritually. He may also heal you physically, if that is His will. Remember, Jesus is also the Divine Counselor! He will comfort you emotionally, and soothe your psychological pain of discouragement, self-doubt, and spiritual depression.

Attending church with other spiritually ill people is part of what connects us to Jesus Christ and each other, regardless of race/ethnicity, gender, age, and more (1 Corinthians 12:13). Dr. Angel M. Rodriguez, Director of the Bible Research Institute, Silver Spring, Maryland, puts it this way:

> The image of the church as the body of Christ designates the unity and the interdependence of believers with one another and with Christ. Such union is reflected or manifested in a life lived in Christ/ in the Spirit. ("Atonement and the Cross of Christ," 2008, Adult Teachers Study Guide, p.146)

Clearly, we cannot base our decision whether to follow Jesus or not on the people sitting in the church pews next to us. However, when we choose to follow Jesus, we must expect that everyone in the church will not be on the same "spiritual level," nor will all church members walk or run at the same pace on their spiritual journey. Some will fully convert, while others will merely be convicted! Others will stagger and fall, barely able to place one foot in front of the other as they seek to remain in this spiritual marathon.

It is through this mixture of "saints" that we find our opportunities to minister, one to another, within God's church. If we cannot show love to our sister in Christ who sits in the same church pew, or treat our brother with kindness and respect, how can we be effective in showing the world outside the church the love of Jesus? 1 Peter 4:8-10, tells us: "Above all, love each other deeply, because love covers a multitude of sins. Offer hospitality to one another without grumbling. Each of you should use whatever gift you have received to serve others, as faithful stewards of God's grace in its various forms" (NIV).

Who Is Responsible for "Peace" in the Church?

I do not believe it is the responsibility of the pastor to make all church members get along and treat one another in a Christ-like manner. Peter suggests it is the responsibility of church members themselves to work together for the good of those who love the Lord. He is telling us that church members have to love one another, forgive one another, and minister to one another.

Showing love to our brothers and sisters, inside and outside the church, means treating each other as Christ would. For example, we cannot expect God to forgive us and show us grace and mercy, only to then turn around ourselves and *not* forgive our fellow men and women. Unfortunately, this is the state of affairs for many within the church. There are still some church members who are far from being able to show love to those around them. Maybe this is because it is impossible to show love for one another when you do not have the love of Jesus Christ in your heart. Too often, we wrap ourselves in our own righteousness (self-righteousness), creating a false confidence that we are inherently good, and therefore, not in need of forgiveness. With this attitude, we withhold forgiveness from others. However, Revelation tells us that, clothed in our own righteousness, we are "wretched, pitiful, poor, blind, and naked" (Revelation 3:17), and that is at our very best. Isaiah describes our righteousness as "filthy rags" (Isaiah 64:6). Clearly, without the love of Jesus, we are not able to consistently love others as we love ourselves. We might be able to be nice to people we like, and tolerate folks we are less fond of, but loving others as Christ loves us? Well, that is quite the challenge!

However, don't be discouraged when you find yourself falling short on the "loving others as yourself" list. Jesus is our role model for how to love others. When asked by the spiritual leaders of his day, "Teacher, which is the greatest commandment in the law?" (Matthew 22:36, NIV), Jesus answered: "Love the Lord your God with all your heart and with all your soul and with all your mind." This is the first and greatest commandment. And the second is like it: "Love your neighbor as yourself." All the Law and the Prophets hang on these two commandments." (Matthew 22:37-39, NIV)

Love for God and love for our fellow human beings brings us that much closer to the loving arms of Jesus. Thank the Lord for the love and the blood of Jesus! For if love covers a multitude of sins, it is because the blood of Jesus covers our iniquities and gives us a spirit of forgiveness toward others; recognizing that we have been forgiven. The lyrics of another favorite song come to mind:

"Cover Me"
By Eleanor Wright

Cover me, oh Lord, with righteousness.
Cover me, and count me with the blessed.
Suffer me, to come to Thee, and hide my nothingness.
Cover me, oh Lord, with righteousness.

Can there be some sin that I've not confessed?
Something in Thy law that I have transgressed?
Let me be, forgiven please, and count me with the blessed.
Cover me, oh Lord, with righteousness.

I have doubted, Lord, cover me with faith
I have hated, cover me with Love
I am wretched, blind, and naked, at my best

Cover me, oh Lord, with righteousness.

Composition/Song Title: Cover Me
Writer Credits: Eleanor Wright
Copyright: © 1979 Eleanor Wright Trust, Publisher
All Rights Reserve. Used By Permission.

We need to ask the Lord to cover us with His righteousness so that we can have a loving and forgiving spirit. It is with a loving spirit that we can be most effective in reaching out to others.

Surely, this is a prayer request that God will honor! It is not easy to accept people who think differently, or live differently than we do. When we attend a church with a diverse group of folks, things can sometimes get misunderstood and mishandled. However, if each of us takes the responsibility on ourselves to be Christ-like (loving, forgiving, kind, and patient), we can mitigate some of the personality issues and disagreements that promote an atmosphere of conflict within the body of Christ. Showing love is the most basic part of this formula, because Jesus is love. He commanded us to love one another: "A new command I give you: Love one another. As I have loved you, so you must love one another. By this everyone will know that you are my disciples, if you love one another" (John 13:34-35, NIV). This is the great challenge for the body of Christ: to demonstrate love for one another. Only then will we be in good practice to go outside the church where, for some, showing love might be even more challenging. It can be done, however, when we allow God to change us from inside out: And have put on a new self, which is being renewed in knowledge in the image of its Creator. Here there is no Gentile or Jew, circumcised or uncircumcised, barbarian, Scythian, slave or free, but Christ is all, and is in all (Colossians 3:10-11, NIV).

The key then to eliminating spiritual depression in our faith communities is learning how to love and forgive. We can do this by first allowing God to change our attitude toward others; seeing the lives of family, friends, neighbors, office-mates, classmates, and even strangers as having as much value as our own. For in God's eyes, all are valued. Eliminating stress and strife between ourselves and others changes our focus from negative thinking to positive thinking. Seeing the best in ourselves and others will lift us from the depths of spiritual depression.

Chapter 7

Spiritual Depression in the Church (Part II): Messages That Encourage

―――――――∞◦⟲⟳◦∞―――――――

"But seek first the kingdom of God and His righteousness, and all these things shall be added to you" (Matthew 6:33, NKJV).

Church Leaders Are Human Too

𝓡epeating our question from Chapter 6: How does spiritual depression manifest itself within churches? There remain a variety of possibilities. For our purposes in this chapter we will look at just three such possibilities: the obvious influence of the faith leader's leadership style; the not so obvious influence of other church leaders who, being human and thus fallible creatures, are not always on the same page as their members, and; still other church leaders who (like some members), are not completely in step with what God expects from them and their religious organization. In essence, they are not in harmony with what Paul repeatedly admonishes in his many letters to the churches. One such letter to Timothy reads:

> Here is a trustworthy saying: Whoever aspires to be an overseer [bishop] desires a noble task. Now the overseer is to be above reproach [blameless], faithful to his wife, temperate, self-controlled, respectable, hospitable, able to teach, not given to drunkenness, not

violent but gentle, not quarrelsome, not a lover of money. He must manage his own family well and see that his children obey him, and he must do so in a manner of full respect. (If anyone does not know how to manage his own family, how can he take care of God's church?) ... (1 Timothy 3:1-7, NIV, brackets added)

Paul provides here a comprehensive list of the preferred characteristics for church leaders. Based on what I know and understand about the character of God's chosen, this is *not* an exhaustive list by any means. These are just the basics, if you will. If we were to break down what Paul considers the prerequisites for being a good spiritual leader, we see at the top of the list: "above reproach" or "blameless." According *to Webster's II New Riverside Dictionary, Revised Edition* (1996) to be *blameless* is to be "guiltless" and "without fault."

Wow! Who is Paul kidding? No human being can live up to even the very first thing on Paul's list! No need to go down the rest of the list. Not one human being who has ever been born, except for Jesus Christ, could get past the first item on Paul's list of prerequisites for leading the church. So we have a church full of diverse individuals who make up all types of families, all carrying a variety of personal and spiritual baggage (i.e. the collection of "average" church members at three different levels of their Christian experience, Chapter 6). They are being led by other human beings (i.e. clergy, faith leaders, ministers, and others) who have all of the same issues and deficiencies as the church members. How can Jesus Christ possibly get anything done within our faith organizations?

The answer, once again, comes from Paul. Paraphrasing Ephesians 2:1-9, Paul sums it up by reminding us that though all human beings fall short of spiritual perfection, in His infinite grace and mercy, God has called a few to lead and guide others on their spiritual journey. It is God's grace, mercy, and forgiveness that allow fallible men and women to lead other fallible people. Clearly, this level of power, influence, and trust comes with huge responsibility, expectation, and a myriad of potential pitfalls.

Since we have already established that "all have sinned, and come short of the glory of God" (Romans 3:23, KJV); there is no need to be harsh with ministers of the gospel who have been chosen by God to lead His church. It is simply a fact that must be considered when one human being, by virtue of position, title, and leadership role, has influence over others. This influence is considerable, and can have both positive and negative outcomes in terms of spiritual depression, depending on the message sent and received.

As leader of God's first Christian church and its first international evangelist, Paul's writings put it out there from the very beginning: We are all in this thing together. God's grace and mercy allow all mankind to be a part of the body of Christ. No one, not even the pastor, can boast about his righteousness. Jesus' death delivered us from our sins, but it is God's continued grace and mercy that allow us to preach, to teach, to minister to one another, and to act as leaders in God's church organization. We must accept the free gift of sacrifice of Jesus' death on a daily basis, so that each day we can begin anew and say to our brothers and sisters: "I face death every day—yes, just as surely as I boast about you in Christ Jesus our Lord" (1 Corinthians 15:31, NIV).

As the first bishop of God's Christian church, Paul understood that only Jesus is blameless and above reproach—only He can save. The blamelessness of Jesus Christ and the blood He shed covers us (all of us "less than perfect" men and women). It is God's grace and mercy that allow us to minister from the highest office in God's church, the lowest office in the church, or those with no office at all. Therefore, it is important for the faith leaders to be on the same page, first, with God. Then they can say with Paul: "But by the grace of God I am what I am, and his grace to me was not without effect. No, I worked harder than all of them—yet not I, but the grace of God that was with me" (1 Corinthians 15:10, NIV).

God-Connected Leaders

After it is established that the leaders of the church are on the same page with God, it is then possible for them to be on the same page as the members. Church leaders who are in constant contact with God, asking for and receiving forgiveness of their own sins (daily) will be led by God to create a firm spiritual foundation on which to build up the spiritual lives of their fellow men and women. I believe

God answers the sincere prayers of His children; especially those He has separated from the masses to minister to His church.

Through daily supplication and constant communication with God, church leaders will surround themselves with members of the church body who can move forward the spiritual programs of God, and those of the church as a whole. For this to happen, the church leader must remind his members what church is really all about (i.e. lifting up the name of Jesus to a troubled world), and help them to stay focused on the important aspects of true worship of Jesus Christ, by doing what Jesus did (i.e. showing love to others and helping those in need by meeting people where they are). It is far more important to provide help, support, and resources to people in need than to try and convince them to convert to a particular religious doctrine. Putting a tangible love into action speaks volumes about the God you share. This is an important reminder for the church body that should be set before them often. Otherwise, it becomes easy to get distracted by all the other things that can take a church, its members, or its leaders off course.

In summary of this point, we can say that based on Paul's prerequisites for church leaders, there are clear expectations for the leaders of God's church. When church leaders do not adhere to staying in constant contact with God, they are susceptible to falling from grace, not being on the same page as God, and creating turmoil within a church that will quickly bring chaos and confusion to the body of Christ, where many will succumb to spiritual depression. It is easy to see how it is possible for a church leader to create an atmosphere primed for spiritual depression, but what about the members themselves? The faith leader can be on the same page with God and still find he or she is leading a group of church members who are not mixing well.

Mixed Messages

We have already established that churches are made up of a variety of people from diverse walks of life. It is easy to see how people hear and receive different messages based on the uniqueness of individual perspectives and perceptions. For one group of people, the members in the church are not central to why they attend, remain consistent, or leave a church. These folks determine what church to attend and how they will serve the Lord based on who the preacher is. This may sound like an obvious no-no to those who know better, but it is an especially common pitfall for "new" believers who may have initially been attracted to the powerful personality who brought them into the church in the first place (i.e. traveling evangelist), and/or those who are, or were, attracted to the "importance" and "prestige" of the minister's platform and/or position in the community.

Church members who are influenced more by the person standing up front are unduly dependent upon the preacher and his/her message, especially if they are "passive" believers who do not study the Word of God for themselves. These individuals are much more vulnerable to falling into spiritual depression, if for any reason, the preacher disappoints them in any way, or puts forth a message that is not conducive to their spiritual growth.

A major cause of spiritual depression in some of our churches is the message being espoused from some of our church leaders. Too often, words from the pulpit have a negative influence on people's lives, not always because of what is said, but sometimes for what is not being said. Sermons can be very effective in encouraging listeners to carry out the mission of true Christianity: Lift up the name of Jesus and address the needs of our fellow human beings by showing love and compassion to those most vulnerable in our society. However, sermons can send messages that are discouraging. For example, a message that those doing poorly financially, physically, and emotionally are in these predicaments due to a "lack of faith" is very destructive, and frankly, largely inaccurate. (This misconception, that a "lack of faith" is responsible for all that ails the poor will be covered in more detail later in this book.). Sermons that focus on the love of Christ and point listeners to a forgiving God are more constructive and impactful than any other message.

Then there are those messages that go in the opposite direction (i.e. trying to preach only "nice things"). Some ministers figure they are more apt to appeal to the masses by preaching feel-good sermons with a softer tone, as these tend to be more palatable for the average listener. Since these listeners are more likely to want to hear such messages, it is likely they will be inclined to give a good offering.

For far too many preachers the priority appears to be getting members to pay an honest tithe and give more offering to the church. Neither of these is a negative idea in and of themselves, but they become less helpful when they become the sole focus of the message. I hear more sermons on how to make money and eliminate debt than I do on how to be saved! So many churches these days, whether on television, radio, or simply doing it the old fashioned way (no media coverage), appear more concerned with acquiring wealth and building ever larger congregations and fabulous buildings! This is not to say that huge churches with affluent and financially successful pastors and members is a bad thing. However, material wealth should not be the primary focus.

It is *not* a bad thing to be blessed by God and have one's hard work pay off financially. It is *not* a bad thing to have impressive bank accounts and the ability to acquire the material things one desires. Plus, the more one has, the more one can give to help others. So having much can be a wonderful resource for faith communities. In fact, many wealthy ministers, faith leaders, and parishioners give unselfishly to others and enhance the world with their gifts. I'm speaking more about a message that seems to be so popular these days, which overemphasizes and pushes financial acquisition over spiritual attainment. I am talking about the popularity of "prosperity preaching" in today's religious organizations. Those who misunderstand prosperity preaching might believe that their condition of poverty is due to their lack of faith, or for *not* having the financial resources to "sow into a leader's ministry," it can be discouraging and foster seeds of spiritual depression.

Misunderstanding Prosperity Preaching

I remember a few years ago, the popular national TV news program, *60 Minutes*, did two shows on the growing trend of prosperity preaching. The show attempted balance in that they interviewed faith-leaders that adhered to a variety of definitions of what true prosperity is, and is not. But the show focused more attention on prosperity messages defined by material wealth. I certainly understand why a message of "wealth" prosperity would be so popular. After all, many individuals and families today are living in desperate financial times. However, what has happened to the focus on love for God and love for one's fellow man? What happened to preaching that points a soul to Jesus and away from pursuing worldly pleasures and piling up material acquisitions and "keeping up with the Joneses"?

I believe that the answer lies somewhere in the fact that preaching that "old-time religion" is no longer popular! "Old-time religion" was simple: "Love God because He first loved you. Love your fellow man as Jesus loves you." There were not a great many "do's and don'ts," or complicated formulas to make sure you were giving enough money to secure a pew in your church. Sermons promoting the basic love of Jesus, His sacrifice to secure our salvation and restoration, and love for our neighbors, have too often been replaced with "how to make money" sermons. Prosperity, it should be noted, is more than having the money to procure the material things one might desire. Prosperity is also physical, spiritual, and emotional!

Admittedly, it makes great fiscal sense if you are the CEO of a large church: If you want to fill the pews in your church building and raise enough money to build a larger, more fabulous edifice, you better come up with a popular message. It should be a message people can easily digest without "spiritual heartburn." You should stay away from any topic that makes folks uneasy and less likely to reach into their pockets when the collection plate is passed. Although I do not personally advocate this sort of thing; I do understand. You cannot have a successful church if the pews are empty! I question whether the best way to keep a church full is to make people feel good about themselves and their lives, by not "stepping on too many toes," and avoiding preaching anything controversial or potentially insulting to your wealthiest or most influential contributors. Again, I am not an advocate of this particular philosophy, but I understand it. If people do not like your message; they will go elsewhere. I only point it out here because I fear that when leaders focus too much on the "bottom-line" of financial growth it can overshadow spiritual growth.

However, I strongly believe we have strayed from the truth with all the feel-good churches with "feel-good" preaching! Most Friday evenings and Saturday afternoons, I watch preachers on television. There are some mighty good speakers, and a lot of very impressive men and women who sincerely promote Jesus as the

God of the universe. They provide comfort to spiritually depressed souls all over the world. They offer prayer and praise to God. They bring together both those still suffering from spiritual depression and those who have overcome it.

It is a wonderful experience to be touched by the presence of the Lord through preaching and music via mass media. I thoroughly enjoy and am blessed by many of the dedicated spiritual leaders on television. I am *not* talking about the majority of churches or the majority of church leaders that do things God's way. Those churches and church leaders are not difficult to identify.

Unfortunately, I also noticed that for every preacher and church that uplifts the name of Jesus, there are others that promote themselves first and spend a vast majority of their time hawking all sorts of items to make money. Jesus Himself guarded against creating a perception that His message was all about Him:

> Jesus answered, "My teaching is not my own. It comes from him who sent me. Anyone who chooses to do the will of God will find out whether my teaching comes from God or whether I speak on my own. Whoever speaks on their own does so to gain personal glory, but he who seeks for the glory of the one who sent him is a man of truth; there is nothing false about him." (John 7:16-18, NIV)

If there is anyone who can rightly, speak "on his own" it is the Son of God! However, Jesus purposely pointed others to God the Father as an example for us to follow. Today's church leaders should do the same.

Again, this is *not* about all clergy or all churches. Most do the right thing and promote a spiritual message, pointing toward God and not themselves. I am currently focusing on those that do not because the result of their behavior is that scores of people are sitting in the pews or have chosen to leave the church (never to return), experiencing spiritual depression. Also, let me say again that there is nothing wrong with making lots of money; especially when God blesses you to do so, and it is not gained dishonestly or by taking advantage of those most vulnerable, bewildered, and desperate (i.e. the poor, the elderly, and others).

These poor souls need to be reminded that the gift of Jesus (redemption of sins/ eternal life) is free of charge. God's mercy and grace cover me, not my financial wherewithal or contribution. God's righteousness covers me, not any great thing

I can do or anything I can purchase. After all, Jesus paid it all with the sacrifice of His life for all people.

Refocus Priorities

I have always felt that the express purpose of a church (and church leaders), was to point others to Jesus. The purpose was not to point people to church leaders who tell people how many Mercedes-Benz cars they have, or how many beautiful homes they own. Jesus Himself tells us in John 12:32: "And I, when I am lifted up from the earth, will draw all people to myself" (NIV). This tells me that Jesus is the key to salvation. He is the "wealth" that we should seek! Spiritual leaders and church members alike have the simple task of lifting up the name of Jesus. The God of the universe will do the rest: We do the lifting; Jesus does the drawing!

When you lose focus on lifting up Jesus first, you may draw men and women to you personally, but that is not what true ministry is about. Salvation is not based on who the minister is, or how successful their self-promotion. Also, all men and women are fallible, so it is most important to make sure you study the Bible for yourself and do not depend solely upon the individual philosophies and traditions of fellow fallible beings. Paul's letter to the Colossians makes it plain:

> See to it that no one takes you captive through hollow and deceptive philosophy, which depends on human tradition and the elemental spiritual forces of this world rather than on Christ." (Colossians 2:8, NIV)

When church members are drawn first to the preacher, the popularity of the message, or the beauty of the church building, there is a disconnect between what God intended and what humans intend. This is fertile ground for spiritual depression.

There is another important issue not so well hidden in this current fad of preaching material wealth over spiritual wealth. *Everyone is not going to be able to acquire the type of earthly riches that many preachers espouse* (i.e. "If you just have enough faith and trust in the Lord, He will give you whatever you ask").

Feeding people this inaccurate line that having enough faith will somehow lead to material wealth directly contradicts what Jesus told His disciples in Matthew 26:11 (see also John 12:8): "The poor you will always have with you, but you will not always have me" (NIV).

Our focus should be on following Jesus' instructions to honor God and love others. We should not waste a lot of time seeking material wealth. For one thing, seeking wealth and fame can be a huge distraction from our true mission (pointing others to Jesus). Also, if the Lord of the universe decides in His will for your life, that giving you material wealth is not the best way to save you, not receiving your desired answer to prayer (material wealth) could lead to disappointment, disillusionment, and yes, spiritual depression!

Jesus does not teach that all men should be wealthy. He teaches just the opposite, in fact. Jesus speaks of sacrificing human pleasures for godly purposes. When Jesus told the disciples to "take up your cross and follow me," He never assured those men of wealth or fame. On the contrary. He assured them of poverty and persecution! Jesus speaks to this effort of going after riches in Matthew 16:26: "What good will it be for someone to gain the whole world, yet forfeit their soul? Or what can anyone give in exchange for their soul?" (NIV).

Please do not misunderstand me. There is nothing wrong with having nice things and being financially wealthy. That is a blessing! However, it may not be a blessing that *everyone* receives. It is easy for the poor to be tricked into thinking that their state of poverty is due to their lack of faith, or to their not having gained the "right relationship" with God. Paul told us to beware of such deceptive philosophies. Paul has more to say on this subject:

> If anyone teaches otherwise and does not agree to the sound instruction of our Lord Jesus Christ and to godly teaching, they are conceited and understand nothing. They have an unhealthy interest in controversies and quarrels about words that result in envy, strife, malicious talk, evil suspicions and constant friction between people of corrupt mind, who have been robbed of the truth and who think that godliness is a means to financial gain.

But godliness with contentment is great gain. For we brought nothing into this world, and we can take nothing out of it. But if we have food and clothing, we will be content with that. Those who want to get rich fall into temptation and a trap and into many foolish and harmful desires that plunge people into ruin and destruction. For the love of money is a root of all kinds of evil. Some people, eager for money, have wandered from the faith and pierced themselves with many grief's. But you, man of God, flee from all this, and pursue righteousness, godliness, faith, love, endurance and gentleness (1 Timothy 6:3-11, NIV)

Again, preaching about acquiring riches and insinuating that a lack of wealth is indicative of a lack of faith is just plain wrong! Our focus and energy should not be on financial gain at the expense of our eternal salvation. God has a plan of salvation for everyone: In this life, accept His *free* gift of salvation made possible by the blood of Jesus. The acceptance of Jesus' sacrifice is what gives you eternal life.

For some, God's blessings while living on this earth will include personal wealth and many nice things. For others, it may not. However, "Do not let your hearts be troubled. You believe in God; believe also in me. My Father's house has many rooms; if that were not so, would I have told you that I am going there to prepare a place for you? And if I go and prepare a place for you, I will come back and take you to be with me that you also may be where I am" (John 14:1-3, NIV). Jesus' resurrection and ascension to heaven to "prepare a place for us" assures us that He is in intercession on our behalf. The decision of whether we are with Jesus in the new home He has prepared rests with each of us through what we choose to focus on, and how we prioritize our pursuits.

Being where Jesus is, is priceless! A time is coming when it will not matter what our financial state was while living on this earth. Fortunately, personal wealth and acquiring an impressive financial portfolio and long list of material possessions will not give you an inside track on receiving the righteousness of Jesus. Hallelujah! This means that everyone—the poor, the working poor, the middle class, and the rich—has an equal opportunity for eternal life. So do not worry about whether you can "afford" salvation. It is free!

In Matthew 6:19-21, Jesus speaks directly once again and addresses where our priorities should be:

> "Do not store up for yourselves treasures on earth, where moths and vermin destroy, and where thieves break in and steal: But store up for yourselves treasures in heaven, where moth and vermin do not destroy, and where thieves do not break in and steal. For where your treasure is, there your heart will be also." (NIV)

"For where your treasure is, there your heart will be also" gives us the true essence of what is important about acquiring wealth: What you focus your attention on and prioritize is what you will spend your time going after. Focus all of your attention on lifting up Jesus and telling others what *He* has done for you, and the rest will take care of itself.

Having your treasure in heaven is not a bad deal at all. We are "treasure" to Jesus! We are the most valuable creatures in all the earth. He wants to save each and every one of us, by any means necessary. If that means that we do not recover from health problems, and God calls us to sleep in Him while others continue to live, then that is what He will do to save us. If it means that we must suffer through some bad choices we made in relationships, and/or live out our days living alone, and He never gives us that "perfect" mate, then that is what He will do to save us. If it means keeping some of us poor financially so that He can make us rich spiritually, just so He can save us; then that is what He will do!

I believe the bottom line for Jesus is that in His quest to save every soul possible, He allows our lives to take twists and turns that will keep us on our knees, and ultimately give Him the opportunity—at precisely the right moment—to step in and save us from ourselves. Peter accentuates this point:

> For you know that it was not with perishable things such as silver or gold that you were redeemed from the empty way of life handed down to you from your ancestors, but with the precious blood of Christ, a lamb without blemish or defect. (1 Peter 1:18-19, NIV)

Jesus sacrificed His life to save ours. With Jesus as our focus, we can then sing with utmost sincerity that old hymn by Rhea F. Miller, "I'd Rather Have Jesus" (1922, *Adventist Hymnal*, p.327):

> I'd rather have Jesus, than silver or gold
> I'd rather have Jesus, than riches untold
> I'd rather have Jesus, than anything
> This world affords today.

That is not to say that the God of the universe is not aware of our most basic physiological needs, our wants, and our desires here on this earth. He is keenly aware of all these things. In fact, nothing gives the Lord more joy than to see His people happy and enjoying what He has provided!

In Matthew 6, Jesus speaks eloquently about His being aware of what we need in this life. He cites examples of how He looks out for the fowl in the air, the sparrow, the beasts of the field . . . and how much more He cares for us. Read Matthew 6:30-34 and allow the detail of just how much Jesus cares for you to sink in. However, after reading the passage, read verse 33 out loud to yourself: *"But, seek first his kingdom and his righteousness, and all these things will be given to you as well"* (Matthew 6:33, NIV). Oh, what a marvelous promise Jesus gives for those who seek Him first! Ours is not to worry about material things. Ours is to trust in the name of Jesus, and let Him do the rest.

When our priority is Jesus, everything else is indeed added as needed. The God of the universe knows what is required for each of us to live and to prosper! The Bible is here to remind us of God's promises and to help people live through and move past life's circumstances that create avenues for spiritual depression to creep in and infect our spiritual strength and stamina. The church should be an anchor for spiritually depressed souls sailing adrift through a life of disappointment, disillusionment, and spiritual doubt! God's people need a safe harbor in which to dock. A place where we can rest, get cleaned up, fueled up, and prepared to go back out across the rough and troubled waters of this life!

Individually, we have talents that serve us well most of the time. However, when we lend our skills and strengths to God's church, we become a powerful and dynamic force to go and connect with the rest of the world of God's people, who may need just what we have to offer: spiritual food for the hungry, hope for discouraged souls, peace for a world in conflict, and the message that Jesus saves. Delivering this message of hope and love is the bare minimum God expects from us as individuals and from His church as a whole. This is the very reason the church exists! However, a message of hope and love must be clothed in sincerity and compassion, delivered by a people who live the message they proclaim:

> *"By this everyone will know that you are my disciples, if you love one another"* (John 13:35, NIV).

Part III

Spiritual Depression in the Individual

———⊸∘⧼⧽∘⊶———

Over the first two sections of this book, we concentrated our attention on the variety of ways spiritual depression affects the family and the church/faith-based community. Families, churches, and communities, of course, are made up of individual people. Therefore, in Part III we will bring our journey of self-discovery full circle by focusing on how the individual can counteract his or her own personal experience with spiritual depression, which affects the other vital areas of life (family, church, community).

In keeping with the established theme of this book, the chapters in Part III will continue to recognize the importance of the physical, cognitive, and psychosocial aspects of our make-up, reference characters and situations in the Bible, and utilize current real-life examples to identify issues common to everyday people seeking spiritual resolution by lifting up the name of Jesus.

Each chapter highlights challenges, obstacles, and victories that build spiritual character and stamina by way of giving hope and reassurance to everyone that Jesus truly saves. I thank you for taking this journey with me. It is my sincere hope that you have been blessed so far, and will incorporate whatever information has been beneficial into your life. And remember: Jesus Saves!

Chapter 8

Trials Come with Blessings

———————— ∞◦⟨∂⟩◦∞ ————————

"Now then, stand still and see this great thing the Lord is about to do before your eyes!" (1 Samuel 12:16, NIV).

Renovation Is a Painful Process

Have you ever watched the demolition of a condemned building? It is a very powerful experience; especially if you are able to witness the process in person. The last demolition I observed was via a television screen. I looked on as the massive structure came crashing to the ground in a thunderous heap. Two metaphors relating to damaged lives and damaged buildings came to my mind. On the one hand, I thought about how a wrecking ball is sometimes used to take down a condemned building. The wrecking ball swings back and forth, striking the building with powerful blows, over and over again, until concrete, iron, and steel eventually succumb to the constant onslaught. In contrast to the wrecking ball scenario, there is another method to take down a condemned building: implosion. In simple terms, this method involves setting explosives around the base of the structure and strategic areas throughout the rest of the building to ensure a balanced and thorough collapse all at once.

In the course of living our lives, many of us can relate to these two metaphors as they represent how damaged we may feel at times. Sometimes, due to no fault of our own, or directly because of poor decisions we have made, we may feel like our life has been "condemned." We sit feeling helpless, or moving, though slowly—the best petrified heart and limbs can muster.

In the wrecking ball scenario, we are the building. The circumstances of life often act as a wrecking ball, pummeling us day after day. And, as with the condemned building, neither the first blow, the second, nor even the third can knock us down. Sure, we may feel parts of our being crumble from the powerful hits, but we are able to stand and deal with a lot. However, eventually, after the continued and constant onslaught, we succumb. It may feel like our lives have become a pile of rubble and debris—no brick resting upon another; our very fabric torn into unrecognizable strips of pain.

For some of us, the damage in our lives may feel more like implosion. Explosive elements are strategically placed in our path, and with one push of the "wrong button," we come crashing down into a heap. When the dust clears, we are left wondering how it all fell apart so quickly.

We can expand on those metaphors by adding that some damaged buildings do not need to be destroyed but simply gutted and prepared for extensive renovation. The story of God coming to free His people from Egypt is an excellent example of the building renovation metaphor in action. The story of Moses and the children of Israel provided such an apt example that we will continue to utilize the rescue from Egypt metaphor throughout this chapter.

An "Egypt Experience" Not of Your Own Making

Most folks who have read the Bible or watched *The Ten Commandments* movie, starring Charlton Heston and Yul Brynner (often shown around Easter time each year), are familiar with the trials and tribulations the Israelites faced individually and collectively as they attempted to leave behind, not just Egypt, the country, but also the gods of Egypt, the food of Egypt, and the very mind-set of Egypt.

In essence, Moses and the children of Israel had the challenge of leaving behind the *culture* of Egypt, and all that entailed. This was a most difficult task because, after being under Egyptian captivity for some 430 years (Exodus 12:40, 41), the Egyptian culture was inbred into the children of Israel. Hence, they were no longer recognizable as God's "chosen people." God would not just take His people out of Egypt. He also had to *take Egypt out of His people*! God had to reverse the brainwashing of the descendants of Abraham, Isaac, and Jacob.

For this "reconstruction project" to be successful, God had to renovate the hearts and minds of His people to make room for His presence to abide within them. He developed a plan to return His people to their original spiritual condition.

The Master Builder formulated a "spiritual blueprint" to reconstruct their belief system and repair the spiritual dilapidation of their souls. He chose to do this by bringing them out of a foreign land and allowing them to wander around in the wilderness for forty years! It should be noted that God did not intend for the children of Israel to wander in the wilderness for forty years! Constant and continuous disobedience on their part forced God to develop an "attitude adjustment plan" via a forty-year detour before the promises to Abraham's generations could rightfully be claimed. The Lord of the universe came to rescue His people, setting them free from bondage. However, He also knew that the Israelites had slipped substantially from the spiritual level of their forefathers, and needed a complete "makeover" if they were to ever again be recognizable as the people of God.

God needed to get the attention of His people. The plagues and miracles God performed against Pharaoh were not just to show Pharaoh who God is, it was also to show the children of Israel that *He* is God (Exodus 5-12). The Lord needed to remind some and state it anew for others, that the God of their fathers was still on the throne. In Exodus 7:3-5, 10:1-2, and 11:9, God explained to Moses why He hardened Pharaoh's heart. The Lord hardened Pharaoh's heart to manifest *His* glory to the Egyptians, the Israelites, and all the neighboring people whose countries shared borders with Egypt (Exodus 7:13-14, 22; 8:15, 19, 32; 9:7, 12, 34-35; 10:20, 27; 11:10; 14:4-5, 8).

God wanted it to be clear to Pharaoh and the children of Israel that the God of Abraham, Isaac, and Jacob was the Almighty Living God whom they should all respect. God wanted to get the attention of *His* people and of those with whom they lived. (What a way to get someone's attention!)

When the Lord announces *His* presence, whether you serve Him or not, it's a very big deal, and you will take notice!

"Egypt Experiences" Often Involve Unusual Circumstances

Using the rescue from Egypt metaphor in our own lives means recognizing that at one time or another, we all have been enslaved to people, places, or things that are not pleasing to the Lord (Galatians 4:9; Titus 3:3). We have all been in need of the Lord coming to take us out of our Egypt experience, and the bondage of our sin, which creates separation from our Lord. God often allows us to be taken through an Egypt experience against our will, or He instructs us to go through an Egypt experience for the purpose of saving us. God loves to receive our praise when He rescues us from challenging situations and circumstances.

To examine the Egypt experience for the children of Israel more closely to see how they ended up in Egypt in the first place, I encourage you to read the whole chapter of Genesis 15. At the beginning of that chapter, Abram is talking to the Lord about not having an heir from his wife Sarah, and how, because he had been blessed with children from one of his wife's servants; one of these children will end up being his heir. The Lord responds to Abram that a servant will not be his heir, and that Abram will become the father of many nations (Abraham)—as many as the stars in the sky. The Bible passage above declares to Abram (whose name was changed to "Abraham") the future of his descendants: a future of captivity (four hundred years, see Genesis 15:13 and Acts 7:6), and a future of inheritance because God made a covenant with Abraham (Genesis 15:17-21). As history can attest, the Lord's word to Abram (Abraham) was true:

> Now the length of time the Israelite people lived in Egypt
> was 430 years. At the end of the 430 years, to the very day,
> all the Lord's divisions left Egypt. (Exodus 12:40-41, NIV)

> So I gave you a land on which you did not toil and cities you
> did not build; and you live in them and eat from vineyards
> and olive groves you did not plant. (Joshua 24:13, NIV)

> Then Joshua dismissed the people, each to their own inheritance.
> (Joshua 24:28, NIV)

Based on the history of unpredictable occurrences recorded in the Bible (and in world history books), and highlighted above, we should not be at all surprised that the actual events which took place to bring into reality the prophecy of the children of Israel in Egypt were those of a most unique nature.

Joseph (son of Jacob, son of Isaac, son of Abraham) had ten older brothers. They hated Joseph and plotted his demise (Genesis 37:18-20). However, the Lord stepped in because he had another purpose for Joseph's life. The Lord already had a plan in mind that would not only save Joseph's life, but the nation of Israel. He would keep His promise to Abraham, Isaac, and Jacob.

Remember, the Lord works in multiples. All of this occurred through a most unlikely and unusual sequence of events:

- Joseph's brother's sold him to some merchants going to Egypt. (Genesis 37:21-36)
- Joseph was falsely accused of a crime and placed in jail. (Genesis 39:1-20)

After all of this, had Joseph begun to feel like his life was one of bad luck or a life condemned, anyone would have understood it. There he was, in jail in a foreign country by no fault of his own. He had gone from being the favorite son of a doting father to being snatched up by his ten jealous brothers in an act of foul play, to ultimately be sold into slavery in a foreign land. He then gained a very good, prestigious job where he was highly respected and had great authority, only to lose it and be imprisoned due to false accusations and broken promises. Yet nowhere do we read about Joseph whining and complaining concerning his fate. I am sure he must have had his own private moments of doubt, discouragement, and even depression. However, there is no recorded evidence that any of these natural human feelings overwhelmed his faith in the Most High God. Joseph must have somehow realized that none of the events that had befallen him was under his control.

God Is in Control

Fortunately, God is always in control, especially when it is obvious that we are not! God used Joseph to reveal Pharaoh's dreams, where others could not, and then interpreted Pharaoh's dreams, creating a vision of the future where Pharaoh knew he needed someone with Joseph's talent, leadership ability, and wisdom to administrate and supervise at the highest level in his kingdom (Genesis 41). Through Pharaoh's dreams, God showed Joseph that Egypt and the surrounding areas were going to go through a seven year famine in the land (Genesis 41:25-32). Joseph needed to implement a plan where workers gathered double the food during across seven years of plentiful crops so that they would have more than enough food to survive the years of famine (Genesis 41:46-57).

Once again, God showed Himself as almighty, and all-knowing. Joseph's brothers, as it turned out, were sent to Egypt to purchase food during the years of famine (Genesis 42:1-5). Joseph created a series of situations that forced his brothers to return to Egypt, bringing their elderly father, Jacob (Genesis 43, 44, 45). Jacob reluctantly brought all his family, cattle, and possessions to Egypt, where he was reunited with his long-lost son, and lived a good life until his death some seventeen years later (Genesis 46). This is how the children of Israel came to be in Egypt: God had multiple plans working, as He saved Joseph for a greater purpose, saved the seed of Abraham, Isaac, and Jacob, and allowed them to multiply as the sands of the sea, keeping His original promise to Abraham.

> And God spoke to Israel in a vision at night, and said, "Jacob! Jacob!" "Here I am," he replied. "I am God, the God of your father," he said. "Do not be afraid to go down to Egypt; for I will make you into a great nation there. I will go down to Egypt with you, and I will surely bring you back again. And Joseph's own hand will close your eyes. (Genesis 46:2-4, NIV)

Notice how God promised Jacob that He would not only be with him as he relocated his family down into Egypt; He also promised to bring His people out of Egypt, even before He sent them there. Not only that; God promised Jacob that his beloved son, Joseph, would be there with him until he died. Our God is thorough!

Whether He allows you to be taken into your Egypt experience, or instructs you to go there voluntarily, God has already worked out your way of release. He will come to rescue you himself! God took the unrighteous plans of Joseph's brothers and turned them into the righteous plans of the Most High God (Genesis 50:19-21)!

When you read stories like that of Joseph and his brothers (the Twelve Tribes of Israel), it is appropriate to recall the old saying, "the Lord works in mysterious ways." The story of Joseph being sold into slavery, taken to Egypt, and then becoming second in power only to Pharaoh, could only be God's plan. No human being could script such a plan and outcome (except perhaps in a movie). However, what about the other ways we sometimes end up in "Egypt experiences"?

Ending Up in "Egypt" Because God Sent You There

Matthew 2:12-15 recounts the Lord sending His angel and instructing another Joseph (and Mary), parents of Jesus Christ, to "Get up." He said, "Take the child and his mother and escape to Egypt. Stay there until I tell you, for Herod is going to search for the child to kill him" (Matthew 2:13, NIV). Once again, we see the Lord working "in mysterious ways" to save His people and preserve the history and purpose of His Son Jesus Christ, to save the world. However, Joseph, Mary, and little baby Jesus had to first go through an Egypt experience before the Lord allowed His plan to manifest for the culmination of His glory.

It is interesting how the Lord works. Jesus was born in Bethlehem, while Herod, King of Israel, sought to find and destroy the Messiah, to whose coming all Israel looked forward. The Lord sent His Son (the Savior of the world) into Egypt, thus fulfilling the prophecy of Matthew 2:14-15.

> So he got up, took the child and his mother during the night and left for Egypt, where he stayed until the death of Herod. And so was fulfilled what the Lord had said through the prophet: "Out of Egypt I called my son." (Matthew 2:14-15, NIV)

Even Jesus Christ, the Messiah, had to endure an Egypt experience. Certainly those of us who would be like Jesus, will have or have had our own experiences of trying to avoid dangerous people, places, or things, feeling captive to life's circumstance, and needing to be rescued from the bondage of this world. We are blessed to serve a God who knows the end from the beginning and coordinates our rescue before we even realize we are in trouble. Jesus understands our need to be rescued from our Egypt experience, because like us, He has been through "Egypt."

Godly Purpose for Egypt Experiences

We see the evidence of an all-knowing God through perfect symmetry, which is demonstrated throughout the Bible. In the Old Testament, He allowed Joseph to be taken into Egypt, and then created a situation where Joseph's father, Jacob, and all his family had to come to Egypt to avoid starvation. He promised Jacob He would make Israel a great nation. He called Moses to lead His people out of their Egypt experience. He had them toil in the wilderness some forty years until they learned to depend upon their God. Moses did everything he could to teach the people under his charge and prepare their generations for the Messiah. Then in the New Testament, God told another Joseph, the earthly father of Jesus, to take the infant into Egypt to protect His life. There He called His only begotten Son out of His Egypt experience to fulfill prophecy stated in the Old Testament.

Moses, you remember, was born in Egypt and raised in Pharaoh's house by his Hebrew mother. Moses grew up in his Egypt experience precisely for his set purpose; *to lead God's people out of bondage*. Joseph was taken to Egypt to fulfill his set purpose; *to feed God's people so they could survive and become a great nation*. Jesus was sent to Egypt to protect Him from premature death. He was called out of Egypt for His set purpose; *to redeem God's people from sin*.

It is amazing to see the similarities in how God brought about these history-making rescues. All three situations involved a series of dreams and visits from angels. Joseph, son of Jacob, had no idea that when he dreamed the dreams that infuriated his jealous brothers (Genesis 37:4-11), it would lead to his being sold into slavery by his own flesh and blood. Nor did he fully comprehend that his propensity to dream dreams would develop into an ability to interpret others' dreams, resulting in the mechanism by which he fulfilled his destiny of becoming the conduit God used to save the descendants of Abraham, Isaac, and Jacob.

The story of Moses is as unlikely as what happened to Joseph. Angels, and then God Himself, visited Moses, to place him on his road to destiny: leader of the great rescue of the Israelites from Egypt.

Dreams also figured prominently in the sequence of events that surrounded the birth and life of Jesus: Mary, mother of Jesus, was visited by an angel and told of her conception of a sacred life. Angels also paid a visit to Mary's fiancé (another Joseph) to make sure he knew and understood his role in raising and protecting the precious gift that was baby Jesus. Finally, the angel told Joseph, Jesus' earthly father, to take the infant Christ down into Egypt to avoid Herod's wrath, thus providing safety to the most important figure known to man. For He would be the Savior of this world, executing the most incredible supernatural rescue in the history of the universe: the redemption of sinners.

These events are much more than symbolism. This is the work of a precise God, who does everything perfectly and in order. No accidents. No coincidences. All that is required of us is to be obedient to God's will, regardless of the circumstances, and trust in His Word.

Your Egypt Experience (Part I)

In the midst of following God's will and trusting in Him, He sometimes requires us to spend time in our own personal Egypt experience so that He can prepare us for His great work. Then, in His time, He will bring us out of Egypt for His honor and glory, and for us to be witnesses of His power, His mercy, His grace, and His love.

We may not understand why we are going through our Egypt experience, but God is so merciful, sometimes He plants a "Joseph" ahead of time to look out for us, supply our needs, and protect us while we're in Egypt. Sometimes we have to wander around in the "wilderness" of life's circumstance while we learn to depend solely upon the Lord. And sometimes we have to remain in our Egypt experience until after the "Herod's" in our lives no longer present any danger.

It is difficult to be patient while going through an Egypt experience because we do not know why we must endure it, nor when it will end and our rescue will be secured. Before being rescued from an Egypt experience, patience and obedience are major requirements, as relief may not come quickly. Being obedient does not always have an immediate payoff. It is often necessary to demonstrate consistency and exercise faith in spite of our current situation.

Take note and highlight the fact that even when Moses followed God's instructions, the burdens on the people increased (Exodus 5). Some may look at this Bible story and think to themselves: *Wait a minute. God hardened Pharaoh's heart, causing him and the children of Israel a lot of unnecessary grief. Then when Pharaoh finally relented and obeyed God, releasing the children of Israel, they experienced a lot of stress and turmoil, wandering through the wilderness some forty years because of disobedience to God. What can we conclude from this?*

First, if we disobey God, we are guaranteed some stress and turmoil. Second, even when we do obey God, we are guaranteed some stress and turmoil. *Wait a minute! Is that right? Is that what the writer meant to say?* Absolutely! We must understand that we live in a very troubled, decadent world where godly men and women are not immune to all things that occur (Matthew 5:45). Third, and most important: When we make the decision to follow God and allow Him to change our lives, we can expect our share of hardships, pain, and disappointment . . . along with more blessings than any of us can imagine or deserve (Matthew 10:22).

Your Egypt Experiences (Part II) Are a Witness to Others

For some, hardships and blessings happen somewhat simultaneously in a sort of rhythmic pattern throughout the lifespan. For others, there may be periods where it seems like all blessings (everything is going well), and then all hardships (everything is going wrong). Some might call this the "roller coaster" of life. At one time or another, we are all passengers on the roller coaster of life. It is a guarantee that troubles will come in life (Matthew 6:34), whether you serve the Lord or not. It is inevitable. So, you may as well serve the Lord. "For my yoke is easy and my burden is light" (Matthew 11:30, NIV). When things get really ugly during your personal Egypt experience, it is good to be on the Lord's side!

Being patient and obedient through our Egypt experience requires total trust in God and acceptance of His will in our lives. Sometimes God tells us to go "here" or leave "there," but then it appears as if He has closed doors—the very doors which, to us, would have allowed our movement. He is testing our faith and willingness to serve Him even under dire circumstances. However, God is also making a statement to all those around us: "I am the Lord, and there is no other" (Isaiah 45:5-6, 18, Joel 2:27, NIV).

Do not become discouraged when it appears as if God has blocked your path to leaving the Egypt experience in your life. Do not despair or remain upset when it seems as though God has sent you on a detour and delayed your escape from the tormentors in your life. Our past experiences with God are designed to increase our present and future confidence in His Word. In those moments when spiritual depression seeps in, it is important to remember that God always knows what is best for us, and He does it *His* way. The victories in our lives are not just for us. God's blessings are designed to have a ripple effect. Like a stone thrown into a still lake, our blessings are sure to reverberate out and touch others, bringing more praise to God in heaven. Remember that God is using your life to make a statement to the world!

God may harden some hearts and not intervene when folks are against you. He may block paths and exits that would appear to get you away from your problems. The Lord may not lift your burdens immediately after you pray. In fact, things could actually get worse before they get better. Hold on! God is making a statement through your faith and obedience. God wants to make a statement through your praise. God wants to show the world, through you, that He is the Alpha and Omega. He is the great Jehovah. He is King of Kings and Lord of Lords. He is your Savior and the Savior of this world (Isaiah 43:3, 11). Be careful when you try and leave "Egypt"! God may use your life to make a statement to your family and friends, co-workers, and anyone else your life touches.

The decision to follow Christ is not for the faint of heart, or for those who seek an easy path. As a child, I remember listening to sermons in which the preachers would tell the congregation that following Christ guaranteed hardship, and often, resentment from even friends and family members who did not believe or accept Christ as the Living God. I used to think to myself: *Wow, this preacher sure isn't selling Jesus very well!* It was not until many years later, when I was a young adult and had experienced the trials and tribulations of this life first hand, that I understood what the preachers meant.

Hold on to Jesus because you will be tested in every way possible. Discouragement is probable at some point during your life journey. Disappointment may occur more often than you ever expected or imagined. Spiritual depression is a possibility no one predicts in life when making the decision to follow the Son of God.

Over the years, as I stumbled and staggered through my own Christian experience, I came to realize that sometimes God allows negative situations to appear so dire and impossible to us that when the situation is resolved, it will be crystal clear to us—and everyone around us—that divine intervention was at work. God makes sure we recognize that we need Him on a day by day, hour by hour, minute by minute, second by second basis!

Just like when God explained to Moses that He intentionally hardened Pharaoh's heart so the situation would appear impossible, and He would be glorified. God's miracles for Moses and his congregation left no doubt who was ruler of the universe. So too, God allows situations in our lives to appear to spiral out of control (out of our control, not His) so that when He delivers us, we can see and feel the magnitude of His power and His love for us, leaving us with no confusion who He is and what He can do in our lives. The Lord wants us to recognize that He is God—and then praise Him!

In God's Time, Not Our Time

It is important to remember (and worth repeating) that all during the time that God was demonstrating His power to Pharaoh, the children of Israel remained slaves and suffered Pharaoh's wrath. It is often the case that God is working on our blessing while we continue to suffer under the weight of the trial. We may be distraught over serious health issues, death of a loved one, or loss of a job. We may feel burdened under a load of stress and worry concerning a troubled marriage, wayward children, or caring for a disabled elderly relative. Sometimes, it may feel as if God is taking too long to address our circumstances. This is a natural human feeling, especially when we are not privy to the inner workings of the Godhead related to our personal outcomes.

Many years ago, I remember a sermon by Elder Henry J. Fordham III, in which he talked about how easy it is to become discouraged as we wait on God to resolve our issues, answer our prayers, and "fix it" the way we want it fixed. Elder Fordham offered an explanation that still resonates in my mind as a reminder to be patient and trust in God, describing Him as someone who knows all about us and the minute details of our needs.

There are certainly many reasons why it may appear that God is taking His time before He lets us in on His will for our lives. It could be that we are ready for the answer, but God is still designing the plan that is ultimately best for us and those around us (remember, our trials and blessings are not just about us). It could be that God's plan is ready and waiting for implementation, but we are far from ready to adhere to His will in our lives. It could also be that God's plan is ready and we are ready, but the Lord is testing our faith and wants us to "Be still, and know that I am God" (Psalm 46:10, NIV).

Regardless of what the particular trial might be, this is not the time to give up. God wants others to benefit from the blessing He is preparing for us.

God deals in multiple blessing moments. He blesses others while He blesses you! Your victory over your trial may be a wonderful example and testimony for those who knew about or witnessed your difficulties. Your victory and subsequent praise are for the purpose of encouraging others to trust in God and serve Him. "Now then, stand still and see this great thing the Lord is about to do before your eyes!" (1 Samuel 12:16, NIV). The postscript to this chapter of "trials come with blessings" is that many of us quickly forget how wonderfully and powerfully God has worked on our behalf. We become discouraged when things turn for the worse and we forget about recent victories and God's faithfulness—just like the children of Israel. There they were, on the banks of the Red Sea after just having been mightily delivered out of Egypt by God, following a series of miracles. When they realized they were being hotly pursued by Pharaoh's army, they cried out to the Lord, asking Him why He had allowed more trouble to come their way. Like them, sometimes when we are just getting comfortable with our last blessing, before we even have time to fully enjoy the victory, trouble comes fast on our heels once again.

As Pharaoh chased after the children of Israel to exact revenge, they panicked and began to question their safety and God's promises. They were fearful and began doubting that leaving Egypt had been such a good idea after all. They began to complain and resent the very thing for which they had prayed—freedom from captivity. The children of Israel wanted the blessing, but not the trial. They wanted God's miracles, but on their own terms. They wanted their request of God to be a smooth transition, from slavery to freedom—no problems in between.

What the children of Israel received was just the opposite of smooth and easy. The God of the universe, as usual, had another plan. God had much more at stake than just freeing His people from bondage. After all, He is God, all-powerful and almighty!

He could have easily shut down Pharaoh and removed His people from Egypt in an instant. However, remember that the Israelites were inhabitants of Egypt for some 430 years. They had developed habits and behaviors which were not of God. They had become comfortable in their state of bondage and had no idea how to handle freedom. Many were not even serving the God of their fathers. If God were to save His people, it was imperative that He first remind them of who He is and what He expects. God's first lesson to His people when they left Egypt: Suffering often precedes saving.

The Lord Keeps His Promises

Even after being saved from the bondage of Egypt and the wrath of Pharaoh, and despite having so recently been the benefactors of God's mercy, grace, and power, the children of Israel questioned the Lord's promises. How often do we turn fearful at the sight of trouble approaching, or panic when caught off guard by the enemy? Far too often, we quickly forget about God's most recent victories (blessings) in our lives and cry out to Him, questioning why He has allowed our trials or why we must fight yet another seemingly impossible battle. Those past victories and blessings should remind us that God is all-powerful! He will take care of us in any situation. God always keeps His promises, yet we have a role to play. The Lord's promises are dependent upon our adherence to His will:

> The Lord is not slow in keeping his promise, as some understand slowness. Instead he is patient with you, not wanting anyone to perish, but everyone to come to repentance. (2 Peter 3:9, NIV)

The Lord has a plan for rescuing us from our "captivity," but we must be willing to trust in Him completely. Why do we doubt the Word of the Lord?

When the Lord brings you out of your Egypt experience, He is a constant guide. When God led Moses and his congregation out of Egypt, He was a "pillar of a cloud" by day, and a "pillar of fire" by night (Exodus 13:21-22, KJV). Our God is very thorough in how He keeps His promises to those that have faith in Him and obey His will. In Genesis 46, the Lord promised Jacob that if he had faith and accepted the Lord's will for him to take his family down to Egypt, He would "surely bring thee up again." Well, in Genesis 47: 28-31, Israel (Jacob) died. He had lived with Joseph in Egypt for seventeen years. Before dying, Israel made Joseph promise *not* to bury him in Egypt, but in the land of his fathers. In Genesis 50, Joseph buries Israel in Canaan, as promised. In this way, as promised, the Lord brought Jacob (Israel) out of Egypt, and he left behind a great nation!

That's not all. Joseph also died in Egypt (Genesis 50:22, 26). This is when the children of Israel became slaves (Exodus 1). The Lord is so thorough that when Moses led the children of Israel out of the land of Egypt, they carried Joseph's bones out with them:

> Moses took the bones of Joseph with him because Joseph had made the sons of Israel swear an oath. He had said, "God will surely come to your aid; and then you must carry my bones up with you from this place." (Exodus 13:19, NIV, see also Hebrews 11:22)

When the Lord makes a promise, it is thorough and complete. He did not leave in the land of Egypt anything or anyone that belonged to Jacob (not even the bones of his descendants!). The Lord made a covenant with Abraham, Isaac, and Jacob, and He stated it often:

> God also said to Moses, "I *am* the Lord: I appeared to Abraham, to Isaac, and to Jacob as God Almighty, but by my name the Lord I did not make myself fully known to them. I also established my covenant with them to give them the land of Canaan, where they resided as foreigners. Moreover, I have heard the groaning of the Israelites, whom the Egyptians are enslaving, and I have remembered my covenant. Therefore, say to the Israelites: 'I *am* the Lord, and I will bring you out from under the yoke of the Egyptians. I will free you from being slaves to them, and I will redeem you with an outstretched arm and with mighty acts of judgment. I will take you as my own people, and I will be your God. Then you will know that I *am* the Lord your God, who brought you out from under the yoke of the Egyptians." (Exodus 6:2-7, NIV)

These words of God: "I *am* the Lord" are echoed throughout the Bible, along with a reminder that God chose the seed of Abraham, made a covenant, and rescued them from their Egypt experience to be *His people* (i.e. Exodus 6:6; 32:11-14; 34:9; Leviticus 11:45; 19:2-4; 22: 32-33; 25:38; 26:40-45; Deuteronomy 4:20, 30-31, 37-39; 5:6, 15; 7:6-9; 9:5, 26-29; 10:17-22; 16:1; 24:17-24; 26:8-19; 29:1-16; 2 Kings 17:34-36; Acts 3:25; 7:34; 13:17; 11:26, 27; Hebrews 6:13-15; 8:8-13; Revelation 21:3).   •

The Lord's covenant is readily available to us even today. God has written it in our hearts and minds (Deuteronomy 30:10-11, 14-16, 19-20).

Moses is telling us that we have the choice of living in God or dying without Him. We must be obedient to the Lord's will so that in keeping our part of His covenant, He will keep His. This is the essence of the metaphor of being set free from your Egypt experience.

Your Egypt Experience (Part III)

Everyone has had an experience where they felt trapped, engulfed, or shackled to a place, situation, or even a person. It could be a job or career path that has someone feeling trapped. Maybe someone is in a relationship in which he or she feels oppressed, abused, or neglected. It could be a circumstance beyond our control that enslaves, discourages, or dismays us. Whatever your personal predicament may be; it is important to listen to what God is trying to tell you through your Egypt experience.

God is telling you that He wants to free you from your bondage. He wants to rescue you from your imprisonment. He wants to release the shackles from your heart, mind, and soul! He wants to lead you out of the land of your Egypt experience—whatever that is for you. However, the Lord is not content to simply rescue you from bondage. The Lord wants to free you from your mind-set of serving other gods. He wants you to stop repeating the same damaging behaviors you picked up during your stay in Egypt. The Lord wants to destroy the gods you became accustomed to while living in Egypt. He wants you to walk away from the gods you brought with you out of Egypt. He wants to be your God!

The Lord wants you to be forever loyal and obedient to the one who created you for your specific purpose, followed you, and kept you safe even when you rejected Him and decided you needed other gods. The Lord wants to take you out of your Egypt experience, but recognizes He must also remove from inside your heart and mind those ungodly things you acquired during your captivity.

However, you must not be confused or naïve about the full impact on your life when you leave Egypt. Be careful when you try to leave Egypt because there is more to it than just being freed from the bondage of your current circumstances. Remember that the Lord works in multiple ways in what may appear to be a singular experience. Once God frees you from your Egypt experience, you may feel the pressure of an "army" of doubt and fear breathing down your neck. You may experience a host of negative influences in hot pursuit trying to keep you from leaving your Egypt experience (including some friends and family). During this time you must exercise strong faith and an unwavering trust in the Lord as He compels you to continue moving forward.

Leaving your captivity and negative existence behind is just the beginning of your journey back to your true, Living God. You will encounter a "Red Sea" of opposition and skepticism just when you think you are safely out of Egypt. It is tough to leave behind a way of life to which you have grown accustomed, even when that life has been full of pain, disappointment, and discouragement. Sometimes people decide to stay in the negative experiences they know well rather than take a chance on seeking new and potentially more positive experiences that lay ahead.

You may grow fearful as you approach the banks of your Red Sea experience because it may appear that the Lord has led you out of one problem only to deposit you on the shores of a big catastrophe. But you must hold on to your faith, raise your hands toward heaven in prayer, and then step forward, knowing that the Lord will make a way out of no way. You must demonstrate your faith and trust in God's will for your life by moving on *His* command. Then watch as the waves of turmoil divide before you, providing a dry path of comfort and stability for you to walk in confidence, knowing that the God of the universe is your support in the midst of even the most impossible situations.

Remember that the journey back to the true and Living God is just beginning, even as you look behind you and see the source of your pain and anguish swallowed up with the wave of God's mighty hand. Your journey back to God is just beginning, though some days may make you feel as if you are wandering in the "wilderness" as God begins the process of purification in your life. The Lord will bring you out of Egypt, and then begin the process of extracting Egypt out of you.

The Lord is patient and just, but He wants to remove all the false gods you brought with you out of Egypt. He wants to destroy everything that held you captive. All of the bad decisions and mistakes of your past were swallowed up in the Red Sea of God's mercy and grace. However, it is human nature to hold on to those things which used to bring temporary comfort or camouflage the reality of a sinful life. The Lord may allow you to wander around in your wilderness of personal and spiritual reflection until all the "demons" in your conscience die off.

God wants to make sure that all your negative self-talk and feelings of worthlessness are buried in the wilderness of your despair. He wants you to emerge from your Egypt experience with an understanding of who *He* is and how much *He* loves you. He wants to strengthen you for the rest of your journey back to Him. There will be some battles along the road back to your God. Mistakes will be made. The Lord may have to chastise, cajole, and comfort you during this journey, but He will never leave you.

The Lord of Abraham, Isaac, and Jacob is also *your* God, and He wants to give you a brand new life. He wants to give you a life of peace—one of real success. He wants to bless your comings and goings in life. He wants to remove you from your Egypt experience and give you a "Canaan experience." The Lord wants to fill your life with a blessed experience, "flowing with milk and honey." He wants to be your God. He wants you to be His son or daughter.

However, there comes a responsibility and an expectation from God when He comes down with an outstretched arm and rescues you from your Egypt experience. God expects loyalty and obedience. He expects recognition and praise. He expects you to understand and tell all with whom you come into contact that you belong to Him. He wants you to humble yourself and admit that your success depends upon Him; that your very life is in His almighty hands. God wants your praise, honor, and love. He wants the glory that comes with saving you from yourself. God wants you to forever be *His* son or daughter!

> But as for you, the Lord took you and brought you out of the iron-smelting furnace, out of Egypt, to be the people of his inheritance, as you now are. (Deuteronomy 4:20, NIV)

If you are currently suffering, keep your faith and trust that your salvation is on the way:

> When you are in distress and all these things have happened to you, then in later days you will return to the Lord your God and obey him. For the Lord your God is a merciful God; he will not abandon or destroy you or forget the covenant with your ancestors, which he confirmed to them by oath. Because he loved your

ancestors and chose their descendants after them, he brought you out of Egypt by his Presence and his great strength. (Deuteronomy 4:30-31, 37, NIV)

Then watch as your blessing ripples through your family, your church, and your community! When the Lord brings you out of the land of your Egypt experience, it is for one purpose: so He can be your God! And you can be His son or daughter! God's perfect plan for your life has already been scripted for success! Give Him praise!

> *"Acknowledge and take to heart this day that the Lord is God in heaven above and on the earth below. There is no other."* (Deuteronomy 4:39, NIV)

Chapter 9

Incarcerated By Sin

———⋄∘≪≫∘⋄———

"The Spirit of the Lord is on me, because he has anointed me to pro-claim good news to the poor. He has sent me to proclaim freedom for the prisoners and recovery of sight for the blind, to set the oppressed free" (Luke 4:18, NIV).

Imprisoned

The man sat there in the dark of night, wondering if the light of day would ever again flash across his sullen face. He was not sure how long he had been in the cramped, dark cell, for very little light came through the Plexiglas window at the top corner of his cell. This man (we'll call him "Steve"), was serving twenty-five years to life for several brutal assaults that were indicative of his life of crime since he was old enough to protect himself. Protecting himself had become a lifelong endeavor for Steve, ever since that fateful day when his mother put him out of her house on Christmas Eve.

Steve was seven years old at the time. He had nowhere to go and no one to turn to. Now, here he was, age 28—an intimidating cut of a man, with strong broad shoulders, a muscular build, and a perpetually menacing glare carved into his rugged face—serving what ultimately could be his final sentence for a life dedicated to hurting others more than they had hurt him. Steve was in "the hole" (solitary confinement) for the umpteenth time for "failure to get along with others." However, something was different this time.

He felt despair as he looked back over the last twenty-one years of his life. The pain of his aborted childhood echoed constantly in his brain as he tried to defend the course of action he had followed throughout his life. He had borrowed the mantra, "Kill or be killed," and had relied on it as a motivating stance on numerous occasions. Yet now he sat alone—remorseful—wondering if there was a God, and if so, where He could be found. Steve had often experienced clinical depression as an abandoned child who grew up as a ward of the state. However, this feeling was different. Steve felt abandoned by God, and his despair was palpable!

Unfortunately, Steve's story is not a novel one. You may be surprised to learn the number of families that experience the reality of incarceration and/or psychiatric confinement. In the United States of America, we incarcerate our citizens more than any other nation in the world. According to *The PEW Center on the States* (2008), more than one in 100 adults is now confined in American prisons or jails. At the beginning of 2008, the American penal system held more than 2.3 million adults. China was second with 1.5 million people behind bars. Russia was a distant third at 890,000 inmates (PEW, 2008).

Prevalence of Mental Illness among Incarcerated Populations

In 1998, an estimated 283,800 mentally ill offenders were incarcerated in the Nations jails and prisons. In recent surveys completed by the Bureau of Justice Statistics, 16 % of State prisons, 7% of Federal inmates, and 16% of those in local jails reported either a mental condition or an overnight stay in a mental hospital. About 16%, or an estimated 547,800 probationers, said they had had mental condition or stayed overnight in a mental hospital at some point in their lifetime (Paula Ditton, BJS, 1999). Current estimates suggest between 7 and 16 percent of those incarcerated in the United States have serious mental illness (Steadman et al, 2009). Among people with severe mental illness, incarceration is five times more likely among those with a co-occurring substance use disorder than among those without a substance use disorder (Steadman et al, 2009). People with mental illnesses face significant clinical, legal, and socioeconomic challenges and are overrepresented among probation and parole populations in the community (Prins & Draper, 2009). Clearly, mass incarceration is a major issue in the United States.

The subject of incarceration and those imprisoned in some form or another is a familiar focus in the Bible, as well as the world in which we now live. In a recent Internet word search of Bible reference resources, I found the word *prison* is identified with 126 Bible verses. In Genesis 39:20, Joseph (son of Jacob) is sent to prison. In Judges 15:10 through 1 Kings 22:27, Samson is tricked into being captured. Throughout the Old Testament, prophets and kings alike were often thrown into prison. From Psalm 68:6 through Psalm 146:7, David often writes of prison, both metaphorically and literally. In the New Testament, John the Baptist, the apostles (most famously, Paul), the disciples, and even Jesus Himself were placed in prison at one time or another. Jesus saw the subject important enough to mention those in prison on several occasions. My favorite reference is when Jesus places Himself in the position of all prisoners throughout history:

> I was a stranger and you did not invite me in, I needed clothes and you did not clothe me, I was sick and in prison and you did not look after me. (Matthew 25:43, NIV)

There are few more devastating circumstances for an individual than involuntary confinement (i.e. incarceration or psychiatric commitment). Forced physical confinement for any reason represents a dramatic level of separation from friends, family, and society as a whole. For some, it feels like one step above the ultimate separation: death. After all, how does one feel "alive" when isolated from those who give one life?

Does this sound too drastic or overly dramatic? In his book, *Margin*, Richard Swenson points to a study that highlights the effects of "aloneness." Swenson reports: "Study after study confirms that a healthy marriage, family, or community support structure yields better health and increased longevity—a kind of buffering system against the pain of distress." It is not a leap, then, to suggest that not having those connections act as a risk factor.

One of the largest surveys followed five thousand residents of Alameda County California, for nine years. The conclusion, after correcting for variables: 'Those who were unmarried had few friends or relatives, and shunned community organizations were more than twice as likely to die during that time than people who had these social relationships" (*Margin*, p. 62). It should not surprise anyone then that for those who find themselves incarcerated or confined to a psychiatric facility, maintaining the type of social relationships ("buffering system") described by Dr. Swenson in *Margin* is greatly compromised (if not nearly impossible). At the least then, many would certainly agree that being removed from those one loves creates a most formidable stressor, and has an impact on individuals physically, emotionally, psychologically, and spiritually.

Regardless of the reasons why an individual is imprisoned or committed, in almost every case, families with loved ones in confinement are temporarily fractured and/or irreparably damaged as a result. And, as is the case with our other "real life" examples of stressors throughout this book, incarceration exerts intense pressure on the three most important components of the human organism: physical (overall health), cognition (thinking), and psychosocial (relationships). Naturally, spiritual depression is a common by-product when any one (or all) of these areas are impaired or grossly compromised.

How Does One Become Imprisoned?

How is it that individuals find themselves in prison in the first place? As children growing up in individually unique environments, we all played the game of asking one another, "What do you want to be when you grow up?" It was a fun, sometimes silly exercise that displayed levels of creativity and uniqueness of culture, which gave a hint to what our minds were exposed to, and what our little hearts desired. We easily rattled off our wish list of career interests. I do not believe that any child who played this game ever wished to be in a psychiatric facility or behind prison walls. Those of us who remember playing that children's game would naturally dismiss such an idea as absurd. So it is safe to say that *no one* ever grew up eagerly anticipating and/or desiring to go to jail or prison and suffer the pain it brings in separation from family, friends, and society. However, many of our brothers and sisters, mothers and fathers, children, aunts, uncles, cousins, and dearest friends have had to walk through the doors of a psychiatric hospital or heard prison gates slam behind them. They ended up in places where hope is certainly fleeting at times, and discouragement, disillusionment, and depression are in great abundance.

The incarceration rates in the United States of America quoted earlier represent definitive evidence that we are a nation of broken individuals, broken families, and broken communities (see Chapter 10). Moreover, justice-involved individuals and those committed to psychiatric facilities at some point all come to understand that they are not the only ones impacted by their imprisonment. Their families are "doing time" as well when those hospital doors lock and those cell bars clang shut. Being incarcerated is a humbling experience, fraught with fear and anguish. For those with severe mental illness, it is also confusing and heartbreaking.

Newly initiated imprisoned persons have every reason to be frightened, frustrated, and fatigued physically, psychologically, emotionally, and spiritually. Those more experienced with being legally confined may appear stronger and more confident on the surface. Nevertheless, having retraced their steps back into confinement yet again (multiple times for some) also brings on a heavy dose of reality: Confident thoughts and stalwart emotions inevitably morph into disappointment, distress—and quite often—spiritual depression. The strain of separation ultimately has the same effect, regardless of which side of the bars you happen to be on: incarcerated or family of the incarcerated.

People who do not have a family member or close friend who is/was incarcerated may wonder how they can possibly relate to those who do have imprisoned family, or who are behind bars themselves. Imagine being separated from those you love as punishment for the poor decisions you have made throughout your life, or due to a condition/disorder that negatively impacts your thought processes, judgment, and behavior.

Try to visualize how it might feel to be locked away from those who gave you life because your internal thoughts and emotions control your external behavior to such a degree that it warrants your removal from society in an effort to protect you from yourself, or protect others from you. It is this same type of empty feeling that occurs between man and God as a result of being "incarcerated by sin."

How Does "Sin" Imprison People Who Appear "Free?"

I must define the term "sin," as it will appear prominently in this chapter. For purposes of our discussion, *sin* is simply *wrong behavior against the laws of God* (i.e. love for God and love for all of God's creation, including animals and nature), which also often coincide with *breaking the laws of man*.

Incarceration is an apt metaphor to describe the spiritual separation we experience from our Creator due to the manifestation of sin. Using the incarceration metaphor not only helps us understand how sin separates us from God; it also provides a realistic example of just how repulsive sin is to God, and how devastating sin becomes for us, His creation, when we fail to recognize that disobedience to God (sin) is the source of our troubles. Consider this:

"God's holiness does not tolerate sin and actively reacts against it" (Dr. Angel Rodriguez, *Atonement and the Cross of Christ*, 2008, Adult Study Guide, p. 12).

"The wrath of God is being revealed from heaven against all the godlessness and wickedness of people, who suppress the truth by their wickedness" (Romans 1:18, NIV).

Sin locks us up, driving a wedge of separation between us and God: "But your iniquities have separated you from your God; your sins have hidden his face from you, so that he will not hear. (Isaiah 59:2, NIV). Our sin is an affront to God's love and destroys the relationship between us: "Because of all their wickedness in Gilgal, I hated them there.

Because of their sinful deeds, I will drive them out of my house. I will no longer love them; all their leaders are rebellious" (Hosea 9:15, NIV).

Those are strong words from God, as given to the prophet Hosea. And there are a plethora of other examples throughout the Old Testament where God's wrath was kindled against His people as a result of their disobedience, and failure to adhere to His commandments. Thank goodness our separation from God, due to sin, is temporary and fixable, depending on our faith and trust in our Creator. God *hates the sin*, but *loves the sinner*.

God has provided ample opportunities for us to reconcile our relationship with Him through His Son: "For through him we both have access to the Father by one

Spirit" (Ephesians 2:18, NIV). However, there is still the chance that, for some, sin will cause irreparable damage to their relationship with God, if they do not accept the free gift of salvation through the death, resurrection, ascension, and intercession (on our behalf) of Jesus Christ our Lord.

Now, before moving forward, we should address the fact that there may be folks who think that using the word "sin" is archaic, does not apply to them, and is not an appropriate term to use in a modern discussion on how the whole human race has become separated from God. Here are a few important reminders that address this form of reasoning:

> As it is written: "There is no one righteous not even one."
> (Romans 3:10, NIV)

> For all have sinned and fall short of the glory of God.
> (Romans 3:23, NIV)

> Surely I was sinful at birth, sinful from the time my mother conceived me. (Psalm 51:5, NIV)

If we are really honest with ourselves, the two Bible texts from Paul's writings in Romans probably make sense to most of us. But what about David's suggestion in psalm 51 that we are not only born into sin, but conceived in sin? How is that possible? Is it also possible that we are born into a "prison" of sin (i.e. the earth)? This may be a difficult concept for many of us to comprehend. So where do we begin our search for a reasonable connection between Paul's examples of the spiritual state of human beings and David's statement? We must go back to the Bible, where all answers exist. And the best place to begin tying together our incarcerated by sin metaphor is, well, at the beginning.

In the Beginning (Part I): Earth (The First "Prison")

"In the beginning God created the heaven and the earth" (Genesis 1:1, KJV). This is the first line of text written in the Bible, so it is a great place to start our search. It is my belief that *nothing* came before God. There is also no indication in this first verse of the Bible (or anywhere else in the Bible) that God created sin. Therefore, we need to keep looking for the origin of sin.

Based on what theologians and biblical historians have shared with us, we can say that God created all life in heaven and in earth. Celestial beings (angels) also qualify as God's creation. It is believed by most theologians that angels in heaven preceded human life on earth. Relying on biblical research and theology, we believe that the most celebrated of all the angels in heaven was Lucifer, a guardian cherub who was magnificently created and shown brightest among all the other angels. Read Ezekiel's eloquent description of Lucifer (Ezekiel 28:12-17) and Isaiah's description as well (Isaiah 14:12-15). These two inspired reports from two respected Old Testament prophets tell us that Lucifer was magnificently created, yet he inherently had some major ego problems in terms of his view of himself compared to the Most High God. Ezekiel is a little more specific than Isaiah, pointing out several important things about Lucifer.

1) Lucifer was "blameless" until wickedness "was found" in him.
2) Lucifer sinned.
3) Lucifer's pride in his beauty and splendor corrupted his wisdom and sealed his downfall.
4) Lucifer was disgraced and expelled from heaven because of his sin and rebellion.
5) Lucifer launched a negative public relations (PR) assault against God and His law.

This is great information because it gives us a pretty good idea of how Lucifer's downfall coincided with the downfall of mankind. Both Isaiah and Ezekiel seem to agree that Lucifer was thrown out of heaven. However, how is it that Lucifer (the angel) ended up inhabiting the earth as Satan (the devil)? The revelation of Saint John can help us here:

> Then war broke out in heaven. Michael and his angels fought against the dragon, and the dragon and his angels fought back. But he was not strong enough, and they lost their place in heaven. The great dragon was hurled down—that ancient serpent called the devil, or Satan, who leads the whole world astray. He was hurled to the earth, and his angels with him. . . . woe to the earth and the sea, because the devil has gone down to you! (Revelation 12:7-9, 12, NIV)

Now we have the full story of how sin first found its way into the earth's atmosphere. Satan did not leave heaven quietly. He put up a violent fight and actually tried to overthrow God and His royal host. Satan lost the war in heaven, but won some support from other celestial beings. Satan's negative PR campaign managed to succeed in convincing one third of heaven's angels to join his insurgence against God (Revelation 12:4). He was successful, in part, by bringing into question God's fairness, God's integrity, and God's love. Satan was successful in creating "the great controversy" (see Ellen G. White) long before his dealings with Job. The focus of the universe on earth is to judge whether God's law is fair, and whether it is even possible to keep the law of God. It seems clear then that Satan's punishment for crimes against God, his disruptive rebellion in heaven—his sin—was to be exiled to the earth. The earth then, in fact, became Satan's prison. Satan was the first creature in history to be incarcerated by sin.

The Rescue Plan

Satan's fall from heaven explains how sin existed in the earth before Adam and Eve were created. However, it does not explain why God went through with His plan of creation, knowing that Satan was sure to challenge His divinity at every turn. The God of the universe created our first parents, knowing they would sin. God could have scrapped His plan to create human life on earth as soon as it became obvious that Satan was out to destroy God's reputation along with anything and anyone He created. Instead, God gave humanity an opportunity to choose to serve Him and choose to love Him without coercion. Why? So that Satan (and his charges against God) would one day be proven false and sin would be forever eradicated from existence.

God obviously had another plan in mind much stronger than the challenge that Satan could put forth. His plan of salvation would enable Adam and Eve, and all the generations that followed, an opportunity to be saved despite their propensity to sin. That plan of salvation, of course, was Jesus taking our place for crimes committed against God by the human race. Jesus, as part of the Godhead (Father, Son, and Holy Spirit), was the architect who volunteered Himself as a sacrifice, should human creation fall to the crafty manipulations of Satan. Jesus, being God, was there at the beginning:

> In the beginning was the Word, and the Word was with God, and the Word was God. He was with God in the beginning. Through him all things were made; without him nothing was made that has been made. In him was life, and that life was the light of all mankind. The light shines in the darkness; and the darkness has not overcome it. (John 1:1-5, NIV)

Jesus, being God, knew that Adam and Eve would fall, yet He willingly consented to the plan of salvation, which involved taking on human form, walking the earth for some thirty-three years as a "light" to mankind, before allowing the most excruciatingly painful and torturous week recorded in human history (ending in his physical death). He also knew that, in Him, victory over sin and Satan was guaranteed. Ever since, this message of victory through Jesus has been pronounced and repeated throughout the history of men. However, as John 1:5 tells us, "The light shines in the darkness, and the darkness did not comprehend it" (NASB).

In the end, Jesus wanted all of us to understand that He already won the battle in heaven. And through His death on the cross, His resurrection, and His ascension back to our Father in heaven (interceding on our behalf), He has already won the war with Satan on this earth, and in life to come. So we are heirs along with Christ because His sacrifice on our behalf made us children of God:

The Spirit himself testifies with our spirit that we are God's children. Now if we are children, then we are heirs—heirs of God and co-heirs with Christ, if indeed we share in his sufferings in order that we may also share in his glory. (Romans 8:16-17, NIV)

As children of God (Romans 8:9; John 1:12-13; 1 John 3:1-2; 1 John 5:19), we too have already won the war against Satan, should we choose to reject sin and embrace salvation. Jesus says to us the same thing He said to His disciples so long ago:

He replied, "I saw Satan fall like lightning from heaven. I have given you authority to trample on snakes and scorpions and to over-come all the power of the enemy; nothing will harm you. However, do not rejoice that the spirits submit to you, but rejoice that your names are written in heaven." (Luke 10:18-20, NIV)

Before even creating the foundations of the earth, God created for us a way of escape because He not only knew the beginning, He knew the ending!

In the Beginning (Part II): Love Conquers All

Creating Adam and Eve was God's crowning jewel during the week of creation on planet Earth. I believe this is so because God waited to create man until after He had created all the heavens, the earth, and all the animals (Genesis 1:26-31). "Then the Lord God formed a man *from* the dust of the ground and breathed into his nostrils the breath of life, and the man became a living being" (Genesis 2:7, NIV, italics added).

The first two chapters of Genesis contain an amazing story of love, kindness, thoughtfulness, and deep consideration. How careful and caring was God, the Creator, to place a being made in His image and in His likeness in a home specif-ically designed for the warmth, comfort, and pleasure of His creation. No wonder the Bible says: "God saw all that he had made, and it was very good. And there was evening, and there was morning—the sixth day" (Genesis 1:31, NIV). To cap it all off, God rested from His work by instituting a day of rest for humankind so they would commune with their Creator, and He with them:

> Thus the heavens and the earth were completed in all their vast array. By the seventh day God had finished the work he had been doing; so on the seventh day he rested from all his work. Then God blessed the seventh day and made it holy, because on it he rested from all the work of creating that he had done. (Genesis 2:1-3, NIV)

My imagination tells me that on that first Sabbath day, God gave Adam a tour of his new home (the Garden of Eden), showing him the river that branched out in four directions, the beautiful precious stones, and the plants and trees that were designated for his unlimited use (Genesis 2:8-16) . . . and just one tree that was "off limits" (Genesis 2:17). It was this "tree of knowledge of good and evil" that would eventually become the center of temptation which would forever mark the human race as "sinners of choice," and result in our past and present state of sin-induced incarceration and separation from God.

The Fall

It should be noted that Adam did not send the fallen human race spiraling down into the "dungeon" of sin all by himself. On the contrary! He had the help and support of his beautiful wife, Eve, whom God created after realizing that all the animals He had created had partners, but Adam had none (Genesis 2:18-22). Unbeknownst to Adam and Eve, they also had to contend with a certain exiled angel who had a bone to pick with God, and a perpetually terrible disposition!

Unfortunately Satan, the originator of sin (1 John 3:8), caught Adam and Eve on a day when they were most vulnerable. I was not there, of course, but I can imagine it had to be one of those days when things were a little slow. Adam and Eve may have been slightly bored and wandered off, looking around the Garden for something new and thrilling they had not seen before. Before they knew it, they had wandered too far away from God and found themselves standing exactly where He told them *not* to be: in front of the tree of knowledge of good and evil.

On the surface, one could understand if our first parents rationalized that simply standing in front of a tree that was off-limits should be no big deal. After all, the tree was planted in the middle of their luxurious home, and they were caretakers of everything in the Garden. Adam and Eve would soon realize the same thing we are usually too slow to appreciate today: The problem is not where one stands, but whom one left to arrive at one's destination of temptation. Adam and Eve left the presence of the Lord—not the other way around. Therefore, they were immediately vulnerable to wherever, whatever, and whoever came across their path. It is the misfortune of the entire human race that Adam and Eve came across Satan, the purveyor of lies and expert in disguise and deceit. He had bad intentions as soon as he laid eyes on them (Genesis 3:1- 3, NIV).

Satan, disguised as a serpent, was able to beguile Eve with the "smoke and mirrors" distraction of his beauty and clever tongue. He delivered the knockout punch using the oldest trick in the book: partial truths:

> "You will not certainly die," the serpent said to the woman. "For God knows that when you eat from it your eyes will be opened, and you will be like God, knowing good and evil." (Genesis 3:4-5, NIV)

How is it that Eve, who before her tragic mistake was perfect in every way (including intelligence), and Adam, who was apparently slightly less intelligent than Eve (evidenced by his giving in to his wife without much objection), fell prey to a fallen angel disguised as a serpent? Dr. Angel M. Rodriguez provides a logical explanation:

> In order for Satan to persuade Eve to disobey God, he sought to attack the character of God. He said, basically that God was fundamentally a selfish being who limits the development of His intelligent creatures, keeping them in a state of involuntary submission through a threat of death. He was not what He claimed to be, a God of love, but was camouflaging His true nature through the appearance of a loving attitude. Satan was projecting onto God His own deceitful nature and the real intentions of his corrupt heart. His attack in heaven against God and God's loving nature was now

being transferred to this planet (Atonement and the Cross of Christ, *Adult Teachers Sabbath School Study Guide*, p. 20).

Satan was the most magnificent of all celestial beings created by God. And, being a guardian cherub placed him in close contact with God the Father, God the Son, and God the Holy Spirit. No being was in a better position to see and witness the omnipotence of the Godhead and to acknowledge God's love for all He created. Why in heaven, and on earth, would the most beautiful, most talented, most intelligent of cherub's willingly rebel against his Creator? Why would he ignore the power of God by attacking His creation on earth, and continue this attack throughout the ceaseless ages of eternity? Again, Ezekiel 28:17, is "exhibit A": "Your heart became proud on account of your beauty, and you corrupted your wisdom because of your splendor . . . " (NIV). Too much pride and selfishness can make even a wise creature behave foolishly. It also makes sense that if your wisdom has been corrupted, your behavior becomes dangerously unpredictable.

Clearly, Satan's perverted, dangerous tendencies help explain his devious interest and determined focus on undermining God by attacking His creation. By subverting Adam and Eve's loyalty to God, he not only hoped to permanently separate man from God, but also (through the stain of sin) to make the case that God's insistence on obedience to His law is unfair, unreasonable, and above all, not based on love, but instead on dictatorial and sadistic power. There it is again, that "evil projection" of Satan's character onto God's character, Dr. Rodriguez addressed.

So, here we have the most beautiful, and intelligent of all God's earthly creatures (woman), trying to match wits with the most beautiful and intelligent of all God's heavenly creatures (angel). The odds of Eve outsmarting Satan, disguised as a talking snake, were about as good then as our odds are today of outsmarting Satan disguised as any attractive person, place, or thing. Our only chance of resisting his "individually wrapped" temptations are to stay close to Jesus, and try to avoid wandering away so far as to find ourselves alone in the midst of the most crafty, life-threatening predator known to man: the devil. Of him, Peter warns: "Your enemy the devil prowls around like a roaring lion looking for someone to devour," (1 Peter 5:8, NIV).

Satan toys with us. He knows our weaknesses. He knows exactly which buttons to push, and which ways to manipulate us. Separating humankind from our God, through sin, has from the beginning of time been a game of seek and destroy for Satan. We are no competition for Satan, the father of lies.

> When the woman saw that the fruit of the tree was good for food and pleasing to the eye, and also desirable for gaining wisdom, she took some and ate it. She also gave some to her husband, who was with her, and he ate it. (Genesis 3:6, NIV)

Game! Set! Match! And the rest, as they say, is history.

Significantly, Adam and Eve were immediately aware of the magnitude of their crucial mistake of choice. They went from . . .

> Adam and his wife were both naked, and they felt no shame. (Genesis 2:25, NIV)

to . . .

> Then the eyes of both of them were opened, and they realized they were naked; so they sewed fig leaves together and made coverings for themselves. (Genesis 3:7, NIV)

This is significant because where there was once no shame, there was shame so visible it caused Adam and Eve to seek cover from God, the Creator:

> Then the man and his wife heard the sound of the Lord God as he was walking in the garden in the cool of the day, and they hid from the Lord God among the trees of the garden. (Genesis 3:8, NIV)

Seeking Independence + Rebellion = Separation

Why on earth would Adam and Eve think that they could hide from the Creator of the universe, their God . . . their friend? It seems to me that we do the same thing today. Our original mistake is veering away from the protective arms of Jesus. Then we fall prey to the temptation of sin. Once we succumb to sin, the Siamese twins of guilt and shame rear their ugly heads to pile on additional emotional burdens. I refer to the combination of negative emotions as Siamese twins because guilt and shame are attached at the hip. You rarely encounter one without the other. And they usually barge into your heart and soul when you are already feeling the lowest.

When we allow guilt and shame to take over our emotions, we exacerbate the original mistake by running further away from our Creator, creating an even wider chasm of separation from our Lord. The act of sin creates an atmosphere of distrust and awareness that we have done something wrong. Then guilt and shame converge to accentuate our immediate certainty of separation from our God, who "cannot tolerate wrong" or "look on evil" (Habakkuk 1:13). We know that the separation is immediate because our relationship with God immediately changes when we sin. Adam and Eve went from walking and talking with God face-to-face (Genesis 3:8), to being confronted by Him (Genesis 3:8-11), put out of their home, and banned for life (Genesis 3:23-24).

Adam and Eve having access to the tree of life would have compromised God's stated promise in Genesis 2:17 concerning what would happen if they disobeyed (i.e. death). So naturally, they had to be evicted. However, being removed from their beautiful Garden home was not the worst thing to befall Adam and Eve as a result of their sin. Of course, not having access to the tree of life began their immediate physical, mental, and spiritual deterioration (they *would* "surely die," but not die immediately, because of a life-saving set of "twins" God's *grace* and *mercy*). Nevertheless, besides eventual death, three other things happened in conjunction with being locked out of the Garden of Eden due to their disobedience:

1) The serpent (Satan) was forever cursed (Genesis 3:14).his fate sealed for eternity (Genesis 3:15, NIV).

2) The human race was cursed (Genesis 3:15), and the woman uniquely punished for her participation in the fall of humankind: To the woman he said, "I will make your pains in childbearing very severe; with painful labor you will give birth to children ..." (Genesis 3:16, NIV)
(Now we know why David wrote what he did in Psalm 51:5, regarding how we are born into a "sinful" world!)

3) The ground (earth) was cursed (Genesis 3:17-18), and the man was uniquely punished for his participation in the fall of humankind (Genesis 3:17-19, NIV).

Wow! What an unfortunate turn of events for Adam and Eve . . . and for all of us who followed! They went from walking and talking with God as one does with a friend, to walking away from His safe and secure presence, to not trusting in His Word, to disobeying at the behest of a clever distraction, to being cursed along with their future generations. Then finally (and no doubt most painfully), they were physically, emotionally, psychologically, and spiritually separated from their life-giving source: their Creator and Savior. As is the case in most separations that result from disobedience, distrust, and dishonesty, the relationship between man and God became impaired, dysfunctional, and grew worse over time.

Even if we all agreed that destroying the trust in a relationship is not a good thing, the punishment for Adam and Eve does not seem to fit the crime. Someone may be wondering: *What's the big deal in eating a piece of forbidden fruit?* We might pose that same question in reference to our own incidents of disobedience and dishonesty: What's the big deal? It was only a little lie." "Why is my wife/ husband so angry with me? I did not hurt anyone but myself when I used illegal drugs?" "Why is my family so hurt and disappointed in me? When I burglarized that home/business I was only trying to be a man and provide financial support for them."

Fill in the blank of the "whys," "it's not fairs," and "the punishment is too harsh" examples from your own life and you may come to realize that it is not the sinful act in particular that separates you from God (and too often, our families), it is the mind-set of disobedience, distrust, and dishonesty that direct our behavior. These then produce the "natural" consequences as a result of going against the laws of nature. The severity of the outcome of sin matches the hurt and disappointment felt by a Creator who gave us eternal life, everything necessary for eternal happiness, and His eternal love.

Dr. Angel M. Rodriguez, once again, provides a fitting perspective:

> Genesis 2:17 ['but you must not eat from the tree of the knowledge of good and evil, for when you eat of it you will surely die.'], was a clear expression of God's love for Adam and Eve and His intense desire to enjoy their fellowship forever. He clearly did not want them to experience death; otherwise, why alert them to the possibility of it? Created as free beings, Adam and Eve had to demonstrate their willingness to enjoy eternity with the Creator. Their obedience to the divine command would show that they were freely choosing to enjoy eternal life with Him. It is that clearly expressed divine will that Satan attacks and opposes, offering instead total 'independence' from God. This was his basic agenda in heaven: independence from the divine command, being his own law without accountability to anyone" (Atonement and the Cross of Christ, *Adult Sabbath School Study Guide,* p. 22).

Independence from God? Is that what our rebellious, deviant, and sinful nature amount to? Does it make sense to any of us that every time we go against the will of God, we are, in essence, demanding our independence from our Creator? Wanting independence from God is like wanting independence from your heart and lungs! God is the life-giver. Seeking independence from God is paramount to wishing/pursuing your own demise. Seeking independence from God perverts our thoughts and behaviors to be sinful, which automatically separates us from God, thereby incarcerating us by sin.

Prolonged Independence/Separation = Captivity/Death

Continued rebellion from God's will ultimately results in death. So, technically, Adam and Eve got off relatively easy (grace and mercy) compared to the actual provision stated in the law of God: "For the wages of sin is death . . ." (Romans 6:23, NIV). God could have destroyed man immediately, right there on the spot and been justified ("… for dust you are and to dust you will return," Genesis 3:19

NIV), but instead, He had a plan of redemption: ". . . but the gift of God is eternal life in Christ Jesus our Lord" (Romans 6:23, NIV). Thank the Lord for knowing us better than we know ourselves, and establishing a plan of salvation long before creating the foundations of the world.

The original fall of humankind was a family affair in every sense of the term in that Adam and Eve *chose* to disobey God's instructions, together. Not surprisingly, this fateful decision of our first parents manifests itself just as it often does for us even today. We become distracted, take our focus off of God, wander away from His protective care, and then meet up with a smooth talking stranger (Satan, our archenemy) who's beauty, sophistication, and style trick us, infiltrating and disrupting our family bond.

Not surprisingly, this master of deceit was unrecognizable to man and woman. He easily duped them into trading their life of eternal love, joy, and connection with their Creator for a life of unremitting pain, misery, and sorrow forever for themselves, and most tragically, for all future generations! Adam and Eve's mistake was one of cosmic proportions because, as is usually the case in many instances, their poor decision impacted more than just themselves. Oh, but praise God! So too, as is often the case, Adam and Eve's redemption and eternal salvation would necessarily impact all future generations as well:

> Consequently, just as one trespass resulted in condemnation for all people, so also one righteous act resulted in justification and life for all people. (Romans 5:18, NIV)

Remember, our trials are not just for us, just as our miracles and praise reports are not exclusively ours. In Jesus' death on the cross, He took the place our first parents rightfully deserved. The purifying blood of the Savior is powerful enough to cleanse each and every person; reaching back to the beginning of time, down through history, to us today, and to future generations to come—regardless of our station in life. All we must do is claim its redemptive power in our lives.

Never Alone

So, how does the redeeming blood of Jesus find its way into the confines of psychiatric hospital rooms and prison cells? When do people stigmatized by society as "patients" and "inmates" realize that their surroundings are evidence that they have lost their way, or that their life plans are well into detour mode? How is it that the committed and incarcerated are able to recognize that they may be suffering from spiritual depression, but many of us who are supposedly "free" do not? This is the miracle of God! Regardless of where we find ourselves in life, we are never alone!

God dwells in places many friends and families hesitate to visit. It was within the prison walls and from behind clanging bars that justice-involved people and those in recovery (stigmatized as "patients" and "inmates") shared with me their hopes and dreams, regret for failures, and disappointment in yet unfulfilled goals. The hearts and minds of the incarcerated and the committed showed me that spiritual depression was as real and as devastating as clinical depression!

For ethical reasons, I obviously could not and would not initiate a religious discussion within a therapeutic setting. However, one by one, patients and inmates relished the opportunity to discuss the *spiritual* aspect of their being. They would come to sessions anxious to reflect on where their lives took a negative turn, how their minds processed the pain, and when their souls began to give up hope. During these sessions those who were considered mentally ill and/or beyond rehabilitation recalled in detail their upbringing in a particular religious denomination, church, mosque, or synagogue . . . and how they remember losing their way, spiritually.

The committed and incarcerated wanted to discuss how it was never their intention to veer off in the direction that cost them their freedom. Listening to these precious souls that were so desperate to be understood, accepted, and forgiven, it dawned on me that God had all the answers. I had none! However, I knew that the God I serve called me (and all of us) to be a vessel. If we allow ourselves to be in service for others, we can take to heart these words of Jesus:

> The Spirit of the Lord is on me, because he has anointed me to pro-
> claim good news to the poor. He has sent me to proclaim freedom

for the prisoners and recovery of sight for the blind, to set the oppressed free. (Luke 4:18, NIV)

So counseling sessions turned into "discussions" about whatever the person in recovery wanted to bring to the table. Therapeutic intervention took on a brand new meaning and the "talking cure" (made famous by Dr. Sigmund Freud) took on a whole new energy. By maintaining appropriate boundaries, we were free to talk about anything and everything! God did us the honor of visiting every discussion.

What we learned during those discussions was that living in a troubled world, poisoned by sin, predisposes us to certain unavoidable trials and tribulations. Sometimes, there is no particular lesson to be learned or specific reason problems occur in our daily lives. They are simply a fact of life due to Satan's untiring quest to turn our thoughts away from God. There will be struggles and difficulties periodically as we journey through this world (Matthew 5:45). If we do not understand that life is full of challenges and obstacles, we set ourselves up for an increased amount of stress by being surprised and upset when problems befall us. The individual expecting a smooth ride through life will not be prepared when things get rough (as they inevitably will). Being surprised, or ill-prepared for life's unpredictability often leads to poor decisions, which lead to painful or distressing consequences, which develop into a lifetime of difficult circumstances.

One thing is guaranteed about all people, and cannot be overemphasized in a chapter about being incarcerated by sin: "There is no one righteous, not even one" (Romans 3:10, NIV). All of us will make mistakes and "fall short of the glory of God." Falling short is what causes many people to become disillusioned and discouraged. Struggling with the same temptations over and over tricks us into believing that obeying God is too difficult a task to accomplish successfully. David's writing in Psalm 51:5 "Surely I was sinful at birth, sinful from the time my mother conceived me" (NIV) reminds us that we are inherently flawed beings. For us, to behave in direct contradiction to God's will is as natural as breathing.

"Learned Helplessness" versus "Classical/Operant Conditioning"

It is this natural inclination to go against God's will that leads to poor decisions, which exacerbates our feelings of helplessness in the face of what we know to be ungodly behavior. Some would call this a vicious cycle. It reminds me of my college Introduction to Psychology class studies of Abramson and Seligman's "learned helplessness" experiments (Abramson et al, 1978; Abramson et al, 1980; Hiroto and Seligman, 1975; Seligman and Maier, 1967; Seligman, 1972; Seligman, 1975; Seligman and Elder, 1985; Seligman and Peterson, 1986). In these experiments, the subjects (dogs) did not realize they could avoid electric shocks by simply jumping over a small partition to safety. After suffering repeated shocks, the dogs would eventually give up and simply resign themselves to their "fate," even lying down on the shock grid in a condition the researchers came to call "learned helplessness." Some of us become so discouraged by our struggles that we just lay there absorbing the "electric shocks" from life's consequences, believing there is no hope, not realizing that all we must do to escape the pain is "hop" over the "partition of trouble" into the loving arms of Jesus.

Jesus has already provided for our escape and rescue from life's suffering. However, when severely tested by the enemy, we tend to forget about our spiritual victories through Jesus. We succumb to the temptations we love the most. And, as we all know, doing something once makes it much more likely we will do it again, especially if we receive pleasure, satisfy a need, or gain some extrinsic or intrinsic reward from the activity. This was illustrated in Pavlov's classical conditioning experiments (again with dogs as the experiment subjects), in which the sound of a ringing bell triggered a salivation response from the subjects because they had been conditioned to expect food at the sound of the bell. Similarly, our natural instinct toward disobedience to God results in conditioned responses that are as predictable as Pavlov's dog: when the "bell of temptation" rings, we respond naturally and without thinking. The consequences from our previous mistakes condition and convince us that we are unable to live up to God's expectations, so we give in to Satan's "ringing bell" of temptation over and over again, salivating at the prospect of engaging once again in our most cherished sins.

Operant conditioning is a little more sophisticated. In operant conditioning, our responses/behaviors/decisions are reinforced based on consequences/out-comes. The consequence/outcome reinforces whether we will repeat our decision/behavior. Consequences/outcomes that result in pleasure or satisfy a need/desire are more likely to be repeated over and over and over again. Operant conditioning in the spiritual sense is further complicated by "temptation" (e.g. "something that entices" us to do evil), which reinforces our natural inclination to go against God. It is complicated because not all temptation resulting in "sinful" behavior/decisions are considered pleasurable by the individuals falling prey to the temp-tation. However, it likely satisfies a desire that is very tempting for a particular individual. Regardless of whether our spiritual challenges are a result of classical or operant conditioning; it is our inability to consistently avoid succumbing to our "tailor-made" temptations that causes us to lose confidence in our ability to choose obedience to God.

Even if/when we try our best not to respond to our "trigger to sin," without the power of Jesus, we cannot avoid our natural weakness to yield to temptation. Even with our best intentions, our inability to do the right thing, at the right time, is not ours alone. Doing wrong when you really want to do right is a condition shared by all humanity. Even Paul, the greatest evangelist and church administrator of all time felt frustrated by this condition:

> And I know that nothing good lives in me, that is, in my sinful nature.
> I want to do what is right, but I can't.
> I want to do what is good, but I don't. I don't want
> to do what is wrong, but I do it anyway. But if I do what I don't want
> to do, I am not really the one doing wrong; it is sin living in me that
> does it. (Romans 7:18-20, NLT)

> I have discovered this principle of life—that when I want to do what is right,
> I inevitably do what is wrong. I love God's law with all my heart.
> But there is another power within me that is at war with my mind. This
> power makes me a slave to the sin that is still within me. Oh, what a miser-
> able person I am! Who will free me from this life that is dominated by sin
> and death? Thank God! The answer is in Jesus Christ our Lord. (Romans
> 7:21-25, NLT)

Hope for the Captive

Like Paul, we may feel trapped inside our own private torture chamber with no hope of escape, handcuffed to our worst decisions and most costly blunders, confined to our dungeon of guilt and shame. Oh, but "thanks be to God—through Jesus Christ our Lord!" There is hope! We can be released from sin. We can be set free from our most damaging mistakes!

This is why the analogy of being handcuffed to circumstances and feeling locked away in the dungeon of spiritual failure and despair is an apt comparison to being incarcerated in prison. In essence, the incarcerated individual has been detained as a result of behavior deemed contrary to the laws of the land. There is a specific price to be paid for all crimes committed. Incarcerated individuals often become contemplative, reflective, and introspective while looking at the circumstances of their lives.

They may ask the question: "How did it come to this?" Just like those individuals who lay awake, staring at the ceiling of their physical imprisonment, we know how we came to our most dreadful spiritual state. It is disobedience to the laws of nature (the laws of God) that insure negative consequences. "Everyone who sins breaks the law; in fact, sin is lawlessness" (1 John 3:4, NIV). Disobedience always leads to behavior that will eventually imprison you on some level or another, whether physically, emotionally, or spiritually.

In the case of disobedience to God (the laws of nature), remember again that the penalty established by God is death ("for the wages of sin is death…," Romans 6:23, NLT). When we sin, we are demanding our independence from God (a death wish), which is not only foolish, but corrupts our minds: "So letting your sinful nature control your mind is death…" (Romans 8:6, NLT). In essence, the human race as a whole has been on death row since the fall of Adam and Eve.

Redemption + Restoration = Freedom and Life

The human race had been incarcerated by sin and circumstance for millenniums without hope of parole, until God allowed His only son to take our place for crimes committed ("… but the free gift of God is eternal life through Christ Jesus our Lord,"

Romans 6:23, NLT). His blood cleanses our minds, restoring our ability to reason ("...but letting the Spirit control the mind is life and peace," Romans 8:6, (NLT). This is the good news of the gospel: Jesus has paid the price for our crimes committed against our Creator, our God, our friend. Regardless of what your sin has led you to do, Jesus seeks to save those who are lost . . . including you (1 John 3:5-8, NIV)!

It matters not whether you are physically free or legally confined. We can all be spiritually saved. God sees to it that His divine love, encouragement, and hope seep through reinforced doors, concrete walls, and iron bars. He allows His mercy and His grace to penetrate hardened hearts and reprobate minds. There is no lockup or lockdown that can prevent anyone from claiming the victory through Jesus Christ. No guilt or shame is stronger than God's forgiveness.

There are no prison walls so thick or impenetrable that they can keep you from reconciling with the Savior of the universe. No background check is necessary—He knows the number of hairs on your head (Luke 12:6-7)! Social status is not important. Jesus saves all who are willing. Approval from others is not a prerequisite. "The Lord will fight for you; you need only to be still" (Exodus 14:14, NIV). One has only to confess one's sin and accept the Lord Jesus Christ as one's personal Savior.

Confused? Bewildered? You are not alone. Remember Paul! We all want to be better and do better. However, we are fighting against our sinful nature: "The sinful nature wants to do evil, which is just the opposite of what the Spirit wants. And the Spirit gives us desires that are the opposite of what the sinful nature desires. These two forces are constantly fighting each other, so you are not free to carry out your good intentions" (Galatians 5:17, NLT). Jesus understands how difficult it is to resist Satan's temptations. He was tempted as we are tempted, in all things, but did not succumb to Satan's power (Matthew 4:1-11). The Lord does not allow us to face temptations that are too difficult for us to handle (with His help, of course):

> No temptation has overtaken you except what is common to man-kind. And God *is* faithful; he will not let you be tempted beyond what you can bear. But when you are tempted, he will also provide a way out so that you can endure it. (1 Corinthians 10:13, NIV)

Jesus understands the difficulties we experience in our lives. He became human so that He could walk this earth and feel what we feel when life is full of hurt and disappointment. He felt physical pain and emotional pain (Matthew 26:37-42; Mark 14:33-36; Luke 22:63-64). Jesus' friends betrayed Him (Matthew 27:1-3; Mark 14:41-72; Luke 22:48, 60). He's been on trial and convicted falsely for crimes He did not commit (Matthew 27:11-37; Mark 14:55-65; John 18; 19-40). Jesus knows how it feels to be disrespected, confined, and tortured. He knows how it feels to be on death row. Jesus knows because He volunteered to take our place just so He could save us!

> What we do see is Jesus, who was given a position "a little lower than the angels"; and because he suffered death for us, he is now "crowned with glory and honor." Yes, by God's grace, Jesus tasted death for everyone. (Hebrews 2:9, NLT)

When we accept the free gift of Christ's salvation, we receive a new identity: overcomers in Christ Jesus! When we accept Jesus as our personal Savior, we become the sons and daughters of God:

> See how very much our Father loves us, for he calls us his children, and that is what we are. (1 John 3:17, NIV)

So, we need no longer walk around as if we are still on spiritual death row. We no longer need to bear the weight of helplessness and hopelessness that leads to spiritual depression. We do not have to conduct our lives as if we remain forever incarcerated by sin or spiritually imprisoned, without hope. We are free! All we must do is say YES to Jesus. Then we must accept the call to service and help those whom the Lord places in our path:

> I, the Lord, have called you to demonstrate my righteousness. I will take you by the hand and guard you, and I will give you to my people, Israel, as a symbol of my covenant with them. And you will be a light to guide the nations. You will open the eyes of the blind. You will free the captives from prison, releasing those who sit in dark dungeons. (Isaiah 42:6-7, NLT)

We must pass on to others the good news that Jesus saves!

Chapter 10

"Ridiculous" Faith (Part I)

———— ∞◦⟨⟩◦∞ ————

"Let the little children come to me, and do not hinder them, for the
kingdom of God belongs to such as these. Truly I tell you, anyone
who will not receive the kingdom of God like a little child will never
enter it" (Luke 18:16-17, NIV).

What Is Faith?

Hebrews 11:1 says, "Faith is the confidence that what we hope for will actually happen; it gives us assurance about things we cannot see" (NLT).

So what's ridiculous faith? Dictionary.com lists the *slang* definition of "ridiculous" as "absurdly or unbelievably good." I'm using the slang for "ridiculous" because sometimes adults need to remember how wild their imaginations were when they were children. As children, we believed our parents could do anything. And, as children, once we learn about God; we surely believe He can do all things! Many of us lose this confidence in God and in ourselves once the challenges and pressures of adult life take hold. Oh, to believe like a child once again.

As a child, I learned most of the complicated concepts contained in the Bible via song. Maybe you did as well. I can still vividly remember how music touched my heart and soul and lifted me to amazing heights of emotional and spiritual energy. It felt good to sing and hear others sing about the wonderful "lamb of

God," and how much "Jesus loves me." Through my love and appreciation for music at an early age, I was able to grasp the complexities of many spiritual concepts, such as love, hope, trust, and faith. One immediate example that comes to mind was a childhood favorite of mine, a song about faith, written and performed by my Aunt Eleanor and Uncle Harold, "Faith Enough to Try." For a child, faith is difficult to visualize and place into an understanding where it can be utilized successfully at a child's developmental level. Their song provided me with a clear understanding of what faith is and how one could embrace a personal connection to what faith means for them. Read the words of the song (below) to see what I mean. Imagine you are about ten or twelve years of age, sitting on the front pew of a small, country church, listening to your aunt and uncle passionately present a song from the very depths of their souls:

Faith Enough to Try
By Eleanor Wright

There's a mountain in the distance, oh-oh my Lord, against a cloudy sky,
All I need to climb that mountain, Lord, is just enough faith to try.
When I come up to the mountain, my Lord and I
Will climb to the top no matter how high.
All I need to climb that mountain is just enough faith to try.
'Cause I've got joy enough to match my sorrow.
And I've got truth enough to light my way.
I've got love enough to make an enemy a friend
And courage enough to obey.
Oh, Lordy, there's a mountain towering high.
And if I don't climb it, I'll know the reason why.
I've got love, truth, joy, and grace; all I need is just a little more faith.
All I need to climb that mountain is just enough faith to try.
There's a river in the valley, oh my Lord, billows are raging high,
All I need to cross that river, Lord, is just enough faith to try.
It's a mighty wide river, but I know that I serve a God
who can make a riverbed dry.
All I need to cross that river is just enough faith to try.
'Cause I've got joy enough to match my sorrow.
And I've got truth enough to light my way.
I've got love enough to make an enemy a friend
And courage enough to obey.

Oh, Lordy, there's a river, hurryin' by and if I don't cross it,
I'll know the reason why.
I've got love, truth, joy, and grace. All I need is just a little more faith.
All I need to climb that mountain is enough faith to try.

I hope you were able to feel just a thimbleful of what I felt as a child when I was able to incorporate the true meaning of this song into my developing spiritual self. It was a wonderful way to grow and learn about Jesus and what it means to be a "child of the King." It was also an excellent tutorial, utilizing metaphor to illuminate faith (a complex concept). However, now, as an adult, I can appreciate the fact that in this life full of challenges, disappointments, and personal triumphs, receiving God's Word through music and preaching brings tremendous comfort, builds spiritual fortitude, and strengthens faith, gently reminding us to continue to trust in an Almighty God.

We live in a complex world where a decision here or there can make the difference between great positive or negative consequences in our lives. As we learn very early in life, there are consequences to all decisions. Even if our decision is to do nothing, this is still a decision—there is still a consequence. We also learn fairly early that sometimes bad things happen to good people, and though there are natural consequences which accompany all actions and behaviors, it is also true that life presents challenges and obstacles that occur due to no fault of our own.

So the big question remains for many people these days, whether they are regular church attendees, believers who do not attend church, or those who have never been interested in attending: What is faith? Two more questions are directly connected to this:

"How do you know if you have it?" and, "How do you know when you've lost it?"

Trying to define and comprehend faith remains a complex undertaking.

Faith That Protects

In keeping with the example of learning about faith developmentally, I want to reflect upon another childhood favorite, a Bible story illustrating faith. Even now, reading about Daniel, and his friends, Hananiah (Shadrach), Mishael (Meshach), and Azariah (Abednego)—the "three Hebrew boys"—brings a smile to my face because of the simple lessons about faith contained in their adventure.

Daniel and his friends were born and raised in the church. They had devoted parents who taught them about God, and how His divine love, mercy, and grace would carry them through any trial or obstacle. Apparently, these boys believed and lived accordingly, even as they grew in stature and knowledge. So much so that when King Nebuchadnezzar was looking for the most intelligent, competent, and honorable young men, he chose from the camp of Hebrew captives within his kingdom. This story is very familiar to many because of what happened when Daniel and his friends were placed in positions of public scrutiny, and were set apart from their peers to serve at the king's request. Their faith in the Living God became the source of testing their loyalty to the king, and to God. (To become familiar with this story, see Daniel 1-3.) Shadrach, Meshach, and Abednego (the names given them by the king), along with the rest of the king's staff and the kingdom at large, were invited to a huge feast to honor King Nebuchadnezzar. They were told that when they heard music signifying the unveiling of the king's golden statute, they were to bow down and worship the king's image. Those who did not bow down would be placed in a very hot furnace and burned alive. This sounds extreme, I know, but King Nebuchadnezzar was quite serious about this. He wanted everyone to bow down and worship his image. Of course, what was left unsaid is that this was all a setup by some of the king's staff who were jealous of the three Hebrew boys' elevated positions within the kingdom. They knew that the king liked and respected these young men very much and they resented them.

If you are over age forty, you may remember the old TV game show, *Let's Make a Deal*, with Monty Hall (another childhood favorite). Well, this situation was similar in that Shadrach, Meshach, and Abednego, had three choices:

Door #1—Bow down and worship the king's image when they heard the designated music (which would have contradicted everything they had been taught and believed as children, and lived as young men: "You must not have any other god but me" and, "You must not make for yourself an idol .... You must not bow down to them or worship them ..." (Exodus 20:3-6, NLT).

Door #2—Pretend that they had back problems and could not bend (while looking for the nearest exit and trying to make a run for it).

Door #3—Refuse to bow down and worship the king's image, whereupon they would be taken quickly and unceremoniously to the fiery furnace.

The three Hebrew boys had some decisions to make. They chose "Door #3" and refused to bow down and worship the king's image.

Naturally, the king's staff, which had orchestrated this very scenario in the first place, had their eyes focused on the three Hebrew boys during the ceremony because they were hoping they had read the boys' character correctly (i.e. they would not bow down). The jealous staff would finally be rid of these "goody two-shoes." The fact that Shadrach, Meshach, and Abednego were raised in the church was not going to save them in this particular circumstance. As a matter of fact, their strength of character, dedication to their belief system, and faith in God could actually lead directly to their death!

The decision Shadrach, Meshach, and Abednego made in refusing to bow down and worship the king's image was not only political suicide but an act of literal suicide (based on their understanding of the stated consequence). It was also a public relations nightmare for King Nebuchadnezzar, because the king had so publicly promoted these young men and showered them with the best of everything the kingdom had to offer. Their public refusal to bow to his image was a slap in the face to King Nebuchadnezzar.

Long story short, the three Hebrew boys were pointed out to the king. After refusing several chances to change their decision and bow to the king, they were taken away to receive their fate. While waiting for the furnace to be brought to full blast, King Nebuchadnezzar asked the most powerful question of all: "Will your God save you from this inevitable outcome?" (Daniel 3:15). Instead of being intimidated, Shadrach, Meshach, and Abednego, simply stated: "We serve a God who is able to save us from the fiery furnace, but if He does not, we will not serve your gods, or worship your golden image" (Daniel 3:16-18). Well, as you might imagine, there was nothing left for the king to say or do after that.

The faith of these three young men had nothing to do with fear, but had everything to do with an unshakeable, "ridiculous" faith and belief in the Living God.

The key for me in this story is not the end result of the boys surviving the fiery furnace, because Jesus Himself stepped into the fire with them (Daniel 3:23-25). That was obviously a fantastic display of God's protective power. To me, it was their statement to the king that they were not going to bow down to an image of a human being because they served the Living God—even if it meant they would lose their lives! These boys exercised their faith to such an extent that it removed the pressure from their shoulders and placed it squarely on the shoulders of the Living God. Their faith had saved them long before being put to the test.

In the example of three Hebrew boys, faith doubled as "supreme confidence" because they had lived life depending on the Living God. Therefore, their faith became the essence of Paul's definition: "Now faith is confidence in what we hope for and assurance about what we do not see" (Hebrews 11:1, NIV). I like how Dr. Gene Donaldson describes Hebrews 11:1: "Hope, in and of itself, indicates that you want something you do not already have, and thereby focuses on future attainment. Yet, being certain of something we do not have, or see, indicates a confidence in the one who has made the promise to provide." Now, that's "ridiculous" faith!

God Specializes in Doing the Impossible

The glory for God was not that He was able to save those faithful servants, the three Hebrew boys. God can do that with the blink of an eye, or the wave of His mighty hand. The glory for God was how, once again, He took an impossible situation that was beyond human control and turned it into a multiple blessing, and everyone witnessed the miracle of the boys who would not burn! Read the rest of Daniel 3:26-30 and you will see what I mean.

Not only did God keep a fiery furnace at room temperature, His display of power provoked King Nebuchadnezzar to testify to the whole host of his royal court that the God of Shadrach, Meshach, and Abednego, is "the most-high God" (Daniel 3:26, KJV).

Then Nebuchadnezzar said, "Praise be to the God of Shadrach, Meshach, and Abednego, who has sent his angel and rescued his servants! They trusted in him and defied the king's command and were willing to give up their lives rather than serve or worship any god except their own God" (Daniel 3:28, NIV). Sound ridiculous? King Nebuchadnezzar ended his testimonial by making a decree to all in attendance that anyone who spoke against the God of Shadrach, Meshach, and Abednego would be put to death, and their homes would be destroyed and covered up with cow manure (seriously!), because no other God can protect and deliver like the true and Living God can deliver (Daniel 3:29).

The king did not want to leave any doubt concerning how he felt about Shadrach, Meshach, and Abednego. And I'm sure Nebuchadnezzar made a big to-do about this decree as well after witnessing the power of the Living God.

Not surprisingly, Nebuchadnezzar promoted these young men to even better jobs than they had before. God is so very thorough in His statements and actions to *His* creation: to those who serve Him and those who do not! The faith demonstrated by the young men in this Bible story is so powerful because they followed God's will to allow *His* glory to be made manifest on a grand stage as a witness to all who observed that day: "Do not be afraid of those who kill the body but cannot kill the soul. Rather, be afraid of the One who can destroy both soul and body in hell" (Matthew 10:28, NIV).

The ability to exercise strength and courage under the direst circumstances is a testimony to having absolute faith in a supreme being: the Living God! Ellen G. White assesses the faith and courage of the three young Hebrew witnesses:

> He who walked with the Hebrew worthies in the fiery furnace will
> be with his followers wherever they are. His abiding presence will

comfort and sustain. In the midst of the time of trouble—trouble such as has not been since there was a nation—his chosen ones will stand unmoved. Satan with all his hosts of evil cannot destroy the weakest of God's saints. Angels that excel in strength will protect them, and in their behalf Jehovah will reveal himself as a "God of gods," able to save the uttermost those who have put their trust in him" (*Prophets and Kings*, p. 513).

Anyone Can Have "Ridiculous" Faith

What would have happened had these church boys not had the support system and spiritual training they received as very young children? Had Daniel and his friends wilted under public scrutiny and peer pressure and bowed down to worship the king, we would not have had such a wonderful illustration of the power of having faith in the Almighty Living God! We would have had one less example of how God takes an impossible situation (for us) and transforms it into multiple blessings for all who bear witness to such a faithful testimony.

There is no age limit to acquire ridiculous faith. As is often the case; young people can lead the way because of their natural affinity to embrace hope regardless of the circumstances. Still, you may be a young person reading this chapter who doubts your ability to believe in a God you cannot see, hear, or touch. You may feel alone with your struggles and want to believe, but are afraid to trust in a being you really don't know well. You know how it is with your friends you *can* see and touch; you need a close relationship with them before you fully trust them—right? It's the same thing with God. You need a close relationship so that you learn to trust Him too.

It's simple, really. Just ask God to be your closest companion and best friend. Tell Him your troubles. Share with Him your joys, hopes, and dreams! Talk with Him in the morning when you wake. Take Him out to lunch. Discuss the day's events with Him before you go to sleep at night. When your life feels like it's spiraling out of control, trust in the relationship you've established with your new best friend. God is all-powerful. He's only limited by the limits we ourselves place on

Him and the amount of faith we have in Him. When it feels impossible; take it to Jesus. When you have ridiculous faith in God, He does the impossible. He does this because He loves you. Give Him praise!

"I am the Lord, the God of all mankind. Is anything too hard for me?" (Jeremiah 32:27, NIV).

Chapter 11

"Ridiculous" Faith (Part II)

———◇○◁⟨⟩◁○◇———

"And he said to her, 'Daughter, your faith has made you well. Go in peace. Your suffering is over'" (Mark 5:34, NLT).

Doubt Crushes Faith

nfortunately, for some people, Chapter 10 was just a children's Bible story. They may think such stories have no real relevance for their life in this present day and age. It is easy to miss the larger point of how having faith in God can carry you past any challenge, and remain skeptical about the details of the miracle of the three Hebrew boys' escape from the fiery furnace. It may even lead to a few burdensome conclusions that the miracle was predictable because Shadrach, Meshach, and Abednego were good, churchgoing boys, and therefore, God's protection was automatic and not predicated on His response to an act of "ridiculous" faith as demonstrated by "exercised faith" from those who believe on Him.

However, adopting that mind-set dismisses the fact that God makes a point of telling adults that they should display a faith like that of children if they want to please Him and enter into His kingdom (Matthew 19:14; Mark 10:14; Luke 18:16). Paul clarifies this point even more when he writes:

> And without faith it is impossible to please God, because anyone
> who comes to him must believe that he exists and that he rewards
> those who earnestly seek him. (Hebrews 11:6, NIV)

Children, it seems, are much more open to the "trust and believe" attitude Jesus so often spoke to in illustrations with His disciples. Instead of dismissing some Bible stories as childish, adults should embrace their lessons for themselves, while teaching them to their children. Still, some attitudes may be more difficult to soften than others. So, in contrast, I'll move this exploration of faith to an adult level, to how trusting in God can heal you.

A reality for so many these days is that their faith is far too often shaken, muted, or completely snuffed out due to the constant onslaught of evil, disappointment, and/or unrealized expectations in this world. Some of us may feel so tired and worn down by problems that they weigh heavy on our chest, threatening to suffocate the very life right out of our souls. We may find no comfort in childhood Bible stories.

It is not surprising then that when you experience the ups and downs of life's roller coaster, it begins to feel like you have lost control, and the anchors in your life have been dislodged. Whether you have a strong religious background, have never really been a consistent participant in a faith community, or just simply accept that we are all spiritual beings and believe and/or acknowledge that God exists, it can be excruciatingly difficult to maintain faith in the midst of what seems like insurmountable odds and trouble around every corner. This seemingly relentless barrage of negative outcomes against us too often breaks us down so much that we begin to get discouraged, lose faith, and lose hope. Some turn away from God altogether. We may sink so low in our personal spiritual quicksand that we even question God's very existence.

However unthinkable the possibility of no longer believing in God may seem to some, I can think of only one thing more confusing, more terrifying, and more painful than believing that there is no God: *knowing* there is a God, but *believing* He does not care about you or your problems! For individuals raised in a religious home where spiritual mores and values all pointed to a strong belief in the God of the universe, such intrusive thoughts can be the most devastating, troubling, and gut-wrenching because they fly in the face of everything they have been taught and held true. Add to this the fear and desperation which accompany such a hollow feeling of helplessness, hopelessness, and intense loneliness, and you get a glimpse of just how fertile the ground can become for planting negative seeds of doubt and self-loathing which too often produce an uncontrollable growth of spiritual depression.

Those who find themselves at the lowest point in their lives are usually shocked and haltingly surprised that it came to this. You do not arrive at a point of hopelessness purely by accident, and usually not overnight. More likely, a succession of circumstances accumulated over time. Red flags went unnoticed and sirens of warning went unheeded or were not taken seriously. Far too often, surviving the journey of life requires a level of coping and resilience that many find overwhelming and almost impossible to navigate successfully without divine intervention. If you are unable to shake this nagging thought of being abandoned by God, or overcome that sense of guilt and shame that cause you to think your life is worthless to the Lord of the universe, you will slip further and deeper into a spiritual depression where, ironically, no one but God can reach you.

It becomes a painful paradox that finding yourself that deep in sorrow and pain, you are square in the middle of spiritual suicide (i.e. isolating yourself from all things "God"). The only one who can reach into the depths of your nightmare and pull you out of its vacuum that threatens to suck the very life from your body and soul, is the same God you may believe has turned His back on you. Needless to say, trapped within you are the feelings of anguish and despair that make anywhere you happen to be the loneliest place on earth. Hold on! You are not the only one. There is hope!

Broken

During the course of my career as a clinical and forensic psychologist, I have treated people who describe their lives in the terms I have outlined above. I have worked with families interlocked with children's services agencies due to child welfare or child safety issues, consulted in cases involving psychological and legal issues for both children and adults, and treated people who felt their only recourse was to attempt to escape their reality through drug and alcohol abuse. I have seen some of the most hurtful and unbelievable things, witnessed some of the most cruel and unnecessary things, and evaluated individuals who have perpetrated some of the most painful and unimaginable things (or those who have been victimized by them). I can tell you without hesitation that we are living in a most difficult time in earth's history.

People are in pain everywhere. People are struggling. They feel broken. Spirits are broken. Psyches are broken. Confidence in our government is broken. Trust in churches and religious leaders is broken. The very will of individuals and families to stay together, remain strong, and move forward is broken. These are certainly "adult" issues. As a result, spiritual depression is common.

The key to any intervention designed to address spiritual depression or behavioral health challenges is a holistic approach; one that recognizes, respects, and supports the importance of the spiritual core of individuals, regardless of whether they belong to an organized faith community or adhere to a specific spiritual philosophy. The spirit in people cannot be ignored, dismissed, or excluded from their whole. We are all spiritual because we are all the creation of *the* Spirit.

So, as has been the focus from the beginning of this book, we embrace the reality that hurt and pain exists. Trials and tribulations are a part of life. Disappointment and discouragement sometimes break us down, yet we look to how we can be made whole. We can access spiritual remedies and heal broken spirits and broken hearts. "Ridiculous" faith is about helping us recognize the cure for spiritual depression lies in each of our hearts through Christ Jesus!

The next section, "Faith That Heals," contains the problem, the answer to the problem, and where to begin our search: the Bible. As we strive to fully understand the concepts of faith, brokenness, and wholeness on an adult level, we must return to that book of ultimate healing: the Bible. For it contains pertinent life examples of those who came before us and serves as teaching, featuring metaphors that show us how to apply healing to our own lives.

Faith That Heals

Another of my favorite Bible stories (not necessarily for adults only) serves as the perfect reference to connect the psychological and spiritual elements needed to understand faith throughout the rest of this chapter:

> Just then a woman who had been subject to bleeding for twelve years came up behind him and touched the edge of his cloak. She said to herself, "If I only touch his cloak, I will be healed." Jesus turned and saw her. "Take heart, daughter," he said, "your faith has healed you." And the woman was healed at that moment. (Matthew 9:20-22, NIV)

There is an intricate connection between faith, brokenness, and healing. A lot of clinical work involves these concepts, or states of being, even if they do not call attention to them specifically. When you provide individual and group therapy, you must decide what approach or model of service adheres to the best practice for the individual's symptoms, condition, and strengths, and also what fits both your personality (comfort level), and your skill set.

For me, the best fit is using a cognitive behavioral model for those patients capable of participating developmentally, cognitively, and psychologically on that level. So when it came time for me to provide therapeutic intervention through individual or group therapy, I used the tools and concepts of cognitive behavioral psychology to guide clients toward making effective changes in their lives.

We can use one such cognitive behavioral concept as we seek to explain effective spiritual change and healing from feeling/being broken. I share this concept with individuals who want to increase their ability to function under stressful conditions and realize effective change using a simple cognitive behavioral construct called the "three A's":

1. *Awareness* that there is a problem
2. *Acquisition* of knowledge concerning the problem (Acceptance)
3. *Application* of the knowledge gained to solve the problem (Action)

These are the three lenses we will use to break down our Bible text and discover how we can be healed from our brokenness. It is important that we spend the majority of our focus on what is going on in Matthew 9:21-22. Here we have the problem (broken body/broken spirit), the desire (wholeness/healing), and the solution ("ridiculous" faith). In these two verses, we have everything we need to effect positive change and increase our ability to not only function, but thrive spiritually in a world of brokenness.

Awareness

We can certainly see that the woman in this Bible story is aware of her situation. How could she not be aware? She has been afflicted with a severe physical malady for some twelve years! No one could be more aware of her condition than she. Maybe you can relate to what this woman must have felt. Maybe you have been broken at some point in your life. We have all been broken at some point in our lives; if not physically, emotionally, or psychologically, then certainly spiritually. After all, we are all facing challenges, from the time we enter this world ("born in sin and shaped in iniquity," Psalm 51:5, KJV). Romans 3:23 tells us "all have sinned, and fall short of the glory of God" (NIV). Spiritually at least, we come out of our mother's womb already in a state of brokenness. And if we are fortunate to grow up and live life, we will inevitably experience hurt, pain, and disappointment, which often lead to feeling broken on a very personal level.

Again, as human beings, our brokenness is made manifest in a variety of ways, across a vast continuum, spread not so evenly across four distinctly "human" categories: physical, emotional, psychological, and spiritual. If you have *not* been broken or felt broken, be patient. You will be broken. If you follow Jesus, brokenness is guaranteed. Read about John the Baptist's beheading, Stephen's stoning, a host of Jesus' disciples and

God's prophets thrown in jail throughout their ministry—it goes on and on. Difficulties in this life are promised, but so is victory: "In the world ye shall have tribulation: but be of good cheer; I have overcome the world" (John 16:33, KJV).

Being aware of one's physical, emotional, psychological, and spiritual condition is the first step toward healing.

Acquisition of Knowledge

Once we become aware of our brokenness, God expects us to seek out information on our condition and what must be done to remedy it. For example, when you go to the medical doctor and she gives you a diagnosis of some terrible illness, like cancer, you immediately become aware of certain fears colliding in your mind, body, and spirit. The first thing you need to do after crying, "Lord have mercy," is to gather some information on your illness. This may include getting a second, third, and possibly a fourth opinion. It may include reading up on all kinds of dietary and nutritional information. Ultimately, you will settle on the fact that this illness is for real, and you may feel broken due to it, not just in body, but also in mind and spirit.

One thing is for sure. You want to find out where you can go for some healing. You want to know what treatment will work best. You want to know where the best doctors and facilities are to treat your illness. You want to know anything and everything that has something to do with healing.

Now, it is likely that the lives of every person on earth today have been in some way touched by cancer or some other dreaded illness. If not you who has been diagnosed, you certainly have a relative or friend who has been. And most of us have at least a cursory knowledge of where to locate resources to educate ourselves about our illness and help us decide on the most clinically appropriate course of action. The same is true for locating information on our spiritual "illness." Note that Matthew 9:22 says, "your faith has healed you." This clearly indicates we have information we can gather about how to best treat our brokenness. Clearly understanding what faith is and where to get it seems to be a key *acquisition of knowledge* for our being healed or made whole.

What exactly does it mean to be made whole? When I looked up the words *faith* and *whole* in *The American Heritage Dictionary* (1996), I was not surprised that faith meant, "confidence or trust in a person or thing; belief that is not based on proof." Nor was I surprised that the word *whole* means, "not broken, damaged, or impaired; intact; uninjured or unharmed; sound." What did surprise me was that the dictionary went on to list this: "pertaining to all aspects of human nature, esp. one's physical, intellectual, and spiritual development."

I must tell you, I got excited when I read that last definition because I knew that is where we could really combine the psychological with the spiritual.

Once you are *aware* that you are broken spiritually, you must seek out information on how you can be healed, just as you would acquire knowledge concerning a physical or mental illness. The Bible provides a wealth of information about physical, psychological, emotional, and spiritual brokenness. You must read up on your illness! You must seek second, third, and fourth opinions. I love reading Matthew, Mark, Luke, and John because they provide similar versions of the life of Jesus on this earth, though from four different individual perspectives. Search the Bible from the Old Testament to the New Testament. Regardless of what you read, it provides consistent diagnosis, treatment alternatives, and a prognosis!

In this day and age, it is commonplace to live in some sort of brokenness. Many societies are morally, culturally, or economically broken. Your brokenness may not be exactly like my brokenness, but what does it matter? We are all broken at one time or another. The Bible contains the information you need to read up on your spiritual condition. In it, you will find treatment options for a cure of your brokenness. We have information in Matthew 9:22 concerning the connection between faith and healing. We also acquired knowledge from *The American Heritage Dictionary,* defining *faith* and *whole*.

Easton's 1897 Bible Dictionary has even more detailed information about *faith* and *wholeness,* emphasizing that our spiritual diagnosis (brokenness), and the cure (faith), really add up to a viable prognosis (wholeness/healing). The challenge, however, is that true faith is trusting in the "unknown."

Having faith is to believe in something, though you cannot see it. "Now faith is confidence in what we hope for and assurance about what we do not see" (Hebrews 11:1, NIV). A demonstration of faith then, is *acting* on that belief *before* it comes to pass. This may sound ridiculous to someone that does not believe in the concept faith, but not to those that have experienced "faith in action." This brings us to the third and final **"A"**: *Application* of what we learn about our spiritual condition.

Application

When we look deeply into this story in Matthew 9:20-22, we see a human being who realizes she is physically, emotionally, psychologically, and spiritually *broken*. She has a *desire* to be healed, and she recognizes a healer when she sees one: Jesus! Against all hope, this broken soul with a broken spirit and a body that no longer functioned as God had designed it, exercised "ridiculous" faith by crawling through a crowd to get to a man she had obviously heard could perform miracles. Now, it is one thing to hear about a man who can heal, but quite another thing to believe so strongly that this healing is possible that you are willing to get on all fours to crawl and struggle through a huge mass of people (keeping in mind you are feeling awful; you've been sick for twelve years). She probably had to lay flat on her belly and chest and rest her face on the filthy ground a few times just to catch her breath, and then gather enough energy to push on through stranger after stranger's smelly feet and dusty sandals, never losing sight of Jesus and where He stood.

Now that's what I call *application* (and, "ridiculous" faith)!

This woman is *aware* of her condition of brokenness. She sought some information from somewhere or someone who must have told her there was a man named Jesus, and He is a healer. Understand, this woman had sought out and been disappointed by the best medical professionals of her time. However, she has done her homework. She *acquired* some knowledge and gathered some information. She read up on her disease. Still, every effort ended the same way: nothing helped her. For twelve years, it had always ended the same way.

So, we must ask ourselves what makes her seek out this man called Jesus? It seems obvious to me that Jesus' reputation had preceded Him. When you look at the early parts of Matthew, you learn that Jesus had been healing folks all over town. If we go back to Matthew 4, before this woman sought out Jesus, we find:

Jesus went throughout Galilee, teaching in their synagogues, pro-
claiming the good news of the kingdom, and healing every disease
and sickness among the people. (Matthew 4:23, NIV)

News about him spread all over Syria, and people brought to him
all who were ill with various diseases, those suffering severe pain,
the demon-possessed, those having seizures, and the paralyzed; and
he healed them. (Matthew 4:24, NIV)

Large crowds from Galilee, the Decapolis, Jerusalem, Judea and
the region across the Jordan followed him. (Matthew 4:25, NIV)

And then, in Matthew 8, Jesus is at it again. He healed a man infected with lep-
rosy, and then told him to go his way and *not* tell anyone what He had just done for
him. (Yeah, right!) Can you imagine? The leper, now healed, did exactly what you
and I would do if/when Jesus healed us! He shouted up and down the street, all the
way home, knocking on doors, shouting, "Come see a man who just healed me!"

Then Jesus runs into the centurion (Roman military commander), who
beseeched Him to heal his servant. Jesus agreed to go to the servant, but the centurion stops Him and says: "Lord, I do not deserve to have you come under my
roof. But just say the word, and my servant will be healed" (Matthew 8:8, NIV).
In verse 10, Jesus responds, "Truly I tell you, I have not found anyone in Israel
with such great faith" (Matthew 8:10, NIV). Even the "church members" didn't
have the kind of faith this man displayed!

Toward the end of Matthew 8, Jesus heals Peter's mother-in-law. Then He
heals two people possessed of demons, sending the evil spirits into some swine that
jumped off a cliff. Then, at the beginning of Matthew 9, before we come across
the woman with the issue of blood, Jesus heals a man who is paralyzed, forgiving
him of his sins (his spiritual disease), and his paralysis (his physical disease).

Whew! Can you visualize all this? Jesus was on a "healing frenzy"! Everywhere
He turned, Jesus was opening blind eyes, strengthening lame legs, making lepers'
clean, restoring life to those who were dead, removing evil spirits, and most importantly, forgiving sins! No wonder the woman was crawling on her belly to get to
Jesus! Through hearing of all these miracles, it must have dawned on her that

wherever Jesus is, there is healing. She must have thought: *If the blind, the lame, and the dead cannot remain the same when in the presence of Jesus, **surely** I will not remain the same if I can just get close enough to touch His clothes.* I will be made whole!

Maybe you can relate. After reading up on your diagnosis, you hear about some special dietary regimen, or a friend calls and tells you about some new discovery or treatment that is "guaranteed" to cure you of your illness. You are likely going to run, not walk, to wherever this cure can be found! So, this woman had to get to Jesus, because she must have felt like He truly was her last hope.

Remember, the question for us in the world we live in today is not, "Will you be broken?" but rather, "After being broken, how can you be healed?" Our reference texts in Matthew 9:20-21, provides the answer: "your faith . . ."

How much faith did it take for this woman to find out where Jesus was going to be, and to somehow get herself to where He was? She saw that there was no way to get to Jesus on foot, so she decided to crawl and believe, crawl and believe, crawl and believe that a simple touch of His clothing would change her life and make her whole. How strong was her faith? She may have come to Jesus because of a physical ailment, but Jesus healed her whole being (body, mind, and spirit).

The text tells us that to be made whole—to be saved—we must exercise faith. When the woman touched Jesus, He perceived virtue to leave His body, hence His question: "Who touched me?" (Mark 5:30). How is it that even in the midst of a throng of loud, boisterous people, pushing and shoving, Jesus took note of a feeble finger brush past the bottom of His robe? There is no one who is insignificant to Jesus! When you exercise faith, Jesus not only takes note, He makes sure that everyone around you notices your encounter with Him as well. Jesus leaves no doubt that He is the source of your miracle. Ellen G. White had this to say about the miraculous healing of the woman with the issue of blood:

> He gave no opportunity for superstition to claim healing virtue for the mere act of touching His garments. It was not through the outward contact with Him, but through the faith which took hold on His divine power, that the cure was wrought.

The wondering crowd that pressed close about Christ realized no accession of vital power. But when the suffering woman put forth her hand to touch Him, believing that she would be made whole, she felt the healing virtue. So in spiritual things, To talk of religion in a casual way, to pray without soul hunger and living faith, avails nothing. A nominal faith in Christ, which accepts Him merely as the Saviour of the world, can never bring healing to the soul. The faith that is unto salvation is not a mere intellectual assent to truth. He who waits for entire knowledge before he will exercise faith, cannot receive blessing from God. It is not enough to believe *about* Christ; we must believe *in* Him. The only faith that will benefit us is that which embraces Him as a personal Saviour; which appropriates His merits to ourselves. Many hold faith as an opinion. Saving faith is a transaction by which those who receive Christ join themselves in covenant relation with God. Genuine faith is life. A living faith means an increase of vigor, a confiding trust, by which the soul becomes a conquering power. (Ellen G. White, "The Touch of Faith," *The Desire of Ages*, p. 347).

We come to Jesus broken in every way, shape, and form. What we are really seeking is total wholeness. We are seeking the ultimate healing of mind, body, and spirit: we are seeking salvation!

How is it that our faith in Almighty God has healing powers for our body, mind, and spirit? It is as simple as recognizing that we are spiritually broken, in need of being made whole. But awareness and recognition of our broken state are not enough. Like the woman who went to great lengths to touch Jesus, we must also have "ridiculous" faith and *do* something! We must seek knowledge of the source of our healing. We must *believe* that there is one who, if we could just see Him, touch Him, be in His presence, and feel His Spirit, we can be healed of our spiritual condition!

We can be healed of the guilt and shame that has plagued our hearts and minds for years without relief. We can be healed of our disgrace, our failures, and the hurt and pain that too often accompany us on this lifelong journey. We have to believe that Jesus will make the difference in our lives. The magnitude of our faith must match the magnitude of our situation!

Saving Faith

We may have to take our faith with us on a "long crawl" to Jesus. However, there may be some of us who are so damaged and exhausted from being spiritually broken that we cannot muster the energy to crawl to Jesus.

Maybe you have some friends like the paralytic in Mark 2:1-12. Remember them? Their faith was so strong, they carried their friend to the house where Jesus was speaking. They had faith that Jesus could heal their friend, so when they could not get in through the door, they tore a hole in the roof and lowered him down to the feet of Jesus (ridiculous, huh?). Do you have friends with that kind of faith? Do you have friends that will carry you when your faith is broken and you are too tired to crawl?

Maybe you think nobody knows you are broken. There are so many people who go through the motions every day, trying to keep their brokenness discreetly hidden from friends, family, and coworkers. I hate to be the one to break it to you this way, but you are not doing such a good job of hiding it! Folks can see it when you are spiritually ill.

They know if you cannot go two days, two hours, or two minutes without having a drink of alcohol. People know if you abuse your wife and kids. They know if you are lonely and feeling like a failure after a divorce. People know when you are suffering, trying to take care of an elderly parent with dementia or Alzheimer's. People know when you lose your job and your house is in foreclosure. They recognize that you are struggling.

How can this be? Broken people can easily recognize broken people! It's one of the things *"saints"* do best. They can sometimes seem to smell your brokenness. They can see it on your face. However, a friend in Christ can sense when you need a lift! A friend in Christ loves you and hates to see you in pain. A friend in Christ always has a word of encouragement for you. A friend in Christ always has some Bible text to share with you to lift you up. And a friend in Christ often has "ridiculous" faith when yours is waning, or just about totally gone.

When you see a real friend in Christ, you look forward to finding some time to spend with them because you recognize that on those days when you are really feeling down, a friend in Christ comes to lift you up, not kick you when you are down. You see, a friend in Christ not only shares words of encouragement, they pray for you right there on the spot. A friend in Christ is not there to get all in your personal business, or rub your nose in humiliation or failure. They simply state: "I have been thinking about you, and the Lord told me to share these Bible texts with you, and pray for you."

There is a sense that God sent the friend your way because He knows when you are broken, and He knows when your faith begins to wane just a bit. It may be during a time when you do not know how much more you can take. You may be paralyzed by fear of the future, stymied by hopelessness in your present, or burdened by guilt and shame due to your past. You may be spiritually paralyzed, unable to move; broken. However, the Lord will not leave you lying on the mat of life, unable to move. He will send some friends in Christ your way to pray for you, lift you up, tear a hole in the roof where Jesus stands, and guide you into the Lord's presence. That's the miracle of having friends or family whose faith may be stronger than yours at a given time. How is it that you can be spiritually *lifted* . . . by being *lowered*? Just like the man whose friends first lifted him, then lowered him to the feet of Jesus, where he was then lifted by Jesus to a state of physical healing and spiritual wholeness, so too can you have the same result in your life! If you know you are broken, but feel too paralyzed to move, I pray that you have some family or friends whose faith is strong enough to lift you up and carry you to Jesus.

Maybe you are too weak and discouraged to crawl. Maybe you do not have friends or family with faith strong enough to carry you. Maybe you are like that thief on the cross in Luke 23:39-43, whose life must certainly have been a disappointment to himself, his family, and to all who knew him. He was not necessarily broken physically (we do not know for sure), but can you imagine his mental state? Can you imagine his guilt and shame? His disgrace? Can you imagine hanging there for the entire world to see what your life had become? We do not know a whole lot about the thief on the cross. His was a short but profitable exposure to the life of Jesus, proving it only takes a second for the presence of Jesus to impact one's life: a touch, a lift, a call, or a thought.

However, because of how his life ended, I can imagine how the thief on the cross may have lived before reaching his moment on the cross next to the Savior of the universe. It would not surprise me if the thief were no different than you and I. He probably had family. It was likely he was employed at some point in his life. Things got tough and he made some poor decisions. Next thing he knew, he was living a life that went against all he was raised to believe and to do. Maybe he was one of those who had lost faith in God. Maybe he sunk so low in his life that he no longer believed that God even knew he existed, let alone cared about him.

We do not know for sure, but if he did feel these things; he was no different than many of us who fall under the weight of spiritual depression. When you fall to your lowest depths, only Jesus can reach you. And, He can reach you *anywhere* you may be "hanging."

One of the biggest fallacies is the notion that you must get yourself together before coming to Jesus. Ridiculous! Only God in us can fix our brokenness! I know from personal experience that even when you are not looking for Jesus, He will reach down and snatch you up from a worse fate. It is especially important during those times to be aware that Jesus is with you wherever you find yourself, and He will lift you up out of out your despair! Just call His name!

Only Jesus can restore your trust and belief in Him! Nothing and no one can make it better until you find the courage to believe what your mind tells you is meaningless: "There is a God, and I still matter to Him." Sound ridiculous? That is why Jesus, the Divine Counselor, was chosen to be our intervention specialist. He knows how it feels to feel abandoned. He knows how it feels to believe that God has forsaken you. Jesus knows how it feels to pray a painful prayer, over and over again, and not hear a response from God (Luke 22:44). He knows how it feels to finally receive God's response, and it is not the response you really want to hear. Jesus knows how it feels to utter the words, "Father if you are willing, please take this cup of suffering away from me. Yet I want your will to be done, not mine" (Luke 22:42, NLT), and still hope God really doesn't allow the loneliness, sorrow, and pain to continue. Jesus was able to have "ridiculous" faith and believe till the end (Luke 23:46) because He had confidence in His Father that everything would be all right if He just stayed in God's will.

Jesus was able to do what we must do: Have faith that your current situation is temporary, apparently necessary, and part of God's will for your life. When it appears that God has abandoned you, it is then that you must reach back into your life experiences and remember all the trials and tribulations God has brought you through. Sometimes, even Christians have selective memory when it comes to forgetting about all the miracles in their lives, and focusing exclusively on life's disappointments.

A major challenge for people who believe in a higher power, God, is how to maintain their faith, trust, and belief in anything or anyone in the face of over-whelming conditions. It is especially difficult for those who have fallen under the load of their burdens and feel crushed by the weight of spiritual depression. It is important to be reminded that people from all cultures, religions, and walks of life are susceptible to developing spiritual depression. Being a lifelong member of a church, religious organization, or family does not protect you from the major ingredients of spiritual depression—feelings of guilt and shame—nor the by-prod-ucts of such if these feelings linger, go unchecked, or are otherwise ignored (i.e. discouragement, depression, or despair).

Membership in a religious organization or faith-based community alone means nothing. You must exercise your faith into action. It is during these times that we must look past what we can see with our eyes and recognize what is sketched in our hearts: Jesus, reaching for us with outstretched arms, saying "Come to me, all you who are weary and burdened, and I will give you rest" (Matthew 11:28, NIV).

I imagine that the thief on the cross must have been "weary and burdened," to say the least. He was most certainly aware that he was broken mentally and spiri-tually, yet able to gather himself, recognize he was in the presence of divinity, and muster enough faith to *believe* that the man hanging on the cross next to him was the Son of God. Moreover, he did not just believe that the man hanging on the cross next to him, Jesus, was the Son of God (ridiculous, considering the circumstance; don't you think?); he did something about his belief. He opened up his mouth and said "Jesus, remember me when you come into your kingdom" (Luke 23:42, NIV).

The thief on the cross did not have time to research the Scriptures or interview those who may have been blessed by Jesus. He had to take action right then and there and rely on his gut feeling that although his life up to that point was not much to speak of, and he was no longer sure that God even cared, there was *something* about this man, Jesus. The thief on the cross had nothing more to lose and everything to gain.

If you are unsure of your place in the heart of God, do not spend a lot of time trying to figure it out. Take action and assume that He is the Living God and wants to save you! Do not beat yourself up emotionally with negative thoughts about your lack of faith. If you know that your faith is weak, just pray the prayer of the father in Mark 9:24, seeking healing for his sick child:

> At once the father of the boy gave [an eager, piercing, inarticulate] cry *with tears*, and he said, Lord, I believe! [Constantly] help my weakness of faith. (AMP)

This is the ultimate in faith!

Lyrics of another childhood favorite on *faith*:

Faith Is the Key
By Audrey Wright Dickerson

After the storm comes the rainbow
After the rain comes the sunshine
It's always darkest just before the light
Never doubt Him always keep Him in sight.

Faith is the key to reach heaven's heights
Faith you will see is the way to win the fight.
Faith the size of a mustard seed
Will move mountains if we just believe.

If you are deep in sin
Fall on your knees and pray to Him
Out of the shadows into the light
Never doubt Him always keep Him in sight.

Faith is the key to reach heaven's heights
Faith you will see is the way to win the fight.
Faith the size of a mustard seed
Will move mountains if we just believe.

Composition/Song Title: Faith Is The Key
Writer Credits: Audrey Wright Dickerson
Copyright: © 1979 Eleanor Wright Trust, Publisher
All Rights Reserve. Used By Permission.

What more do *you* have to lose? What do you want to gain? If you are going to believe in someone, believe in one who accepts your mustard seed-sized-faith and sincere effort to believe. This is the ultimate in "ridiculous" faith!

The ultimate in healing is to be saved into God's kingdom.

Your faith can make you whole, but you must be willing to get to Jesus any way you can: crawling, carried on the back of a friend, or simply opening your heart and asking Jesus to remember you when He comes into His kingdom!

"Ridiculous" faith will save you!

Thank you, Jesus! Thank you, Lord!

Chapter 12

God's Been Bragging on You Again: Surviving Your Job Experience

—————o⟨⟩o—————

Then the Lord said to Satan, "Have you considered my servant Job? There is no one on earth like him; he is blameless and upright, a man who fears God and shuns evil" (Job 1:8, NIV).

The Test

*D*o you ever wonder, *Why me?* or think to yourself, *Why does life always seem so challenging and difficult?* And, have you ever thought, *Is it me or do these trials and tribulations seem to pop up at the most inconvenient times?*—particularly when they interrupt a smooth part of the road on life's journey you were enjoying? Ever had times when it feels like you just can't catch a break? Well, I certainly have! It used to be a mystery to me until I was blessed to hear a sermon delivered by Dr. Rupert Bushnell. Dr. Bushnell planted a thought in my mind that day which I shall never forget. He described a scene familiar to those of us who have ever sat in a school classroom: "Jesus as teacher; brings us to class (life), provides the textbook (Bible), and all the materials we need to be successful and 'graduate' when the 'school of life' has ended. However, it is the prince of evil (Satan) who is allowed to administer the test, in the form of temptation." Sound unfair? Well, here's the part that stuck immediately in my mind, and has given me hope whenever I feel like I cannot pass the next test, or I have already "failed" it: *"During the test, God is somewhere bragging about you!"*

Dr. Bushnell went on to remind listeners that Satan cannot tempt us beyond what God has already calculated we can bear:

> No temptation has overtaken you except what is common to mankind. And God is faithful; he will not let you be tempted beyond what you can bear. But when you are tempted, he will also provide a way out so that you can endure it. (1 Corinthians 10:13, NIV)

The test is set up so that we have the advantage every single time. All we have to do is remember that when evil, temptation, or difficult tests come our way, look up to God and say: "Oh, I get it—you've been bragging on me again!"

By the time Dr. Bushnell finished that sermon, I was walking out of church with my chest puffed out, feeling like Paul: "I consider everything a loss because of the surpassing worth of knowing Christ Jesus my Lord, for whose sake I have lost all things. I consider them garbage, that I may gain Christ" (Philippians 3:8, NIV).

Receiving that particular sermon during that time of my life was extra special timing on God's part! I was going through a series of complex problems and felt overwhelmed, inadequate, and spiritually depressed, for sure. Not so coincidentally, my younger sister (who lived next door at that time) was experiencing her own brand of life's difficulties, and we were both quite discouraged. I remember standing in the driveway one day, telling her that my life was so wrought with challenges and obstacles that I was beginning to feel "like Job, in the Bible." We shook our heads, laughed, and eventually agreed that although we were both going through some very difficult tests, we were nowhere close to enduring what Job had to endure.

However, it occurred to me that day in the driveway that each of us, in our own individual ways, is confronted with trials and tribulations so painful and so discouraging to us that we often feel as bad as Job must have felt.

So where does this theory of God "bragging on us" originate? Anyone who has ever studied the Bible or attended church (in Western culture, especially) at some point in their lives is likely familiar with, or has at least heard of, the story of

Job, "God's good and faithful servant." Regardless of how difficult life becomes, few of us would trade places with Job. It is fitting, however, that we take a closer look at his story, because after all, it is the life of Job that many reference when life seems most difficult. His story stands the test of time as a perfect example of what it means for God to "brag on you," and how knowing and remembering this can help encourage you while you survive your "Job experience."

Let's take a quick look at the basics of this phenomenal biblical lesson on having faith and trusting in God.

The stage is set for Job's "adventure" in the first two chapters of the book of Job. Job was "perfect and upright" and "feared God and avoided evil" (Job 1:1). Job was blessed beyond measure (Job 1:3); he had a large family (Job 1:2). Job was righteous. The things of God were constantly on his mind and reflected in his daily behavior. He even made sacrifices of atonement to the Lord on his children's behalf just in case they "sinned," or "cursed God in their hearts" (Job 1:5). Here is where things began to get interesting:

Job's First Test

> Then the Lord said to Satan, "Have you considered my servant Job? There is no one on earth like him; he is blameless and upright, a man who fears God and shuns evil."

> "Does Job fear God for nothing?" Satan replied.
> "Have you not put a hedge around him and his household and everything he has? You have blessed the work of his hands, so that his flocks and herds are spread throughout the land. But stretch out your hand and strike everything he has, and he will surely curse you to your face." The Lord said to Satan, "Very well, then, everything he has is in your power, but on the man himself do not lay a finger." (Job 1:8-12, NIV)

It is clear to me when I read this passage that Job was minding his own business, living well, blessed beyond measure, and more, when God Himself, volunteered Job to Satan, as an example of one that was perfect (Job 1:8). This is the verse that set off the chain of events which changed Job's life so abruptly, causing it to spiral (seemingly) out of control. This is the verse where God "brags on Job" and holds him up to Satan, to be tested in the "school of life."

Job's story is so famous that one does not need to be a Bible scholar, or even a regular church attendee to be familiar with all the carnage that befell him. I've seen Job's story referenced in a variety of ways across American culture, from game shows (*Jeopardy* and *Family Feud*) to clichés. For example: He escaped just "by the skin of his teeth" (Job 19:20); is often used to describe a "close call" or "avoiding danger" or some other negative circumstance or outcome.

After God issued His challenge to Satan to "consider my servant Job," Job had a run of unprecedented misfortune. When Satan "considers" you, this means he is focusing all his time and energy just on you, because God has been bragging on you!

Job's life served as the model for "Murphy's Law" ("Whatever can go wrong, will go wrong") long before Murphy existed. Notice that after being "considered" by Satan, everything connected to Job's life began to crumble and die, including the death of his children. The only restriction God placed on Satan during Job's first test was: "but on the man himself do not lay a finger" (Job 1:11).

What is often missed when recounting the story of Job and all his calamities is that Job was not suffering alone through this series of tests. Just as we may feel like we are the only one's suffering when we go through tests and trials, whatever happens to us affects those we love and those who love us. Job was not living in a vacuum, or some laboratory, in solitude, while God and Satan acted out the "Great Controversy" (see Ellen G. White, 2005) with Job as the pawn. Remember, Job had a wife and family. Job's wife suffered through everything he suffered. When Job lost all his financial wealth (i.e. houses, investment properties, and more), his wife also lost those things. When Job had to face the horrible, tragic death of every one of their ten children, his wife also absorbed this pain. And based on what we know about the bond between mother and child, we can assume that Job's wife felt an even greater sense of loss for her family.

More compelling is the fact that even after these tragedies in Job's life took place one painful blow after another (Job 1:13-19), the Bible says, "In all this, Job did not sin by charging God with wrongdoing" (Job 1:22, NIV). Job's response to his life falling apart, bit by bit, and losing everything, was: "Naked I came from my mother's womb, and naked I will depart. The Lord gave and the Lord has taken away; may the name of the Lord be praised" (Job 1:21, NIV). This is an amazing response, even for someone as righteous as Job! I would not venture to guess how many of us today could suffer such horrific personal loss and respond by praising the name of the Lord.

Obviously, this is a time for celebration and hallelujah's, right? Because Job has passed the test of Satan, he can now continue on with his life and Satan can go and "consider" someone else, right? Not so fast. When you take a look at chapter two, you may be shocked to learn that Job's test was not over:

Job's Second Test

> Then the Lord said to Satan, "Have you considered my servant Job? There is no one on earth like him; he is blameless and upright, a man who fears God and shuns evil. And he still maintains his integrity, though you incited me against him to ruin him without any reason."

> "Skin for skin!" Satan replied. "A man will give all he has for his own life. But stretch out your hand and strike his flesh and bones, and he will surely curse you to your face." The Lord said to Satan, "Very well, then, he is in your hands; but you must spare his life." (Job 2:3-6, NIV)

Wait! Is it just me, or did God "brag on Job" again in chapter two, verse three? Wow! Either God has a twisted sense of humor, or He really has a lot of confidence in Job's confidence in *Him*! I am positive in the latter explanation, because remember, God allows trials and tribulations in our lives so that *His* glory can be manifested in our circumstances, and *His* name will ultimately be praised. It may seem like a game between Satan and God, but the stakes are not a trivial matter. On the line are God's integrity, His love for us, His mercy, His grace, and our salvation! All of which are constantly being questioned and challenged by Satan.

Satan's response is also telling, in that he plays the role of "devil's advocate" (pun intended) before such a cliché' became vogue! He basically argued with God that he still was not impressed with Job's righteousness because "A man will give all he has for his own life" (Job 2:4). However, if confronted with some major health problems, Satan is sure that Job will not be so righteous the next time around and curse God to His face (Job 2:5). Amazingly, God once again gives Satan permission to "consider" Job, but specified that Satan must spare his life (Job 2:6). "So Satan went out from the presence of the Lord and afflicted Job with painful sores from the soles of his feet to the crown of his head" (Job 2:7, NIV). Surely, Job would not be able to remain strong and faithful to a God that allowed him to lose every material possession he had—as well as his children—and then allowed Satan to attack his body with disease!

No Man Is an Island

The amazing thing to me about the life of Job was that the Lord allowed Satan to take everything but Job's life (Job 1:12; 2:6) and Job's wife! It is clear that Mrs. Job was still by his side, even after experiencing all the same losses as Job, save the loss of her healthy skin. In Job 19:17, Job says: "My breath is offensive to my wife; I am loathsome to my own family" (NIV). This tells me that Mrs. Job was not only still in the picture; she was still experiencing all of the trauma that impacted Job! Maybe Job's wife even helped him scrape the sores on his body (Job 2:8). Of course we do not know for sure, but my imagination tells me that Job's wife was a good woman because the Lord allowed her to live and stay by Job's side through all of the tests that befell her husband. Remember, the Lord works in a myriad of ways to test and bless others through your trials and through your miracles.

The focus was on Job, but the Lord allowed Job's wife to be a witness to all that transpired. And, just as she felt all the same pain and loss as her husband, Mrs. Job stood to gain all the blessings and redemption that came with holding on to faith, standing by her significant other, and praising the Lord through her adversity!

With all this in mind, you might find it strange to learn that the only words recorded from Mrs. Job, over forty-two chapters of physical, psychological, emotional, and spiritual intensity, are these: *"Are you still maintaining your integrity? Curse God and die"* (Job 2:9, NIV)! It seems harsh that these are the only words recorded from Mrs. Job. I am sure she must have had other things to say during this test of attrition between Satan and God, with her husband squarely in the middle.

Can you imagine how Mrs. Job must have felt? She was experiencing every loss her husband felt, plus she must have felt badly, watching her husband go through all that he endured. What wife could stand idly by and watch her husband's hard work, dreams, and self-esteem be taken from him right before her eyes? Mrs. Job was hurting just as bad, yet she chose to stand by, unable to lift a finger to help her husband in any way, as God allowed him to be broken. How painful this must have been for her to watch!

In today's world of mental health diagnosis, it seems clear to me that Job and his wife must have suffered from post-traumatic stress disorder (PTSD), and major depression. A couple of things lead me to this assumption:

1. Very few people could have survived the accumulation of tragedy and trauma which Job and his wife endured, without experiencing some increase in emotional arousal, and decrease in level of psychological function.
2. Job's response to his wife's declaration that he should, "Curse God and die!"
3. Job's response to his three "friends" who came to "comfort" him.

Job's reply to his wife's suggestion to "Curse God and die":

> "You are talking like a foolish woman. Shall we accept good from God, and not trouble?" In all this, Job did not sin in what he said. (Job 2:10, NIV)

Job's response to his wife gives us a hint that Mrs. Job was *not* behaving like her usual self. Notice Job did not declare that his wife was "foolish," nor did he "call her out of her name." He expressly mentioned that his wife was "talking like" a foolish person.

Apparently, Mrs. Job was acting and speaking out of character for how she normally spoke. The Job's were experiencing something far beyond "normal." It seems reasonable to think that Mrs. Job just wanted the pain to stop! She wanted to see the man she loved relieved of his pain. It was *their* pain—a shared pain! And Job himself wanted to die just to end the pain. Carefully read Job's soliloquy:

Job Speaks

> After this, Job opened his mouth and cursed the day of his birth. He said: "May the day of my birth perish, and the night that said, 'A boy is conceived!' That day—may it turn to darkness; may God above not care about it; may no light shine on it. May gloom and utter darkness claim it once more; may a cloud settle over it; may blackness overwhelm it."

> "That night—may thick darkness seize it; may it not be included among the days of the year nor be entered in any of the months. May that night be barren; may no shout of joy be heard in it. May those who curse days curse that day, those who are ready to rouse Leviathan. May its morning stars become dark; may it wait for daylight in vain and not see the first rays of dawn, for it did not shut the doors of the womb on me to hide trouble from my eyes."

> "Why did I not perish at birth, and die as I came from the womb? Why were there knees to receive me and breasts that I might be nursed? For now I would be lying down in peace; I would be asleep and at rest with kings and rulers of the earth, who built for themselves places now lying in ruins, with princes who had gold, who filled their houses with silver."

> "Or why was I not hidden away in the ground like a stillborn child, like an infant who never saw the light of day? There the wicked cease from turmoil, and there the weary are at rest. Captives also enjoy their ease; they no longer hear the slave driver's shout. The small and the great are there, and the slaves are freed from their owners."

> "Why is light given to those in misery, and life to the bitter of soul, to those who long for death that does not come, who search for it more than for hidden treasure, who are filled with gladness and rejoice when they reach the grave?"

"Why is life given to a man whose way is hidden, whom God has hedged in? For sighing has become my daily food; my groans pour out like water. What I feared has come upon me; what I dreaded has happened to me. I have no peace, no quietness; I have no rest, but only turmoil." (Job 3:1-26, NIV)

Wow! As a professed lover of poetry and prose, I admit to being smitten by the beauty in the writing, while vicariously feeling the pain of the writer. That was how Job was feeling after only three chapters of being "considered" by Satan! He had thirty-nine more chapters left in this horrible experiment of what can happen when "God brags on you" to Satan! Even the most righteous and staunch Christian could be forgiven for feeling just a little bit down and discouraged after dealing with the sequence of events which threatened to topple the Jobs! Reading Job's words in chapter three almost overshadows the "good news" in chapter two, verse ten, which ended with another victory for Job (and God): "In all this, Job did not sin in what he said" (Job 2:10, NIV).

"Friendly" Comfort?

What Job wrote was poetic, to say the least. But, it was also telling in that he wrote this "prose" after his three "friends" came by to "comfort and support" him (Job 2:11-13). These friends started by weeping, crying in a loud voice, tearing their clothes, and sprinkling dust on their heads (traditional response for that era), as they looked toward heaven (Job 2:12). After that, they sat down on the ground with him for seven days and seven nights, not saying a word, because they could see that he was gravely sorrowful (Job 2:13). Oh, if only they could have remained silent!

How different were Job's friends from the friends of the man we spoke of in chapter 11 ("Ridiculous" Faith), who was stricken with paralysis (Mark 2:1-12). Remember? Those friends' faith in God was so strong, they lifted him up, carried him to where Jesus was, and then tore a hole in the roof so they could let him down at Jesus' feet. Talk about being careful to choose the right friends! (But, that's another story.) For now, suffice it to say the friends Job had were painfully lacking in administering the proper elements of comfort and support.

From Job, chapters four through thirty-two, we have a front row seat to a dramatic play of intimate relationships among so-called friends. In Job, chapters four and five, his three "comforters" question everything from Job's integrity to his righteousness. And Job's response to them in chapter six, once again solidifies his utter anguish and spiritual depression:

> Oh, that I might have my request, that God would grant what I hope for, that God would be willing to crush me, to let loose his hand and cut off my life! Then I would still have this consolation—my joy in unrelenting pain—that I had not denied the words of the Holy One. What strength do I have, that I should still hope? What prospects, that I should be patient? (Job 6:8-11, NIV)

Clearly, Job remains discouraged and confused about why he is experiencing so much misfortune (Job 7:20-21; 10:2-3, 18). However, he is not confused about the less than adequate attempts at comfort and support from his three friends. Job addresses them as well:

> "Anyone who withholds kindness from a friend forsakes the fear of the Almighty. But my brothers are as undependable as intermittent streams, as the streams that overflow when darkened by thawing ice and swollen with melting snow, but that stop flowing in the dry season, and in the heat vanish from their channels. Caravans turn aside from their routes; they go off into the wasteland and perish. The caravans of Tema look for water, the traveling merchants of Sheba look in hope. They are distressed, because they had been confident; they arrive there, only to be disappointed. Now you too have proved to be of no help; you see something dreadful and are afraid." (Job 6:14-21, NIV)

More than telling his friends they are not very helpful, Job goes a step further and shares what he would do if their circumstances were reversed:

> "I have heard many things like these; you are miserable comforters, all of you! Will your long-winded speeches never end? What ails you that you keep on arguing? I also could speak like you, if you

were in my place; I could make fine speeches against you and shake my head at you. But my mouth would encourage you; comfort from my lips would bring you relief." (Job 16:2-5, NIV)

When you are down and out, and feeling like the Lord has turned His back on you, the last thing you need is a group of friends (or family) who come around and try to figure out for you (or for themselves), what you must have done to bring this on yourself, or why God is so angry with you. It is almost as if Job's friends had waited for this day to come so that they could express some form of their own resentment toward Job, who held himself out to be so righteous. In my profession, we call what Job's friends did, "blaming the victim." Young folks might say that Job's friends were "haters"! Either way, I think we can all agree with the old cliché: "With friends like these, who needs enemies?"

However, before we are too hard on Job's friends, we should consider the historical context and customs in which Job lived. It is a historical fact that Job lived during a time when it was commonplace for misfortune, be it physical illness or disease, loss, destruction of property or livelihood, and more, to be attributed to having been "cursed" by God, and/or receiving punishment for sin. Yet, in the case of Job's friends, they took it to an amazing level, for an extended period of time.

They not only were less than helpful; Job's friends became part of his problem. They didn't think to say to Job: "Hey, maybe God has been bragging on you again." Nor did they offer up any intercessory prayers on Job's behalf. They hung around and tortured Job with their words and smothered him with their sarcasm, blaming, and unsympathetic attitudes. Not once did any of the three try to lift Job's spirits by lifting him up to God. Instead, they blamed Job! Some customs are less helpful than others.

Naturally, the constant needling and unrelenting interrogation from Job's friends compounded the problem and took an even greater emotional toll on his psyche and spiritual confidence. I think it safe to say that the attitude of Job's friends only exacerbated Job's spiritual depression. Think about it. Job was under intense pressure from the "great experiment" between Satan and God, and also had these three irritants "pouring salt" into his wounds, as it were. It is a true testament to Job's faith in the midst of turmoil, and the strength of God's hand protecting those whom He chooses to manifest His glory, that Job was able to remain faithful to God even in his measured retort to his friends (Job 19). Toward the end of Job's statement, he utters words I'm sure echo the thoughts and feelings of people today who suffer spiritual depression and feel alone:

> "Have pity on me, my friends, have pity, for the hand of God has struck me. Why do you pursue me as God does? Will you never get enough of my flesh? Oh, that my words were recorded, that they were written on a scroll, that they were inscribed with an iron tool on lead, or engraved in rock forever!" (Job 19:21-24, NIV)

Still clearly depressed, and in pain, Job says:

> I know that my redeemer lives, and that in the end he will stand on the earth. And after my skin has been destroyed, yet in my flesh I will see God; I myself will see him with my own eyes—I, and not another. How my heart yearns within me!" (Job 19:25-27, NIV)

Here is where I see Job getting his "second wind." Sure, he is still down and disturbed, but as his anger pushes him to confront his tormentors and their comfortless words; he is simultaneously being revived to continue his fight. As emotions go, *anger* often gets a bad rap. There is nothing inherently wrong with being angry. It is just an emotion like any other. The focus from outside observers is more often on *what we do* when we feel anger. Anger that is out of control (e.g. "rage") is a catalyst for destructive behaviors, which usually result in negative outcomes. However, anger can also be a catalyst for motivation. How does this relate to Job's situation?

In her work on grief and loss (*On Grief and Grieving*, 2005), Elisabeth Kubler-Ross identified "The Five Stages of Grief." The second stage is anger. She states: "Underneath anger is pain, *your pain*" (p.15). This is clearly what Job felt during his traumatic experience, and what many of us feel today when our own circumstances seem too difficult to bear. However, Kubler-Ross provides encouragement as well, that "anger is strength and it can be an anchor, giving temporary structure to the nothingness of loss" (p.15). Maybe you can relate. Whether you are grieving the loss of a friend/loved one due to death, or grieving the loss of a cherished relationship, loss of employment, or any other loss, your initial grief may feel like being "lost at sea" with no connection to anything. Then you get angry at someone and they then become the focus of your anger. Kubler-Ross describes this as "the anger becomes a bridge over the open sea, a connection from you to them" (pgs. 15-16). Anger signals an opportunity for greater focus and "is a necessary stage of the healing process" (p. 12). Just like Job's anger helped him to focus, regroup, and motivated him to get in touch with God; so too, our anger in response to our difficult circumstances can be used as a catalyst to draw us closer to God as we seek understanding (not answers) and comfort in the midst of trials.

Surviving Your "Job" Experience

Job was able to vent his anger toward his three tormentors (a cathartic experience, I'm sure), and then regain his focus on praising God in the midst of his trial!

Job 19:25 says it all: "I know that my redeemer lives, and that in the end he will stand on the earth" (NIV). It is marvelous to watch as this dramatization closes in on its pinnacle. In the end, Job has faith that God will be vindicated, and therefore, whether it is in life or in death, Job is assured he will see God. That's the beginning of a testimony that will break you out of your spiritual depression!

In chapters 26-31, Job appears to be settling in on acceptance of his plight. He has silenced his three friends, and no doubt convinced them that he is not so weak as to accept an emotional pounding from them while continuing to receive, what Job thinks, is chastisement from God. Here is where things really begin to get interesting, because a fourth observer, younger than the other three, offers his opinion to Job (Job 32-37).

In chapters 36-37, in particular, the younger observer speaks "on God's behalf," and puts forth quite an impressive argument. However, the most impressive, inspiring, mind-boggling set of prose in this whole chapter comes from chapters 38-41, where God answered Job out of a storm. I recommend you read those chapters in their entirety because, outside of the book of Psalms and Song of Songs

(Song of Solomon), the book of Job presents some of the most awe-inspiring poetry and prose ever written. Reading the chronicles of God's handiwork toward creation of earth, man, and beast, will make you fall on your knees in honor and praise for the Lord God Almighty!

God's confrontation with Job and his three friends did not end with the Lord simply reminding them that *He* is the Creator and caretaker of this world. He is so merciful and just to forgive that He gave Job another opportunity to respond:

> Then Job replied to the Lord: "I know that you can do all things; no purpose of yours can be thwarted. You asked, 'Who is this that obscures my plans without knowledge?' Surely I spoke of things I did not understand, things too wonderful for me to know. You said, 'Listen now, and I will speak; I will question you, and you shall answer me.' My ears had heard of you but now my eyes have seen you. Therefore I despise myself and repent in dust and ashes" (Job 42:1-6, NIV).

It is important to note two things about Job's response to God's challenge to "answer" Him:

1. Job was smart enough to realize that he could not argue with God about his own "righteousness" as he had done with his three antagonists.
2. Anytime you see God for yourself, you will confess your unworthiness and repent.

In Job 42:5-6, Job clearly states that now that he has seen God, he abhors himself and wishes to repent in dust and ashes. Job's reaction to seeing God, or even being in His most holy presence appears to be a common one throughout the Bible (e.g. Exodus 20:18-19; 33:18-23; 34:28-35; Judges 13:20-22; Isaiah 6:5; Revelation 1:17).

So Job's reaction of feeling unworthy in the presence of God was understandable, as was the anxiety that accompanied his sense of self-preservation. As we discovered in Chapter 9 ("Incarcerated by Sin"), God cannot dwell in the presence of sin because His natural inclination is to destroy anything sinful. Therefore, God does us a great favor by not allowing us to see Him face-to-face. Visiting us in dreams, or vision (Abraham), in a cloud, in a pillar of fire (Moses), or in a windstorm (Job), is another sign of His love for us—by not destroying us on sight. Even Job, in all his righteousness, could not stand toe-to-toe or face-to-face with God. That's #1 on the list in surviving your "Job" experience: acknowledging your weakness in the presence of God's strength.

God Provides Shelter Before He Prepares a Storm

The story of Job is a classic reminder that when we have storms in our lives, we must seek the shelter that God provides. The beautiful thing is that God prepares our shelter in the time of storm long before we encounter the rain in our lives. Regardless of how hard it rains in our lives, God covers us with the protection of His love and righteousness. No matter how difficult the storms become in our families, our churches, on the job, in school—whatever life has in store for us— God has designed a plan for us, so we need not fear being swept away in the current. Jesus Himself will walk across the floodwaters of our lives, reach down, and make sure we do not drown in self-pity, discouragement, and spiritual depression.

So often we watch the news, waiting to hear what the weather is going to be that day or for the weekend as we try and plan for holiday or a day out in the sunshine. It is not unusual to be disappointed when we hear that the forecast includes rain showers and possibly a rainstorm, because this will likely disrupt, postpone, or completely cancel our plans. Very rarely do you hear people talking about how happy they are to have a rainstorm (the exceptions being farmers and those living in areas with frequent droughts). Well, the same is true with plans for our lives. We do not like having our life plans interrupted or cancelled due to the rainstorms in our lives. We want only sunshine to greet us every day, and even the hint of a small rain shower or the slightest crack of thunder cause many of us to think negative thoughts and complain: "Why does it always seem to rain in my life?"

It may do us some good to think like the farmer thinks, as she looks over the crops that she grows to support her way of life and provide food to the world. What might the farmer be thinking as she looks out across the vastness of her fields and sees the rain caressing each leaf and forming small puddles in the troughs between plants? Maybe her thoughts go toward praising God because she knows that although rainstorms may interrupt holiday plans or a day at the beach, rain provides the moisture and nutrients needed for crops to grow and fulfill their purpose of feeding her family and the world.

Or perhaps we should view a rainstorm as those who live in arid, desert-like areas. What might the folks who live in such climates be thinking when they look up and see water pouring down from the sky? Maybe their thoughts and praise ascend toward heaven because they realize that when it becomes too dry, living things can wither up and die.

In the Midst of the Storm

The rainstorms in our lives can be viewed as a blessing or a curse. This depends entirely upon the perceptions of each and every one of us. It all depends on how *you* choose to see things, which reminds me of a story.

One relaxing summer Sunday afternoon, I was sitting on our living room floor playing with our two-year-old son. It had been raining earlier that day, but nothing overly dramatic or problematic. We had just gone through a very hot, very dry period in the Philadelphia area, so many welcomed a little rain. My young son loves to go outside, and periodically he will go to the shoe rack by our front door and bring me his shoes, indicating he wants to go outside. The rain sprinkles had stopped, so when he brought me his little shoes, I dutifully put them on his little feet and prepared to take him outside.

All of a sudden rain began to pour down. I apologized to my son and explained that we could not go outside while it rained so hard. He pointed to the sliding glass door and grunted! The little fellow rarely chose to grace our ears with any words at that point (though we were sure he could talk); probably because he received pretty much whatever he wanted by pointing and grunting.

I took my son out on the balcony which faced a beautiful public golf course and pointed to the rain. I then pointed to the golfers huddled under trees, seeking protection from the powerful storm. I stuck his arm out so he could feel the rain. I talked about what rain is and how God brings it from heaven to water the trees and soothe the dryness in the earth. (Fascinating stuff for a two year old, I'm sure!) We turned to go back inside and continue the game we had left before the rain began. Suddenly, a booming crack of thunder grabbed our attention. My little boy jumped into my arms, terrified by the unfamiliar sound. As he shook in my strong embrace, I tried to comfort him and explain that sometimes when God brings the rain, He allows thunder and lightning to come along as well. I found myself explaining to a two-year-old child what I did not always realize in my own life: rain provides cleansing and growth, and thunder and lightning, which—although terrifying—often provide nothing more than a "special effect" to the storm.

Meteorologists have said that if you are caught in the eye of a storm, you are actually in the safest place possible. While the winds and rain swirl around your life, and the special effects of thunder and lightning make a lot of noise that may frighten you into giving up on God, you must remember to run into the arms of your Heavenly Father who is more powerful than the storms in your life! He has a strong embrace. Jesus will comfort you through your storm. He will remind you that the rain is a necessary component for spiritual growth and the cleansing of your soul. Your Heavenly Father will show you the dry and arid spots in your life that need spiritual rain. You must be patient in the midst of your storm. When you slow down and begin to breathe easily again, your heart will fall back into its familiar rhythm as your faith and trust in God is restored. Jesus will simply say to the storm in your life: "Peace be still!"

Like many stories in the Bible, Job's story is there to remind us that God rewards our faith and our trust in Him by having our back when life is a struggle and times get tough (as they inevitably will). There comes a point in everyone's life when we go through our "Job experience." It is a compliment from God to our faith in Him, that He is so willing to "brag on us," knowing that with His help, we will make it through. In the end, God blessed Job and his wife "more than his beginning" (Job 42:12, KJV). He blessed them with ten more children: "seven sons and three daughters" (Job 42:13, KJV). After all that befell Job and his family, the Lord allowed him to see his children grow up, and "even four generations" (Job 42:16, KJV).

When you find yourself at your lowest point, think about what Job endured. When just getting up and going outside become a struggle, think about God's restorative power made manifest in the life of Job and his family. When you are in the eye of your storm you may not be able to see a positive outcome. Fight the urge to dismiss your blessings and focus only on your problems (selective memory).

Instead, make a list of the blessings you receive on a daily basis. Start with waking up and seeing the light of day. Assume that the involuntary action of your heart beating and your lungs taking in air is affirmation that God has ordained your life that day for His purpose. Leave space on your list to include the fact that God's blessings more than trump the trials and tribulations you experience.

Think about how merciful God is to allow rainstorms in your life when your faith becomes dry and brittle and your soul becomes arid from spiritual depression. Soak in the lyrics of the song below and make them your testimony when you find yourself in the eye of the storm, safely in the arms of Jesus:

In the Midst of the Rain
By Victor W. Caldwell, Cedric J. Caldwell, and BeBe Winans

Now every time I lift my eyes to the sky, I'm reminded of a time in my life
When all the dark clouds hung over me, I was lost, in search of a key.

I remember loved one's being so kind, saying things
would get much better with time
And I admit sometimes they did for a while,
then I'd find myself back under the cloud.

Right in the midst of the rain, my heart was so full of pain.
You came and rescued my soul, and then your love took control.
Right in the midst of the rain, you caused me to smile again.
My life was awesomely changed, right in the midst of the rain.

When it comes right down to just you and me,
there's nothing better now these eyes can see.
And tell me what compares to all that you are? You are everything,
yes, my morning star.
My mind, my heart, my soul, I now give to you.

I'm under your control, so what can I do?
Cause I surrender all, all that I owe, and will follow you wherever you go.

Right in the midst of the rain, my heart was so full of pain.
You came and rescued my soul, and then your love took control.
Right in the midst of the rain, you caused me to smile again.
My life was awesomely changed, right in the midst of the rain.

Be thankful for what God provides. Before you know it, you will be laughing and singing, and lifting up the name of Jesus as you suddenly recognize that your troubles are no comparison to what brother Job endured. Stay faithful and trust in the Lord in the midst of the rain, and even through your storm. God will show Himself in your life beyond measure. Then praise the name of the Lord for His mercy and His grace:

> *I will extol the Lord at all times; his praise will always be on my lips.*
> *I will glory in the Lord; let the afflicted hear and rejoice.*
> *Glorify the Lord with me; let us exalt his name together. I sought the*
> *Lord, and he answered me; he delivered me from all my fears.*
> (Psalm 34:1-4, NIV)

Chapter 13

Finding Joy in Your Cross (Part I)

———————⋙⋘———————

"Consider it pure joy, my brothers and sisters, whenever you face trials of many kinds, because you know that the testing of your faith produces perseverance. Let perseverance finish its work so that you may be mature and complete, not lacking anything" (James 1:2-4, NIV).

Everyone Has a Cross to Bear

Regardless of what life throws at you, there is comfort in knowing that God is so full of mercy and grace that He supplies us with *joy* in the midst of trial and tribulation. Trial and tribulation are not words we normally associate with *joy*! As a matter of fact, we have spent the better part of this book identifying Jesus as the "cure" to counteract spiritual depression, which so often develops when our lives are constantly filled with trial and tribulation. There is an old saying: *"We all have our cross to bear."* After studying the Bible over the years, and doing research specifically for this book, I believe a stronger statement can be made, especially for those of us seeking the face of Jesus, the redemption of our sins that comes with believing on Him, and accepting His free gift of salvation and eternal life. It is this: Bearing our cross is a prerequisite!

We are passengers on the roller coaster of life, and as such, we willingly accept God's grace and mercy in allowing joy here and there between peaks and valleys.

However, I would guess that very few of us find *joy* in bearing our cross. I will go a step further and state that no one actually volunteers to carry a cross in the first place, except of course, our Lord and Savior, Jesus Christ. It is difficult to picture any of the rest of us willingly carrying a cross, let alone finding it joyful to do so. However, if that old saying is true—that we all have our cross to bear—then a most important question remains: How do you find joy in your cross and not succumb to spiritual depression in the process? As has been our custom, we will look to biblical Scripture to see if we can sort this out. Let's consider our theme text in detail:

> Consider it pure joy, my brothers and sisters, whenever you face trials of many kinds, because you know that the testing of your faith produces perseverance. Let perseverance finish its work so that you may be mature and complete, not lacking anything. (James 1:2-4, NIV)

The word "joy" seems a bit out of place at the beginning of these two verses because of what follows: trials of many kinds, testing of faith, perseverance, and more. Joy doesn't seem to fit within the context of what normally comes to mind when one thinks of trials, testing of faith, or perseverance. Somewhat confused, I searched the *The American Heritage Dictionary, 3rd Edition* (1996) to make sure I truly understood the meaning of *joy*. This is what I found: "intense or elated happiness" (noun), "a source of great pleasure" (noun), "to rejoice" (verb). So, this text in James is telling us that we should have intense or elated happiness when we have trials and tribulations. What? In essence, our "cross" should be a source of great pleasure. Come again? Said another way, we should *rejoice* when God tests us! Whoa! I must admit this is a view I had not considered before taking up the challenge of writing this book.

On the surface, the concept of finding "joy" amongst difficulties does not seem to make much sense! Should I be elated and happy in the midst of trials and tribulations? Is it possible to get pleasure from my cross? Does it *really* seem logical to *rejoice* when God puts my life to the test? Yes, yes, and yes! We highlighted this reality of God testing us in Chapter 12, which focused on the life of Job and his wife ("God's Been Bragging on You Again"). There was not a lot of visible or tangible joy recorded in the process of God testing Job. We will have to wait until we make it to heaven to interview Mr. and Mrs. Job, to learn how they were able to stay faithful to God during their most difficult times, finding joy in their cross.

The "What," "Why," and "How" of "Cross-Bearing Joy"

The idea of finding joy in your cross begs the question: How? Before we can answer this and find joy in our cross, it is important to answer two other questions: What does the cross represent? Why must you and I carry a cross? The answer to the first question is easy. The cross represents Jesus paying the total price for our rebellion via His crucifixion: Redemption! Restoration! Salvation! Eternal life!

The "why" question requires a little more thought. If Jesus already carried the cross and died on it for your sins and mine, why must we carry our *own* cross? Matthew 16:24 provides a partial answer: "Then Jesus said to his disciples, 'Whoever wants to be my disciple must deny themselves and take up their cross and follow me'" (NIV). Okay. So now we know that if we expect to be a disciple of Jesus, we must first *deny self* (restrain ourselves from self-indulgence), and then *take up our cross* and *follow Jesus*. Well then, what does it mean to be a disciple? The dictionary can help us with the second "what" question. A disciple is *"one who embraces and assists in spreading the teachings of* another" (*The American Heritage Dictionary,3rd Edition,* 1996).

However, what if you do not want to be a disciple, per se, and you do not want to spread the teachings of Jesus? What if you just want to accept Jesus' free gift of salvation and follow Jesus, but without carrying your cross? What if you want to skip the part about "take up their cross and follow me" and just hang out with Jesus for the rest of eternity? I mean, you know, discipleship is not for everybody, right? Okay. That's three more "what" questions, so we need to return to the Bible for help here. Matthew 10:38 says: "Whoever does not take up their cross and follow me is not worthy of me" (NIV). Oh my! It seems clear that if you plan to follow Jesus, you must include the carrying of a cross in your plan. Otherwise, you are not worthy to be in the presence of Jesus.

So, now we have established the "why," the necessity of carrying a cross to spread the message of Jesus. And we have established "what" makes carrying your cross a necessity: to spread the message of Jesus. Amazing that the reasons for "why" and "what" are identical. No surprise here: the cross (your cross) is all about Jesus! We have emphasized throughout this book that our trials and tribulations are not just for our benefit. Neither are our blessings and praise. *When we accept the fact that following Jesus requires us to carry our cross, we will have a testimony to share with others. This means, in essence, we are "spreading the message" that Jesus saves, which in turn, makes us disciples!*

The added benefit of willingly carrying our cross is that Jesus will be under the load, carrying it with us! Then and only then can we gain the knowledge and experience (read: "wisdom") of what Jesus can do for our broken lives and how He can turn our pain into gain, hurt into healing, and sorrow into *joy*! Only after carrying our cross can we grasp what it really means to be solely dependent upon Jesus (i.e. ". . . the testing of your faith develops perseverance. Let perseverance finish its work so that you may be mature and complete, not lacking anything" James 1:3-4, NIV). Once God is satisfied that the testing of our faith has produced the right amount of character in us worthy to be disciples, He will give us opportunities to share His love for us with others. As a matter of fact, when Jesus bends down low and steps underneath your cross and helps you carry your load, you will not hesitate to spread the message that Jesus saves!

Hopefully, we are in agreement: There can be no following Jesus or being in His presence without carrying our cross! We have answered "why" and "what." We can move on to answering the "how" question: How do you find *joy* in your cross? In keeping with the tenor of this book, we will utilize the life experiences of people in the Bible to draw parallels with modern-day experiences, which reflect wonderful examples of what it means to find *joy* in your cross.

Finding Joy in Your Cross in Personal Triumph

Exhibit A: Hannah

The first Bible story I want to highlight is Hannah, the wife of Elkanah, and mother of Samuel, one of Israel's greatest men of God. Her story is found in 1 Samuel 1-2:26.

There may be those of you not familiar with what Hannah ("the graceful one") had to endure. Hannah's "cross" was being unable to conceive children. Those of us who grew up in church, or are history buffs, are probably just familiar enough with biblical history to recognize that a woman being unable to bear children back in Hannah's day was quite a dishonor. There was immense public shame and private anguish for any woman known to be "barren." And it was not good enough to simply have children. In those days, it was even more important to have a male child. Hannah had neither.

To make matters worse, Elkanah, Hannah's husband, apparently grew impatient with Hannah's inability to conceive, because he married another woman, Peninnah ("the fertile one"), who gave birth to many children, including many sons. This was all legal back in those days, so Elkanah didn't break any laws, but his actions certainly broke Hannah's heart. After all, Hannah was Elkanah's first wife, and according to the Scriptures, he loved her very much (1 Samuel 1:5).

Now, the second wife, Peninnah, may have produced many children for Elkanah, but she was still very jealous of Hannah. This tells me that Elkanah probably made it no secret that he really loved Hannah more than Peninnah. Needless to say, this was a bad situation. Two women living in one house, married to the same man, in any day and age has got be challenging, to say the least! Add to this the fact that the first wife (the incumbent, if you will) is childless and wants a child more than anything in the world. The other wife (the new recruit) has given birth to several male children, and will not let the first wife forget it (1 Samuel 1:6). Peninnah literally prances by Hannah at every opportunity, parading her children in Hannah's face. Hannah is so distressed and depressed that she refuses to eat and she cannot sleep (1 Samuel 1:7-8). She's looking sickly, worn out, and worn down! Said another way, Hannah is not finding any *joy* in her cross. However, Hannah is a firm believer in the Most High God!

Hannah went to the temple and prayed her heart out (1 Samuel 1:10). She begged for God to hear her and to answer her cries for a male child. Notice that Hannah didn't pray some selfish prayer, like, "Lord, please give me some children so I can finally shut the mouth of that nasty woman living down the hall." Instead, she promised the Lord that if *He* would grant her this one *joy*, she would bring that child to the temple and give him back to the Lord, and leave him at the temple to live, grow, and work as a priest (1 Samuel 1:11). Even in distress, Hannah's request involved giving back to God and to His people (the community in which her future son, Samuel, would grow and flourish). All the while Hannah prayed to the Lord, Eli, the high priest, observed her supplication and took notice of how she prayed:

> Hannah was praying in her heart, and her lips were moving but her voice was not heard. Eli thought she was drunk and said to her, "How long are you going to stay drunk? Put away your wine." (1 Samuel 1:13-14, NIV)

Hannah must have been quite a sight to behold in her sorrow for the priest to believe she was drunk. Her lips were moving, but no words could be heard. I can only imagine that Hannah must have been on her knees, rocking back and forth, or maybe laying prostrate on the ground; bowing, then rising, bowing then rising, head and hands pointed toward heaven as she pleaded her case to the Lord! Hannah, no doubt, was a woman experiencing spiritual depression at the gut level. However, she also knew where to go when life had her down. She took her "cross" to the feet of the only one who could understand how she felt, and had the power to step under her cross and lift her up. Hannah answered Eli:

> "Not so, my lord," Hannah replied, "I am a woman who is deeply troubled. I have not been drinking wine or beer; I was pouring out my soul to the Lord. Do not take your servant for a wicked woman; I have been praying here out of my great anguish and grief." (1 Samuel 1:15-16, NIV)

The priest blessed Hannah and told her, "Go in peace" (1 Samuel 1:17, NIV).

Now, here is another important piece: When Hannah rose up from her knees and was finished crying and praying, praying and crying, the Lord lifted her spirits immediately. Not after a few days, or a few weeks, but right then and there! The Bible says she rose up, felt better, and "did eat" (1 Samuel 1:18). Notice that when Hannah rose from praying she was *not* suddenly nine month's pregnant! Hannah's spirits were lifted immediately because of her *belief* and *faith* that God *would* answer her prayer. And God did answer Hannah's prayer. She had a son, who she named Samuel, which sounds like the Hebrew word for "God heard" but is actually related to "asked of God." Hannah explains the name: "Because, I asked the Lord for him" (1 Samuel 1:20, NIV).

After Hannah had weaned Samuel (about age three), she kept her promise to the Lord and took the little boy to Eli, the head priest. She said to him, essentially, "Remember what I promised the Lord. Here is my son" (1 Samuel 1:26-28). The conclusion of Hannah's story is a joyful one:

> And the Lord was gracious to Hannah; she gave birth to three sons and two daughters. Meanwhile, the boy Samuel grew up in the presence of the Lord. (1 Samuel 2:21, NIV)

After living for years in want of a child; and forced to watch in sorrow as a rival bore a "basketball team," the Lord gave Hannah a house full of children! Hannah found *joy* in her cross! More importantly, she did not forget to keep her promise to the Lord, by giving Him back the special gift He gave to her: Samuel, who would become a prophet of the Lord and serve God and the community the rest of his life. Then she gave the Lord resounding praise in public, through her prayer of thanksgiving. In 1 Samuel 2:1, we read the beginning of Hannah's prayer:

> Then Hannah prayed and said:
> "My heart rejoices in the Lord;
> in the Lord my horn is lifted high.
> My mouth boasts over my enemies,
> For I delight in your deliverance." (NIV)

Take time and read all of Hannah's prayer of praise and thanksgiving to the Lord. It will inspire you and hopefully remind you to give the Lord praise in public when He lifts your burdens and adds His broad and ample shoulders underneath your cross!

Hannah presented a wonderful example of what it means to "find joy in your cross," because of how she carried herself in the midst of her sorrow and depression. She did not strike out against her nemesis. Neither did she curse the Lord for her unfortunate circumstance. Instead, Hannah carried her cross directly to the feet of the Most High God, and presented herself to Him as a faithful witness to His limitless power, mercy, and grace. This is what each of us must do when we are feeling the weight of our cross:

1. Take your cross to the feet of Jesus; understanding and accepting that it is not just about you.
2. Believe and have faith that God will not only answer your prayer; He will help you carry your cross.
3. Share your praise report with friends/family and the community.

Following this simple (but challenging) process will help you find joy in your cross.

Finding Joy in Your Cross for His Honor and Glory

There are so many examples in the Bible of people experiencing challenges and overcoming obstacles. Although the actual stories occurred long ago, the truths and principles within these stories are apropos for current and future generations.

For some of us, the weight of our cross may come in the form of persecution from a rival, as it was with Hannah. Sometimes we are faced with a nemesis at work, at school, and far too often, even in our own homes! Nothing has changed in today's world. Following Jesus still has a price. That price includes carrying your own cross. Carrying your cross likely includes persecution of some kind or other, for lifting up the name of Jesus. The word "persecution" may seem archaic and overly harsh, but simply describes the diversity in challenges (testing of faith) we face in our lives. Persecution, as stated previously, can come in a variety of forms: oppression on your job or in your home; pressure at school; or political pressure from federal, state, or local governments. It is important to remember that God allows difficulties so that *His* glory and honor can be made manifest.

> Dear friends, do not be surprised at the fiery ordeal that has come to you to test you as though something strange were happening to you. But rejoice in as much as you participate in the sufferings of Christ, so that you may be overjoyed when his glory is revealed. (1 Peter 4:12-13, NIV)

So then, we should not be surprised when persecution and/or trials befall us. Peter tells us that Christians, in particular, should actually expect painful experiences in this life; especially those situations and circumstances that challenge our faith and trust in God. Peter also seems to agree with Paul's statement to "consider it pure joy my brother, whenever you face trials of many kinds," because the benefits in Christ Jesus far outweigh the difficulties in this life.

A great example of how God allows testing of faith through trials and tribulations for His glory and honor, is the story in John 9, where Jesus heals a man blind since birth.

Exhibit B: Ex-Blind Man

This is a fascinating story on so many levels, but what caught my attention was not the miracle of healing a blind man (which was impressive, to say the least). It was the reason Jesus gave for the blind man's circumstances: "that the works of God should be made manifest in him" (John 9:3, KJV), and the overall purpose for allowing the blind man's physical, mental, and spiritual condition to become a public spectacle: "Do you believe in the Son of Man?" (John 9:35, NIV)

As is almost always the case, Jesus was using the life circumstance of a human being—in this case, physical blindness (his cross)—to make a much larger statement to the world at large about what is really important above and beyond what is on the surface: faith in God, which enables you to find joy in your cross. The healing of the blind man in John 9 was a means to draw attention to the power of Jesus Christ to both heal physical infirmity (restore the vitality of life), and forgive sins (restore eternal life).

If that is not impressive enough, then we should spend a little time on how this act of healing, and the public controversy which ensued as a result, necessitated that Jesus be publicly acknowledged as the Son of Man/God, in essence, spreading the message of Jesus/discipleship.

First of all, Jesus' disciples unwittingly played the part of "setup men" by asking the question: "Rabbi, who sinned, this man or his parents, that he was born blind?" (John 9:2, NIV). The assumption in that day was that anyone who suffered from physical or mental disability must have committed some terrible sin and was being punished by God through their infirmity (see Job, in Chapter 12, "God's Been Bragging on You Again").

To say that the disciples, and the dominant religious culture at this time in history, generally displayed prejudice and discrimination openly, would be quite the understatement. It was not unlike our current generation, as "learned" and "civilized" as we often pretend to be, where it seems we still "blame the victim" more often than not. (Although, it was still early in the disciple's education at the feet of Jesus, so let's not be too hard on them.) They were expressing the popular thought of the day (as we do, still).

The "lesson" begins, not just for the disciples, but also for everyone within sight and sound of Jesus' response:

> "Neither this man nor his parents sinned," said Jesus, "but this happened so that the works of God might be displayed in him. As long as it is day, we must do the works of him who sent me. Night is coming, when no one can work. While I am in the world, I am the light of the world." (John 9:3-5, NIV)

These words are quite profound, and to those listening at the time, quite bold I am sure (if not somewhat confusing), even bordering on arrogance!

Jesus dismisses the disciple's (and the audience's) cultural prejudice in his first sentence, essentially saying, "Your assumptions about this man are wrong!" Then

He explains that the man was born blind so that God can show up and show off in this man's life. And then, seemingly off the subject, Jesus starts going on about "day" and "night," and "working for him who sent me," and how He (Jesus) is the "light of the world." If Jesus did not have everyone's attention when He spoke, He certainly had all eyes on Him when He made His next move:

> After saying this, he spit on the ground, made some mud with the saliva, and put it on the man's eyes. "Go," he told him, "wash in the Pool of Siloam" (this word means "Sent"). So the man went and washed, and came home seeing. (John 9:6-7, NIV)

There are a few things to notice here. First, before healing the blind man, Jesus presented His mission ("we must do the work of him who sent me"). Second, He included in that mission those around Him ("*we* must"). Third, He proclaimed His authority (*He* was *sent*, and while *He* is in the world, *He* is the "light of the world"). Jesus had captured the undivided attention of the throng with His words, first, and then amazed them with His follow-through. The blind man came up from washing off his "mud pie facial" with twenty-twenty vision! It's not bragging, Jesus, if you can back it up.

Now that the man who had been blind since birth can see, he became a bit of a spectacle around his neighborhood. Everyone wanted to know if this was the same blind guy they remembered walking past and stepping over as he begged for money along their streets. Some claimed that it was the same fellow, while others weren't so sure. However, all agreed on asking this most compelling question: How did it come to be that he could now see (John 9:8-10)? The man's response was so direct and simple, one would think there could be no way to confuse what he said:

> He replied, "The man they call Jesus made some mud and put it on my eyes. He told me to go to Siloam and wash. So I went and washed, and then I could see." (John 9:11, NIV)

That's exactly what happened! So what could possibly be the problem?

The story goes on to tell us that those who were inquiring about his healing and whether he was actually the blind man in question (or was ever *really* blind in the first place), took him to the Pharisees (religious leaders of that time). There was a big to-do about Jesus making the mud and placing it on the blind man's eyes on the Sabbath day (John 9:13-16). The religious leaders thought that they had an opening into finding fault with Jesus, so they interrogated the beneficiary to Jesus' miracle of healing.

The ex-blind man gave the religious leaders the same story he presented to his neighbors and other witnesses to the event. These antagonists still did not accept the man's word, so they had the man's parents brought to them to see if they could find someone, anyone, to refute his testimony and a neighborhood full of corroborating witnesses (John 9:17-19).

It is starting to become clearer now for those of us who were confused by Jesus' words at the beginning of this story. Now that the whole neighborhood and town leaders are investigating how this man came to receive his sight, the glory and honor of Jesus Christ is being lifted up! The man's parents cannot, and will not, refute the miracle. But they also do not want to admit that it was Jesus who was responsible for their son receiving his sight, because they were afraid of persecution or of being excommunicated from the synagogue. And, as it turned out, the parents were right to be concerned, for the Pharisees had already decided that "anyone who acknowledged that Jesus was the Messiah would be put out of the synagogue" (John 9:22, NIV). So, the man's parents told the religious leaders to go and ask their son what happened, insisting he was old enough to speak for himself (John 9:20-23).

Through the life of this man, the stage had been set to draw attention to the power of Jesus to both restore the vitality of life and restore eternal life, which demonstrated that Jesus was/is the Messiah. By that point, I am sure the ex-blind man, his parents, and the observing witnesses were wondering why the Pharisees were trying so hard to discredit Jesus. Why couldn't the religious leaders be as happy as they were and praise God for this man's miracle of sight? Why were they interrogating innocent bystanders, and persecuting this man and his parents for his having been the beneficiary of much needed healing? By now, you know the answer: God will display His work in our lives.

Those who would tear down Jesus and the people who believe in Him were about to witness the power of God when He is displayed in a life! It is not only the miracle of physical healing Jesus highlighted here, but also the miracle of spiritual healing! Remember our "mantra" throughout this book: "Your trials and tribulations (your cross) are not just for your benefit, and your healing/blessing (*joy* in your cross) is not just for you alone. Your public praise for God working in your life will bless others." Sins Forgiven = Joy in Your Cross = Testimony = Spreading the Message that Jesus Saves!

Watch what happened next. When the religious leaders brought the ex-blind man before them a second time, they accused Jesus of being a sinner, and told the man to "give glory to God" for his miracle. The insinuation being, Jesus was an impostor, and *not* the Son of God, as He claimed. The man, who was once blind, knew the stakes involved here: If he admitted that Jesus was the Christ, and therefore responsible for his healing, he would be persecuted or excommunicated from the synagogue, and quite possibly worse things could transpire, considering the apparent desperation with which the Pharisees moved against Jesus. The man, now with perfect vision, responded to the religious leaders in this way:

> "Whether he is a sinner or not, I don't know. One thing I do know.
> I was blind but now I see!" (John 9:25, NIV)

Hallelujah! Thank you, Jesus!

This guy is a man of few words. You have to love that in a witness. Any good lawyer will tell you to "answer only the question asked; don't add anything more." Can you imagine how the Pharisees must have taken this bold testimony? His simple retort must have really enraged those who were trying to indict Jesus by intimidating the one who benefited most from His healing power. Pay attention to what happened next, and how the Pharisees digested the man's testimony:

> Then they asked him, "What did he do to you? How did he open
> your eyes?"

He answered, "I have told you already and you did not listen. Why do you want to hear it again? Do you want to become his disciples too?" Then they hurled insults at him and said, "You are this fellow's disciple! We are disciples of Moses! We know that God spoke to Moses, but as for this fellow, we don't even know where he comes from." (John 9:26-29, NIV)

This part is beautiful:

The man answered, "Now that is remarkable! You don't know where he comes from, yet he opened my eyes. We know that God does not listen to sinners. He listens to the godly person who does his will. Nobody has ever heard of opening the eyes of a man born blind. If this man were not from God, he could do nothing." (John 9:30-33, NIV)

Hallelujah . . . twice! What a powerful witness for the Lord this man turned out to be. Did you notice how the man asked the Pharisees if they wanted to be "his disciples too?" The Man implies that *he* is already a disciple of Jesus. When you testify to what Jesus has done for you; how He has given you *joy* in your cross, other folks will assume you have been with Jesus (Acts 4:13). They may assume you are one of His disciples. Sharing your testimony is a major step toward becoming a disciple of Jesus! So, how does one qualify? First, we must demonstrate the ability to find *joy* in our cross, and then spread the message of Jesus! The man in John 9 who was born blind and then healed was the perfect candidate to be used by God in this particular instance because he:

1) Was tested by God with a disability from birth (bore his cross)
2) Exercised faith by following Jesus' instructions to wash off the mud in the Pool of Siloam (obedient)
3) Received his sight and a platform to testify (found *joy* in his cross)
4) Gave God the glory, honor, and praise for his healing (praise testimony)
5) Stood up for Jesus, and stood his ground when persecuted by those who refused to believe that Jesus is the Christ (spreading the message to all that Jesus saves)

The Lord sees the potential in each of us for His will to be made manifest in our lives. We only need be willing to see beyond our cross and exercise *obedient faith* (Chapters 10 and 11, "Ridiculous Faith"). Standing up for Jesus will help us find joy in our cross, but it may not mean that our lives will be without distress or incidence, going forward. Hannah found joy and then returned her son to God by leaving him to be raised by the priest. That was a tough decision, especially for a woman who had been childless!

The man in John 9 was jeered, publicly scorned, and thrown out of the synagogue even though he did nothing wrong but be a witness for Jesus (John 9:34). That is the wonderful thing about standing up for Jesus: Regardless of what our fellow man does to us, or what our circumstances happen to be, Jesus simply lowers a shoulder and gets underneath our cross with us. Jesus tells us not to worry when others try to hurt us: they cannot control our destiny (Matthew 10:28). He rewards our faith in Him by giving us something worth so much more than anything we could attain on this earth. He gives us a free gift of salvation. He gives us eternal life!

Hannah's joy was evident through her prayer of thanksgiving, and the man in John 9 received a reward beyond obtaining his vision. Read John 9:35-41. It is a stunning account of what lengths Jesus goes to in order to save us, and how His message and intentions are so much deeper than what appears on the surface. Jesus heard about the man being excommunicated from the synagogue and went looking for him (as he does each of us today). When Jesus found him, He simply asked the man, "Do you believe in the Son of Man?" Once Jesus stood face-to-face with this man and introduced Himself the man said, "Lord, I believe," and eagerly worshipped Jesus. Now that the man could *physically* see His healer/redeemer, it was a no-brainer to worship Him because of having already seen Jesus, *spiritually*. Except for the fact that, through history, we have a better vantage point by which to closely scrutinize Bible texts, the words that Jesus used toward the end of this story may seem as confusing as those at the beginning:

> Jesus said, "For judgment I have come into this world, so that the blind will see and those who see will become blind." Some Pharisees who were with him heard him say this and asked, "What?

Are we blind too?" Jesus said, "If you were blind, you would not be guilty of sin; but now that you claim you can see, your guilt remains." (John 9:39-41, NIV)

The mystery of Jesus' words are captured in the phenomenon of physical blindness versus spiritual blindness.

How poignant were the words of Jesus concerning those who have eyes but are spiritually blind, versus those who may be physically blind, yet able to see that He is the light of the world. The juxtaposition of physical blindness versus spiritual blindness was certainly common during the years of Jesus' ministry, and most definitely so, the last week of His life. That last week of Jesus' life was the epitome of spiritual blindness on the part of those who participated in His mock trial and crucifixion. However, it was also spiritual blindness on the part of all mankind who rejected Jesus from His birth to His death. People not recognizing the "light of the world" while He is right in front of them began in a manger (a barn) in Bethlehem. Not coincidentally, the birth and death of Jesus was also our most paradoxical example of "carrying your cross."

He bore our transgressions, took the punishment that is rightfully ours, and suffered the most undignified and horrific death known to humankind. Yet, He was completely innocent of wrongdoing! Odd then, that we, in our most flawed and human state, think we should escape the trials and tribulations that come tailor-made for each of us. Jesus' example was a literal and complete action of suffering, death, resurrection, and eternal life! He died so that we might live! Unlike Jesus, for us, carrying our cross is a metaphor indicating the real fact that life is often difficult. As each of us travel along life's journey; it is important to understand that the road is not always smooth. There will be delays, detours, and discouragement. Stay on the path that God has ordained for your life no matter what challenges you must confront and conquer. Share your testimony of struggle and triumph. Your victory will encourage and inspire others in the struggle. Carry your cross with dignity and appreciation for what Jesus did for you! Doing so makes you a disciple of Jesus Christ.

> *"He personally carried our sins in his body on the cross so that we can be dead to sin and live for what is right. By his wounds you are healed"* (1 Peter 2:24, NLT).

Chapter 14

Finding Joy in Your Cross (Part II)

———————◇○◇———————

"We can rejoice, too, when we run into problems and trials, for we know that they help us develop endurance. And endurance develops strength of character; and character strengthens our confident hope of salvation." (Romans 5:3-4, NLT)

A Deeper Purpose for Our Struggles

Throughout this book we have emphasized that trials and tribulations in life are multifunctional. Sometimes we forget that our trials are not just about us. So often, our trials are allowed as an opportunity for us to witness about the glory of God. The stories of Hannah (1 Samuel 1 and 2), and the ex-blind man (John 9), are wonderful reminders of how God uses our lives to touch others. There are many more examples of this type of witness recorded in the Bible to prepare God's people for rejection, harassment, arrest, and persecution (Matthew 10:17; Acts 5:40; 12:1). These are not joyful situations, to be sure. However, Jesus teaches us that it is not what happens to you, but how you handle yourself during trials and tribulations.

Jesus wanted His followers to be clear about what they would encounter when they lift Him up to the world. Persecution of some sort is a certainty. It is the same today. Another way to look at one's trials and tribulations, even persecution, is that God is testing your faith as you are given an opportunity to speak a word for the Lord. In the book, *The Desire of Ages*, Ellen G. White writes:

> Persecution will spread the light. The servants of Christ will be brought before the great men of the world, who but for this, might never hear the gospel. The truth has been misrepresented to these men. They have listened to false charges concerning the faith of Christ's disciples. Often their only means of learning its real character is the testimony of those who are brought to trial for their faith. Under examination these are required to answer, and their judges to listen to the testimony borne. (*The Desire of Ages*, p. 354)

Some of you may be concerned about what you should say to others when you witness for Jesus and share how the Lord has changed your life. You may feel ill-prepared to speak, or feel shy because public speaking or addressing those with whom you are unfamiliar is not your strongest suit. We all have different talents and abilities, and talking to others about Jesus (in public or private) is not so easy, especially with those who challenge one's faith and/or belief system. One thing I know for a fact, through personal experience and through God's promises in His Word: You need not worry about what you should say because the same God who chose Moses and put words in His mouth (Exodus 4:11-12, 15) chose you and will bless you with all you need so that the work of God might be displayed in your life.

When the apostle Paul was called on to be a witness for Jesus Christ, he received power from the Holy Spirit to speak what was necessary (Acts 1:8; 18:9-10). When the servants of God were brought before governors and kings, they did not need to worry about what to say at that time. Jesus said: "But when they arrest you, do not worry about what to say or how to say it. At that time you will be given what to say, for it will not be you speaking, but the Spirit of your Father speaking through you" (Matthew 10:19-20, NIV, see also Mark 13:11). Ellen G. White provides additional clarity concerning the support from heaven witnesses for Jesus will receive when needed:

> God's grace will be dispensed to His servants to meet the emergency. . . . The servants of Christ were to prepare no set speech to present when brought to trial. Their preparation was to be made

day by day in treasuring up the precious truths of God's word, and through prayer strengthening their faith. When they were brought to trial, the Holy Spirit would bring to their remembrance the very truths that would be needed. (*The Desire of Ages*, pp. 354-355)

The example of the disciples enduring harassment, arrest, even persecution for Christ's sake, while providing a testimony and a witness that Jesus saves, should create a different picture in our minds concerning our own trials and tribulations. It is now more clear than ever that our life difficulties, just like our blessings, are not just about us. It is also clear that the burdens and challenges in our lives are allowed for more than just character building:

Not only this, but we also rejoice in sufferings, knowing that suffering produces endurance; and endurance, character; and character, hope. (Romans 5:3-4, NET)

Imagine that. When you learn to rejoice in your sufferings it produces hope! Hope is the one thing a dying world needs. And believers in Jesus Christ possess an abundance of hope to share with the world.

Rest assured; there will be some who hear your witness and accept the miracle God has made manifest in your life. Others may be skeptical and need extended time to observe how God is working in your life. And still others will not accept your witness whatsoever, and may go as far as trying to shut you up through a variety of means that fall under the broad definition of persecution. Whatever your cross is to bear, understand that you can find *joy* in your cross by staying faithful and obedient to God. And when the miracle in your life is made manifest, your trials and tribulations will give you *joy* as you recount for others how Jesus saved you right in the midst of your trials. Never forget: Sharing your triumph over your trials with others as you give praise to God is the most important phase of finding joy in your cross. Your "praise report" will not only encourage others who are struggling; it will strengthen you spiritually as well!

So, in essence, the character acquired by way of suffering and perseverance makes you depend on Jesus, and Jesus brings hope. In your troubles, God is providing an opportunity to stand up and witness of His mercy and His grace. Your trials and tribulations place you in unique positions to speak a word for the Lord to people who may never have had the opportunity to hear it, but for you. What an amazing way to view the problems in your life! It kind of makes you want to think back to past difficulties in your life and try and remember how you handled them: *Did I complain and take the "woe is me" approach, or did I see an opportunity, in my trial, to praise the Lord?*

So often we miss our opportunities to praise the Lord because we are too focused on our problems (our cross). We miss the opportunity to spend ample time studying God's Word, gain strength through prayer, and prepare for our "breakthrough moment" when God asks that we stand up and speak a word for Him. How often do you miss these opportunities, and by focusing on your difficulties and disappointments, allow others to miss an opportunity to be blessed through your testimony?

Remember, when the time comes to speak, you need not worry about what to say (Exodus 4:11-12, 15; 2 Samuel 23:2; Jeremiah 1:9; Matthew 10:19; Mark 13:11; Luke 12:11-12; Acts 1:8; Acts 18:9-10). However, we do need to maintain a daily relationship with Christ, so that the Holy Spirit has something to draw from our preparation and our memory. Ellen G. White, referring to Christ's disciples, writes:

> A daily, earnest striving to know God, and Jesus Christ whom He has sent, would bring power and efficiency to the soul. The knowledge obtained by diligent searching of the Scriptures would be flashed into the memory at the right time. But if any had neglected to acquaint themselves with the words of Christ, if they had never tested the power of His grace in trial, they could not expect that the Holy Spirit would bring His words to their remembrance. They were to serve God daily with undivided affection, and then trust Him. (*The Desire of Ages*, p. 355)

Thus, we can conclude with confidence that, not only are our trials allowed for a testimony for more than just us, God has already taken care of the success of our witness. It's sort of like academic study, or preparation for a presentation at work: the Lord cannot bring something back to memory that we never placed in our minds in the first place. Our job is to prepare daily through prayer and study, exercise faith, trust in the Lord by asking for all that we need in His name ("it will be given to you," Matthew 7:7 and Luke 11:9), and endure till the end. If we do this, we can begin to see our trials as opportunities to persevere and build character, so that our witness brings hope to others. In this way, we find *joy* in our cross and the seeds of spiritual depression are uprooted with our praise to God!

Remember God's Promises

Knowing that we can speak a word for the Lord should bring a smile to our face and help us find joy in our cross. Disciples are able to do this, and Jesus reminds us of the promise we will receive if we stay faithful till the end: "So do not throw away your confidence; it will be richly rewarded. You need to persevere so that when you have done the will of God, you will receive what he has promised" (Hebrews 10:35-36, NIV).

It is one thing to understand that we will be tested in our faith by being required to speak before "governors and kings" of the saving grace of Jesus Christ. It is quite another to be able look at some of life's other challenges as opportunities. Illness, death of loved ones, divorce, financial crisis, unemployment, and just the daily grind of life can undo many of us, and send us spiraling down a path of spiritual depression. Even in the midst of enduring some of the most unpleasant circumstances life has to offer, we must still remember that God allows burdens for the express purpose of manifesting His glory within us. Our lives will produce a magnificent witness to the world at large. To do this, we must follow Paul's lead and stand up for Christ in the midst of our trials:

> So never be ashamed to tell others about our Lord. And don't be ashamed of me, Either, even though I'm in prison for him. With the strength God gives you, be ready to suffer with me for the sake of the Good News. For God saved us and called us to live a holy life. He did this, not because we deserved it, but because that was his plan from before the beginning of time—to show us his grace through Christ Jesus. And now he has made all of this plain to us by the appearing of Christ Jesus, our Savior. He broke the power

of death and illuminated the way to life and immortality through the Good News. . . . That is why I am suffering here in prison. But I am not ashamed of it, for I know the one in whom I trust, and I am sure that he is able to guard what I have entrusted to him until the day of his return. (2 Timothy 1:8-10, 12, NLT)

You too, cannot be ashamed of the gospel of Jesus Christ! "But rejoice inasmuch as you participate in the sufferings of Christ, so that you may be overjoyed when his glory is revealed" (1 Peter 4:13, NIV).

When it appears that there is no way out of your situation, and you feel your cross is too much to bear, resist the temptation to give up in despair; for that is not the voice of Jesus urging you to quit. The voice of Jesus tells you to trust in Him because He has already triumphed over evil:

"I have told you these things, so that in me you may have peace. In this world you will have trouble. But take heart! I have overcome the world." (John 16:33, NIV)

Jesus is telling you to get up one more time, place one foot in front of the other, and He will help you carry your cross. Bearing your cross is not supposed to be a pleasant or easy experience. Overcoming immense obstacles that generate a testimony of praise rarely is. The significance and symbolism of carrying a cross speaks volumes of what we must endure in this life to reach our ultimate goal of salvation and seeing Jesus face-to-face. It is during your moments of deepest despair that you must reflect upon the sacrifice Jesus made for you:

Keeping our eyes fixed on Jesus, the pioneer and perfecter of our faith. For the joy set out for him he endured the cross, disregarding its shame, and *has taken his seat at the right hand of the throne* of God. Think of him who endured such opposition against himself by sinners, so that you may not grow weary in your souls and give up (Hebrews 12:2-3, NET)

You must hang on to your faith in God and trust in His ability to deliver you from any trial, for "the Lord knows how to rescue the godly from trials" (2 Peter 2:9, NIV).

Being willing to carry your cross is not enough. Also important is *how* you carry your cross. Representatives of Jesus are not to walk around looking down and discouraged, openly whining and complaining about how unfair life is, or how terrible it is that, "My cross is heavier than your cross." Words of discouragement and dismay not only have a negative effect on those in the sound of your voice; they also increase your own feelings of spiritual depression.

Remember that the ultimate purpose for carrying your cross is to be a witness, spreading the message that following Jesus brings *joy* and an assurance of eternal life. Sharing that message from deep in your heart makes it possible for you to declare, as Paul declared, that you count all earthly things "but loss" for the *exquisite joy* of knowing Christ Jesus as Lord (Philippians 3:7- 8).

When you can find the joy in your cross, you are better able to witness to others that though the road is sometimes hard, and the way is often painful, *you would not have it any other way*, because it is worth it, just having the Lord in your life! Read closely the words to this song. Contemplate whether you can consider that your present sufferings are not worth comparing with the glory that will be revealed in you (Romans 8:18, NIV):

I Wouldn't Have It Any Other Way
By Eleanor Wright

As I look back upon my life, and I survey
The rugged road I've had to travel day by day,
There's been many a hill to climb
And many a storm to brave.
But if I reach heaven
And that's all I have to pay
I wouldn't have it any other way.
I would not have it any other way.

I wouldn't have it any other way.
I wouldn't have it any other way.
I don't have to be a prophet just to see

That God would only lead me down the road that's best for me.
And if I let him take control
I will surely reach my goal.
And if on the way I have to suffer
I just want to say
If that's the only way
I can be saved, you know
I wouldn't have it any other way.
I would not have it any other way.

I think of all those sleepless nights I spent in prayer.
Poverty and hunger taught me how to share.
I've learned how to sympathize
Thru' my suffering day by day.
There's been such a change in me
That's why I can truly say.
I wouldn't have it any other way.
I would not have it any other way.

Rejoice in the Lord always. I will say it again: Rejoice! Let your gentleness be evident to all. The Lord is near. Do not be anxious about anything, but in every situation, by prayer and petition, with thanksgiving, present your requests to God. And the peace of God, which transcends all understanding, will guard your hearts and your minds in Christ Jesus. (Philippians 4:4-7, NIV)

•

Chapter 15

The Miracle in You

---◇○⟨⟨⟩⟩○◇---

"Dear friends, since God so loved us, we also ought to love one another. No one has ever seen God; but if we love one another, God lives in us and his love is made complete in us." (1 John 4:11-12, NIV)

What Does Love Look Like?

I saw him standing on the corner. The same disheveled figure of a man I see every morning as I exit the building where I work to hit the convenience store for a hot beverage and breakfast sandwich. I'm usually in a hurry; especially when it's wintertime. No time for niceties and conversation with street beggars. I mean, we all have our own struggles and problems, so it's none of my business why he's always standing on this corner, asking folks for money. This particular morning, I didn't cross the street when I saw him. I walked close enough to him to make eye contact.

He said, "Good morning."

My conscience (i.e. my mother in my head) reminded me that I had manners and jolted a hurried reply of, "Mornin' to you too!" Then suddenly, without warning, I felt compelled to stop, turn around, and walk back to the familiar stranger and ask his name.

"Jerry," he mumbled.

"Excuse me?" I said, straining to hear.

"Uh, Jerry," he said, a little more audibly.

I told him my name. "Getting cold out here, huh?" I said, trying to make conversation by stating the obvious.

"Uh, yeah, it is," Jerry replied.

"You hungry?" I managed to get out before saying something else about the weather. "Sure, I could eat," Jerry replied.

As we walked to the nearest "food on wheels" establishments (prominent on the city streets in Philadelphia), I could see that Jerry had a pronounced limp. His clothing was mismatched and not adequate to keep him warm standing outside in the elements. The coat he wore was torn in the sleeves and had a hood with fur lining in it, partially hiding his forehead, but I could see his eyes. Sad eyes. Kind eyes. Eyes weary from life's difficulties. He had a straggly "salt-and-pepper" beard that protruded prominently above the matted scarf wrapped around his neck.

I told Jerry to order whatever he wanted. He only wanted a meat and egg sandwich, and a hot cup of coffee. He thanked me, over and over. He couldn't remember my name. So he kept calling me, "Kind sir." I was embarrassed, hearing this moniker, because I knew that I walked across the street every day to avoid the very encounter I was having at that moment. Still, it felt good to see someone in need feeling good. I felt "human."

No longer in a hurry, I asked Jerry, "You here every morning?" (though I already knew the answer).

"Yep!"

"Okay," I said. "See you tomorrow."

Hence, a relationship that began on the heavy side of reluctance morphed into my looking forward to meeting Jerry every morning for breakfast. Jerry never remembered my name. I made sure I called him by his name each time we met. Once the weather warmed up, I didn't see Jerry on his usual corner. I wondered where he might be. Was he eating? Was his health holding up? I missed the daily gift Jerry gave me: a reminder of what it means to love strangers. To see all humanity as God's children—my brothers and sisters. Thanks, Jerry.

Key Ingredient #1: Getting God's Love Inside You

Sometimes the stressors in this life keep us moving in rapid, hurried motion, rarely taking time to notice the plight of others. After all, everyone really is in survival mode; especially in the United States, where we are assuredly an individualistic culture ("cultural values such as independence and self-expression" versus collectivistic culture, which is "cultural values such as obedience and group harmony," Arnett, 2012). How does one enmeshed in an individualistic culture relate to our theme text in this chapter? Well, the simple answer is that we must learn to trust in a power stronger than our natural independent and individual motives, and thought processes. More complicated; we must allow the love of Jesus to enter our hearts and its influence to set up shop in the deepest part of our souls. We must give God permission to intervene in our hectic, time warp schedules, and implement "the miracle in you" that will heal ourselves as well as those with whom we come into contact.

The key component to access the spiritual energy of this miracle is whether you really believe that Jesus has the power to come into your life. More importantly, it is whether you have the courage to invite our Lord and Savior into your life. It takes courage because, once you invite Jesus into your life, you will never be the same! You will have the number one key ingredient to cure spiritual depression in yourself and others as you find strength in your struggle.

Wondering how this is possible? After all, no one has seen the face of God (1 Timothy 6:16; Exodus 33:20), and Jesus has not appeared "in person" since showing Himself to His disciples and followers before ascending back to heaven and sending us a counselor, the Holy Spirit (John 14:16, 26; 15:26; 16:7).

As we learned in the preceding chapters, it is not an easy thing to trust your troubled soul to a supernatural being whom you have never seen, while also in the midst of trials and tribulations. Nor is it an arbitrary decision to seek Jesus when life seems to be crumbling all around you. First John 4:7-17 helps explain how we can trade in our trouble filled souls for souls filled with the love of Jesus. Hence, we can implement the miracle of Jesus Christ—a profound and immeasurable love—into our lives by loving others as Jesus loved us:

> Dear friends, let us love one another, for love comes from God. Everyone who loves has been born of God and knows God. Whoever does not love does not know God, because God is love. This is how God showed his love among us: He sent his one and only Son into the world that we might live through him. This is love: not that we loved God, but that he loved us and sent his Son as an atoning sacrifice for our sins. Dear friends, since God so loved us, we also ought to love one another. No one has ever seen God; but if we love one another, God lives in us and his love is made complete in us. (1 John 4:7-12, NIV)

How do we know that God can come into us, cleanse our souls of sin, and fill our hearts with His Spirit?

> This is how we know that we live in him and he in us: He has given us his Spirit. And we have seen and testify that the Father has sent his Son to be the Savior of the world. If anyone acknowledges that Jesus is the Son of God, God lives in them and they in God. And so we know and rely on the love God has for us. God is love. Whoever lives in love lives in God, and God in them. This is how love is made complete among us so that we will have confidence on the day of judgment: In this world we are like Jesus. (1 John 4:13-17, NIV)

So the key ingredient to discover the "miracle in you"—in addition to exercising faith and belief in the love of Jesus Christ for you—is to love as God loves. In this way, "love is made complete" in our lives and with those within the immediate vicinity of our reach: family, church, the community (our fellow human beings), and others.

Spiritual Depression Weakens Love

You may also be wondering if you are really capable of loving your family, church, and community the way Jesus loves you. For trouble filled souls, it is certainly a mighty tall order, because being able to love others starts with being able to love yourself. The same goes for being able to forgive others—it begins by forgiving oneself. This is the difficult thing about allowing the miracle in you to manifest: a spiritually depressed soul has little confidence, is short on energy and motivation to change, and finds it difficult to trust in themselves, let alone others. Peter tells us that we can trust in Jesus and love Him even though we cannot see Him with our physical eyes:

> Though you have not seen him, you love him; and even though
> you do not see him now, you believe in him and are filled with an
> inexpressible and glorious joy, for you are receiving the end result
> of your faith, the salvation of your souls (1 Peter 1:8-9, NIV).

Peter's words indicate a level of confidence in how we should feel about Jesus that many of us may not believe we possess. Naturally, a constant barrage of problems can be a nagging source of discouragement, and the stress of feeling like you are swimming upstream can wear you down, leaving you in a state of bewilderment, doubt, and despair. Peter's words are meant to encourage us by reminding us of our natural and reciprocal love for Jesus (we love Him because He first loved us) and the glorious joy that fills our souls when we think about our ultimate goal of salvation. It is a reminder that despite whatever you may be going through, this is not the time to give up. It is not the time to give in. It is not the time to turn away from the love of God.

Unfortunately, the reality for so many is to allow spiritual depression to drive them away from the essence of God's love. Spiritual depression, like the waves of the ocean, beats against the walls of our souls, gradually eroding our faith and belief in God's love, chipping away at the mortar of our self-esteem, weakening our spiritual foundation. It is brittle faith and broken belief in self that ultimately undermine our hope and trust in God. After all, if we do not feel that we are worth saving, how can we possibly believe that a divine being exists, who is invisible to our eyes and intangible to our touch, yet one who loves us enough to give His life for us? Our lack of love for self compromises our ability to love others, driving a wedge between us and our Lord and Savior, Jesus, and between our fellow man and us.

In short, spiritual depression acts as a psychological and spiritual "gatekeeper," which blocks our belief that we are worthy of love, thereby negating our ability to accept the unconditional love of Jesus into our lives. Our failure to recognize the hand of Jesus reaching out to us in the midst of our struggles produces a "boomerang effect" where feelings of unworthiness, anger, fear, and sadness keep coming back to strike us every time we try to rid ourselves of His still small voice. The more we attempt to move away from God and hide ourselves from the relentless pursuit of His love, the more our emotions cycle through a continuous "loop" of guilt and shame. If unchecked, guilt and shame festers into self-loathing, and ultimately, self-imposed isolation. Isolation, of course, is the "emotional death knell" of spiritually depressed souls!

Those experiencing spiritual depression may perceive that "everything" they try fails. Their greatest difficulty may come when they face the possibility that their inability to recover and/or bounce back from their dungeon of despair is due to their faith having been dislodged or temporarily disrupted. Their belief system has been turned upside down!

In an earlier chapter we discovered that there is nothing more emotionally painful and spiritually damaging than believing that God doesn't care about you. There is nothing more spiritually debilitating than fearing you have been cut off from the source of spiritual power that *is* God, and are no longer privy to His love, His mercy, and His grace! God does not place these negative thoughts in our minds. Negative thoughts are a result of fear, past disappointment, and disillusionment; which ultimately can lead to feelings of hopelessness. God does not give us a spirit of fear (2 Timothy 1:7).

Spiritual Depression Creates Doubt and Fear

When you are caught in the throes of spiritual depression, you have not only lost faith in God; you have also lost faith in yourself and your ability to know what's up, what's down, and where you fit in this vast universe. You start to wonder if what you have been taught all your life about God (that He is merciful, kind, and loving, and more) is really true. You begin to question everything you thought you knew and believed about God, about life, and about yourself. You lose sight of all the miracles God has performed in your life up to that point (selective memory). You wonder if He brought you all this way to leave you (He will be with us wherever we go; Joshua 1:9); forgetting that God gave us His Word that He would never leave us or forsake us (Deuteronomy 31:6; Hebrews 13:5). You may feel yourself slowly drifting out of control, seemingly tossed about by a gust of wind, experiencing a strange sensation of floating aimlessly about until landing in the middle of life's scrap heap; discouraged, damaged, and discarded. These types of feelings accurately describe the symptoms of spiritual depression.

Spiritual depression can become so devastating to a person that he or she begins to show the signs and develop the symptoms of clinical depression. And, as stated throughout this book, for these individuals I recommend an immediate and thorough medical exam and subsequent referral to a mental health professional. God has provided us help in the form of women and men who are skilled professionals in a variety of careers, including those in the medical and mental health profession. Prayer works miracles too! So, never stop praying. Pray especially for those professionals who are providing your medical and/or mental/behavioral health services. Sometimes our fellow human beings initially guide us to begin again to believe in self, and hopefully, eventually return to our belief in God.

It is through God's generosity that miracles come through those individuals placed on this earth for the exact purpose of providing comfort, medical care, mental health care, treatment for drug and alcohol dependence, social services, and more. Said another way:

> What human power can do divine power is not summoned to do. God does not dispense with man's aid. He strengthens him, co-operating with him as he uses the powers and capabilities given him. (Ellen G. White, *The Desire of Ages*, p. 535)

However, there are also times when even medical and mental health professionals are at a loss for how to best help someone. This is not a failure on God's part to "bless" the hands of professional caregivers. I see this as God reminding us that He is sovereign and rules our world. It is the will of God that decides when, how, and why. We may not always agree with how He goes about handling the world we live in, or how He chooses to address our individual and personal requests for divine intervention.

God does not always "snap to it" when we demand that He intercede for us in the way we believe He should. For instance, though we may prayerfully seek professional medical and/or mental health assistance, we may still find that using prescription medication and/or treatments (i.e. antidepressant, anti-anxiety, anti-psychotic, and more) does not always eliminate our problems. Also, there are occasions when counseling and/or other "evidenced-based" interventions are not immediately effective for a select group of people. We may continue to feel help-less and/or hopeless, even after seeking professional help (God's will decides the when, how, and why).

More often than not, the best interventions work in tandem. For example, "best practice" treatment for clinical depression and anxiety is a regimen of antidepressant/antianxiety medications in tandem with psychotherapy. Moreover, I think most people would agree that when all else fails, we tend to call on the God of the universe as an emergency solution to heal what man, and man-made medications could not. Untreated spiritual depression is an emergency as well. So, naturally I strongly recommend going to God first, and enlisting prayer without ceasing *while simultaneously* seeking professional help. This is absolutely the "best practice" — utilizing all the resources God has provided.

Still, when life feels like a constant struggle and the weight of life's burdens is heavy, it is difficult for even the strongest of spiritual legs not to buckle. The daily grind seems to exacerbate problems. The cumulative effect adds pounds exponentially to the personal baggage strapped to already rounded and wilting shoulders. Spiritually depressed individuals dismiss the struggles of all those who came before them as somehow different than what they must endure. We forget that life on this earth holds trials and tribulations. Even Jesus guarantees us a life of difficulty when we pick up our cross and follow Him (Matthew 10:22; John 16:33, Matthew 16:24).

We overlook the fact that there are no "smooth roads" in this life, just roads. We fail to remember that there is no perfect life, except for Jesus Christ's. And though He struggled with all we face today, He paved the way for us to receive redemption and claim salvation (the end of Matthew 10:22 [NIV], " . . . but the one who stands firm to the end will be saved," and; the end of John 16:33 [NIV], "But take heart! I have overcome the world").

Perfect Peace: A Reachable Goal

Since there is no perfect life after that of Jesus Christ, our goal can be refined to strive for perfect peace!

Perfect peace is possible by "re-tooling" your belief system to understand that life is often difficult, and the consequences harsh. Reality is not for the faint of heart, but for those who realize that perfect peace is only possible through Jesus Christ. It is in this combination of belief in the possibility of perfect peace, and trust in the only one who can provide it, where hope is revived. It is coming to an understanding that God believes enough in you to allow only those struggles you are equipped (through Him) to handle (1 Corinthians 10:13). It is being confident in knowing that God has blessed you with talents and abilities that are more than sufficient to help you navigate your way through the obstacle course of life. It is being able to face your difficulties with determination, knowing that troubles often accomplish God's goals for our lives (to save us), and strengthen character (Philippians 4:13, "I can do all things through Christ who strengthens me," NKJV). It is being able to stand against evil (as did Job) and look toward heaven with a wry smile, knowing that "God has been bragging on you again!"

The only sure way I know of to receive perfect peace is by willingly receiving Jesus Christ into one's life. We must be willing to open ourselves up for the Prince of Peace to enter into every aspect of our beings: physical, mental, and spiritual. We must be willing to step out on faith and recognize that what we have been doing up to this point is clearly not working out in our best interest. We must invite Jesus into our hearts, minds, and souls so that He can make sure we receive His free gift of redemption, salvation, and eternal life. In short, we must be willing to create space in our whole being and set it aside especially for Jesus Christ to come in and fill the vacuum in our lives, replacing struggle and conflict with peace and harmony.

Key Ingredient #2: We Are Changed by Eating with Jesus

This brings us back to the question posed at the beginning of this chapter: "Why must I allow Jesus to come into my life?" The most direct response I can give comes from Paul, in Romans 8:8 (CEB), "People who are self-centered aren't able to please God." I believe that the majority of people in God's creation want to see Him face-to-face. We want to ask God questions about our journey in this life, and more. We will not be able to see the face of God if we remain self-centered in nature; same as we were born. The only way to rid ourselves of our self-centered nature is to allow the Spirit of Jesus Christ to dwell within us (Romans 8:9-11).

By allowing Jesus to live within us, we have access to the same power source upon which the Son of God relied while He walked this earth!

The apostle Paul gives his personal testimony of how his future was forever changed simply by accepting Jesus Christ into his life as a permanent resident. In Galatians 2:20, Paul shares:

> I have been crucified with Christ and I no longer live, but Christ lives in me. The life I live in the body, I live by faith in the Son of God, who loved me and gave himself for me. (NIV)

Those who remember the story of *Paul* (whose name before meeting Christ was *Saul*) should be impressed that this man who was once a highly motivated and eager persecutor of the early Christians could be transformed into a man who would later write: "For it is God who works in you to will and to act in order to fulfill his good purpose" (Philippians 2:13, NIV). If Jesus can enter the life of Saul, a notorious persecutor of Christians, and change him into Paul, the greatest evangelist for Christ, then I am confident that God is powerful enough to change your life for the better in ways you probably cannot imagine!

Now, you are probably wondering how is it possible for Jesus to actually enter into your body and soul, and live within you. The answer is surprisingly simple:

all you have to do is ask. Jesus makes it even easier by willingly standing close by so that we do not have to go too far in search of Him: "Here I am! I stand at the door [of your heart] and knock. If anyone hears my voice and opens the door, I will come in and eat with that person, and they with me" (Revelation 3:20 NIV, brackets added).

Jesus is so anxious to be invited into your life that He sticks close by you, never venturing far, just so He will be right there in case you choose to answer His knocking at the door of your heart, and invite Him in. Not only is Jesus anxious to come into your life so He can "eat with that person [you], and they [you] with me," He has already planned and prepared the meal you will eat when you sit down with Him:

> Jesus said to them, "Very truly I tell you, unless you eat the flesh of the Son of Man and drink his blood, you have no life in you. Whoever eats my flesh and drinks my blood has eternal life, and I will raise them up at the last day. For my flesh is real food and my blood is real drink. Whoever eats my flesh and drinks my blood remains in me, and I in them. Just as the living Father sent me and I live because of the Father, so the one who feeds on me will live because of me. This is the bread that came down from heaven. Your ancestors ate manna and died, but whoever feeds on this bread will live forever." (John 6:53-58, NIV)

Now this is a strange saying, isn't it? How do we "eat" the flesh of Jesus, and "drink" His blood? Jesus has talked liked this before. He often used parables (metaphor) and symbolism when communicating difficult concepts to clearly present His message in terms His audience could understand. However, this saying of Jesus, about eating His flesh and drinking His blood is difficult to understand, no matter what. When Jesus instructed His disciples on how they must "believe in Him whom He [God] sent" (John 6:29, NKJV, brackets added). Jesus said to them,

> "Very truly I tell you, it is not Moses who has given you the bread from heaven, but it is my Father who gives you the true bread from heaven. For the bread of God is the bread that comes down from heaven and gives life to the world." (John 6:32-33, NIV)

Also, when the disciples asked Jesus for some of this bread, He declared: "I am the bread of life. Whoever comes to me will never go hungry, and whoever believes in me will never be thirsty" (John 6:35, NIV).

Jesus prompted a similar conversation earlier in John 4, when He confronted a Samaritan woman at Jacob's well (John 4:5-30), and asked her for a drink of water. Stop and read the whole fascinating story. In short, the woman questions Jesus about His breaking the rules of the day, by His—being a Jew, and male—speaking with and associating with her—a Samaritan, and a woman. "Jesus answered her, 'If you knew the gift of God and who it is that asks you for a drink, you would have asked him and he would have given you living water.' 'Sir,' the woman said, 'you have nothing to draw with and the well is deep. Where can you get this living water?'" (John 4:10-11, NIV). "Jesus answered, 'Everyone who drinks this water [Jacob's well] will be thirsty again, but whoever drinks the water I give them will never thirst. Indeed, the water I give them will become in them a spring of water welling up to eternal life'" (John 4:13-14, NIV, brackets added).

Jesus tells us in John 6:48, "I am the bread of life" (NIV). In John 6:51, Jesus says: "I am the living bread that came down from heaven. Whoever eats this bread will live forever. This bread is my flesh, which I will give for the life of the world" (NIV). In John 7:38, Jesus says: "Whoever believes in me, as Scripture has said, rivers of living water will flow from within them" (NIV). So, eating the "flesh" of Jesus is tantamount to eating the "bread of life," and drinking Jesus' "blood' is like drinking "living water" that will cause a perpetual stream of water to flow from within us, quenching our thirst forever! What Jesus is communicating is that for us to be changed and become consistently loving and forgiving to self and others; we must first spiritually ingest all that He is and believe that His love can save us.

Key Ingredient #3: Have Jesus As Your "Roommate"

When Jesus stands at the door of our hearts, waiting for an invitation, He is not coming empty-handed! He carries in His nail scarred hands salvation and eternal life.

258

He is waiting patiently for an invitation to come inside and fill us with the bread of life, living water, and the abundance of His love. However, you and I control whether an invitation is extended to the Savior of the universe. He will not force His way into your heart, or into your life.

Jesus does not just want a standing invitation by which He can "visit" at your convenience, or when some special event is going on in your life. The King of Kings and Lord of Lords wants you to allow Him to "move in" permanently, filling up the space in your whole being with His everlasting joy, His will, and His love.

Jesus wants to be your roommate! He wants to live with you while you are on this earth so that He can provide you with perfect peace until He can take you to live with Him in His glory for all eternity.

I know that this all sounds unbelievably wonderful. And, I also know that when you are spiritually depressed, it is difficult to focus on positive things, and even more difficult to *believe* that anything wonderful can, and will, happen in your life. When life feels like a constant struggle, it is *not* unusual to be blinded by the magnitude of your current circumstances. It is difficult to remember the victories and miracles from your past, and even more of a stretch to envision good things in your future. When this happens to you, go to the story in Mark 9:17-27, where the father brought his son to Jesus, because the disciples were not able to help the boy. Then, focus on Mark 9:23-24:

> "'If you can'?" said Jesus. Everything is possible for one who
> believes." Immediately the boy's father exclaimed, I do believe;
> help me overcome my unbelief!" (NIV)

It is the difficulty of *believing* that hampers most of us from maintaining a strong foundation of *faith* when under extreme stress or duress. The evil one waits until our very weakest moment to try and throw a "knockout blow" to our emotional, psychological, and spiritual psyche. It is during those times when we are hanging by a thread that "your enemy the devil" swoops in "looking for someone to devour" (1 Peter 5:8 NIV).

It is at precisely these moments when we should fall on our knees in earnest supplication to the one who understands exactly what we are going through. Jesus understands that life is often difficult. He has experienced all the trials and temptations that we go through (Hebrews 4:15). Jesus got tired and hungry. He was mistreated. Jesus has felt our hurts, pains, and sorrows. He knows the feeling of being disappointed by friends and family. Jesus knows what it is like to be rejected and betrayed by those closest to you (Isaiah 53:3); denied and left hanging by those who were supposed to "have your back." It is these experiences and more that make Jesus one with us!

The wonderful thing about inviting Jesus into your life is that He has already made arrangements for your victory party (John 14:1-3). Jesus knows and understands that sometimes you have to be creative to find the "silver lining" that surrounds the dark clouds in your life. He knows that sometimes the best way to find strength in your struggle and feel better and move past your troubles, disappointments, hurts, and pains is to reach out and help someone else through their difficulties. If you stay too focused on your own problems you may miss the opportunity to be a blessing to others!

Key Ingredient #4:

Intercessory Prayer—Becoming a "Change Agent" for Others Changes You

I implore you to try this little secret for successfully moving past your problems: After you pray to the Lord to revive your strength and help you to hold on a little longer, pray for someone else you know who is suffering through the ups and downs of life. Intercessory prayer is said to be a most powerful prayer; one which God listens to in earnest (Sheets, 1996). Not only will God honor your intercession for others, He will also give you strength to make it through your own trial.

When we are feeling down or become discouraged, we often become too obsessed with what we do not have and what we cannot do. This is the perfect time to pray for someone else.

Take a look around. You may see someone who needs *your* prayers. You may see someone who needs exactly what God has given you. No matter how little you may think you have to offer, it may be just the thing and just the right amount for someone God has sent into your path. Give of your talent. Give the best you have to God and to others. If the best you have is just a smile and a hug, give a smile and a hug. It could be worth more than money to a wayward, discouraged soul who believes no one cares.

There is always someone doing worse than you. The Lord might just send them your way to provide you with some much needed perspective. There is always someone suffering through difficulties similar to yours. The Lord may send them your way so that you realize you are *not* the only one. Certainly, some problems are more monumental than others. However, problems and trials always seem biggest to the individual who is personally going through them. Intercessory prayer will bless you and the people you lift up to Jesus.

In John 17, Jesus provides a perfect example for us to emulate when faced with adversity, spiritual depression, and even impending death. Before going into the Garden of Gethsemane to face the intense pain and overwhelming magnitude of what lay ahead—betrayal, judgment, torture, and death—Jesus first prayed for Himself (John 17:1-5, NIV). Then Jesus prayed for His closest followers, the disciples (John 17:6-19, NIV). And then, Jesus prayed for *you* and me (John 17:20-26, NIV).

Key Ingredient #5: Your Witness of God's Love

How marvelous to know that Jesus Christ, the Son of God, prays for us! Jesus is our High Priest in heaven; ministering, advocating, and pleading our case before the Father on our behalf (Hebrews 4:14-16; 8:1-2). The very thought of Jesus taking the time, in the midst of His trials, tribulations, and impending death, to look down through history into the twenty-first century and beyond—to pause and send up a special intercessory prayer with a lasting warranty that is redeemable throughout the ceaseless ages of eternity—well, it sends chills down my spine! My heart erupts with everlasting joy when I realize that my life is that important to the Savior of this world!

What does it feel like for you? What goes through your mind and heart when you sit down in the midst of all the difficulties this life guarantees, and focus on what Jesus has truly done for you? Does it make you want to get up, shout

"Hallelujah!" and praise the name of Jesus? Does it make you want to run outside and tell somebody—anybody—what the Lord has done for you? I hope that it does. And I pray that you will be able to find the joy in your cross. I pray that you will cling to that "ridiculous" faith that heals. I pray that you will stay strong in the midst of your trial and tribulations, knowing full well that "the Lord disciplines those He loves," and that the obstacles and challenges life offers are just spiritual signs to let you know that God has been bragging on you again. We know that the miracle in each of us *is* Jesus Christ, because we know that we would not be alive today without the miracle of His mercy and His grace. It took a miracle for Jesus to come down to earth in human form just to suffer the indignity of our sins and to pay with His own life the price we should have paid. It took a miracle for God to allow His Son to take our part, die on the cross, and lay in the grave for three days. It took a miracle for Jesus to raise himself from the grave with All power in His hands! And it took a miracle for God to claim each of us as His sons and daughters; heirs with Jesus for the reward of salvation and eternal life. Please read the words of another childhood favorite:

It Took a Miracle

My Father is omnipotent
And that you can't deny
A God of might and miracles
'Tis written in the sky.

It took a miracle
To put the stars in place
It took a miracle
To hang the worlds in space.

But when He saved my soul
Cleansed and made me whole
It took a miracle of love and grace.
It took a miracle of love and grace.

The Bible tells us of His love
And wisdom all way thru

And ev'ry little bird and flow'r
Are testimonies too.

It took a miracle
To put the stars in place.
It took a miracle
To hang the worlds in space.

But when He saved my soul
Cleansed and made me whole
It took a miracle of love and grace.
It took a miracle of love and grace.

By John W. Patterson (1921); L. M. Montrose, J. W. Patterson (1948)
Adventist Hymnal, p. 111.

It took a miracle for Jesus to love us enough to die on the cross for our sins. And it took a miracle of love and grace for Jesus to take time out of His suffering in Gethsemane to say a prayer for His followers and future generations. However, how will we know if and when Jesus' prayer in John 17 (for Him to reside in each of us, and we in Him) to His Father on our behalf is answered? First John 4:13, 15 tells us;

> And God has given us *his* Spirit as proof that we live in him and he in us. All who confess that Jesus is the Son of God have God living in them, and they live in God. (NLT, italics added)

This is our assurance that Jesus has already worked out a plan for our salvation. The Son of God gave His life on Calvary's cross so that you and I could live with Him forever. He made the plan. He prayed for us to accept His plan and His sacrifice. And then He paid the price! The only thing left to complete the success of God's plan is for you to invite Jesus into your life and acknowledge that He *is* the Son of God. Once you allow Jesus into your life, it is a brand new day, for the rest of eternity! Perfect peace comes with Jesus: "But these are written that you may believe that Jesus is the Messiah, the Son of God, and that by believing you may have life in his name" (John 20:31, NIV).

Key Ingredient #6: Minister to Others with Your Spiritual Gifts and Talents

As you have come to learn in this book, I have a favorite songwriter. She wrote songs from a vantage point of having perfect peace in the midst of her trials and tribulations. She wrote about "A Singing Storm," "A Better Day," and how she "Wouldn't Have It Any Other Way." She penned the lyrics to one of my favorite prayers in song of all time: "Cover Me." She allowed God to use her gift of music to minister to others. You too have a gift, and sharing it with others will help cultivate the miracle in you.

Allowing God to use you to encourage and inspire others will soon become a positive cycle of behavior, which takes your focus off of your own problems and places it on Jesus and His using you to help someone else. Take the time to read the brief example of Peter's mother-in-law, found in Matthew 8:14, Mark 1:29-31, and Luke 4:38-39. This is the first miracle recorded by three of the Gospel writers.

Immediately after being healed, Peter's mother-in-law rises up and ministers to those in her household who accompanied Jesus and Peter. After being very ill with a fever for many days, it certainly would have been understandable if Peter's mother-in-law had simply continued to rest a bit, and her guests would likely have understood completely. However, when Jesus touches you, the reaction is just the opposite: you want to get up immediately and minister to others. Using your spiritual gifts and talents in service to others is an excellent way to say. "Thank you, Lord." It sends praises from your grateful heart to the ear of God Himself!

God has blessed each and every one of us with unique gifts—talents and skills—He expects us to return to Him so that He can continue to bless others through them. Your talent may or may not be singing or writing music. It may not be preaching, painting, or playing an instrument. However, whatever talent you have inside you is placed there by God, entrusted to you for His exact purpose. If you do not know what your talent is, find out by prayerfully asking God to reveal it to you. God will not ignore this prayer. He wants you to know about your special gifts. Once you discover the miracle in you, allow God to use you to help others. You will be surprised to discover that somewhere deep inside your struggle lies strength and a miracle of perfect peace.

If you are blessed to wake up each day, you have been given a gift. That gift is yours to do whatever you like for that one day, because tomorrow is not promised! Most of us are familiar with the mantra: "One day at a time." If/when your eyes open each day, this is an opportunity to renew the gift of life from Jesus Christ.

Use your daily gift of your renewed life to make someone else's day a blessed day! Someone has blessed you at some point in your life. Use your "today" to give of yourself to others. God expects us to give *back* and give *forward* to touch someone else's life. If for some reason you cannot give back to the person or persons who were a blessing in your life, then give forward!

Giving forward means opening your eyes to those around you in your daily life experiences. This is a rare opportunity to give of yourself to those with whom you may not have an existing relationship: people in your community with whom you normally do not cross paths or spend a lot of time. Every day, real people in your real life present an opportunity for you to reach out and be a blessing in their life. It may be a complete stranger, a coworker, a family member, or a friend. It may be someone in dire straits, someone in need of an advocate, someone with health issues, someone burdened with grief, someone disappointed and discouraged, or someone simply in need of a hug and a smile. When you can find the strength and courage to turn away from your own troubles and reach out to someone else, you will clearly see the silver lining encircling your clouds. By giving of yourself, your talent, and your time, you will find strength in your struggle, and someone will clearly see the miracle in you!

> *Now to him who is able to do immeasurably more than all we ask or imagine, according to his power that is at work within us, to him be glory in the church and in Christ Jesus throughout all generations, for ever and ever! Amen. (Ephesians 3:20-21, NIV)*

Thank you, Jesus! Thank you, Lord!

> *We must let go of the life we have planned, so as to accept the one that is waiting for us. (Joseph Campbell)*

Appendix A

References

Books

Abramson, L.Y., Garber, J., and Seligman, M.E.P. (1980). Learned helplessness in humans: An attributional analysis. J. Garber and M.E.P. Seligman (Eds.), Human Helplessness. New York: Academic Press, 3-35.

Amato, P. R. (2006). Marital discord, divorce, and children's well-being: Results from a 20-year longitudinal study of two generations. In A. Clarke-Stewart & J. Dunn (Eds.), *Families count: Effects on child and adolescent development* (pp. 179-202). New York, NY: Cambridge University Press.

Amato, P. R. (2000). Diversity within single-parent families. In D. H. Demo, K. R. Allen, & M. A. Fine (Eds.), *Handbook of family diversity* (pp. 149-172). New York, NY: Oxford University Press.

Arnett, J. J. (2012). Temperament: Emotional and social Development. *Human development: A Cultural Approach*, (pp. 160-162). Upper Saddle River, NJ: Pearson Education, Inc.

Bellah, R. N., Madsen, R., Sullivan, W. M., Swidler, A., & Tipton, S. M. (1985). *Habits of the heart: Individualism and commitment in American life*. New York, NY: Harper & Row.

Chess, S., & Thomas, A. (1984). *Origins and evolution of behavior disorders*. New York, NY: Brunner/Mazel.

Clarke-Stewart, A., & Brentano, C. (2006). *Divorce: Causes and consequences*. New Haven, CT: Yale University Press.

Books (cont.)

Collins, R. D. (2007). *The Trauma Zone*. Chicago, IL. Moody Publishers.

Collins, W. A., & Laursen, B. (2004). Parent-adolescent relationships and influences. In R. M. Lerner & L. Steinberg (Eds.). *Handbook of Adolescent Psychology* (2nd ed., pp. 331-361).

Couden, B. (Ed.) (1999). *Understanding Intimate Violence*. Review and Herald Publishing Association, Hagerstown, MD.

Diagnostic And Statistical Manual of Mental Disorders, Fourth Edition, Text Revision (DSM-IV-TR, 2000). American Psychiatric Association. Arlington, VA.

Dobson, J. (1993). *When God Doesn't Make Sense*. Wheaton, IL. Tyndale House Publishers.

Gibbens, J. L. , & Stiles, D. A. (2004). *The thoughts of youth: An international perspective on adolescents' ideal persons*. Greenwich, CT: IAP Information Age.

Goldsmith , H. H. (2009). Genetics of emotional development. In R. J. Davidson, K. R. Scherer, & H. H. Goldsmith (Eds.), *Handbook of affective sciences* (pp. 300-319). New York, NY: Oxford University Press.

Goosens , I., & Luyckx, K. (2007). In J. J. Arnett, U. Gielen, R. Ahmed, B. Nsamenang, T. S. Saraswathi, & R. Silbereisen (Eds.), *International encyclopedia of adolescence* (pp. 64-76). New York, NY: Routledge.

Greene, E. & Heilbrun, K. (2014). Wrightman's Psychology and the Legal System, 8th Edition. Wadsworth. Belmont, CA.

Hart, D., & Atkins, R. (2004). Religious participation and the development of moral identity in adolescence. In T. A. Thorkildsen & H. J. Walberg (Eds.), *Nurturing morality* (pp. 157-172). New York, NY: Kluwer.

Hetherington, E. M., & Kelly, J. (2002). *For better or worse: Divorce reconsidered*. New York, NY: Norton.

Koenig, H., King, D., & Carson, V. B. (2012). *Handbook of Religion and Health*, 2nd Edition. Oxford University Press.

Koenig, H. (2005). *Faith and Mental Health: Religious Resources for Healing*. Templeton Foundation Press.

Kubler-Ross, E. & Kessler, D. (2005). *On Grief and Grieving*. New York, NY: Scribner.

Kunzman, Kristin A. (1990). *The Healing Way: A Guide for Recovery from Childhood Sexual Abuse*. Hazelton Educational Materials. Center City, MN.

Plomin, R. (1990). *Nature and Nurture: An Introduction to Human Behavioral Genetics*. Pacific Grove, CA. Brooks/Cole.

Rodriguez, Angel. M. (2008). Atonement and the Cross of Christ. *Adult Teachers Sabbath School Bible Study Guide*. Office of the Adult Bible Study Guide, General Conference of Seventh-day Adventist. Silver Spring, MD.

Seifert, Kevin, L., and Hoffnung, Robert, J. (1997). *Child and Adolescent Development*. Fourth Edition. Boston, MA. Houghton Mifflin Company.

Seligman, M.E.P. (1975). *Helplessness: On Depression, Development, and Death*. San Francisco: W.H. Freeman. ISBN 0-7167-2328-X

Seligman, M.E.P., and Elder, G. (1985). Learned helplessness and life-span development. In A. Sorenson, F. Weinert, L. Sherrod (Eds.), Human development and the life course: Multidisciplinary perspectives. Hillsdale, NJ: Erlbaum, 377-427.

Seligman, M.E.P. (1975). *Helplessness: On Depression, Development, and Death*. San Francisco: W.H. Freeman. ISBN 0-7167-2328-X

Seligman, M.E.P., and Elder, G. (1985). Learned helplessness and life-span development. In A. Sorenson, F. Weinert, L. Sherrod (Eds.), Human development and the life course: Multidisciplinary perspectives. Hillsdale, NJ: Erlbaum, 377-427.

Seligman, M.E.P., and Peterson, C. (1986). A learned helplessness perspective on childhood depression: Theory and research. In M. Rutter, C.E. Izard, and P. Read

Books (cont.)

(Eds.), *Depression in Young People: Developmental and Clinical perspectives*. New York: Guilford, 223-249.

Sheets, D. (1996). *Intercessory Prayer: How God Can Use Your Prayers to Move Heaven and Earth*. Ventura, CA. Published by Regal, from Gospel Light.

Smetana, J. G. (2005). Adolescent-parent conflict: Resistance and subversion as developmental processes. In L. Nucci (Ed.), *Conflict, contradiction, and contrarian elements in moral development and education* (pp. 69-91). Mahwah, NJ: Erlbaum.

Smith, C., & Denton, M. L. (2005). *Soul searching: The religious and spiritual lives of American teenagers*. New York, NY: Oxford University Press.

Stark, E., & Flitcraft, A. (1996). *Women At Risk: Domestic Violence and Women's Health*. Thousand Oaks, CA. Sage Publications, Inc.

Swenson, R. (2014). *Margin: Restoring emotional, physical, financial, and time reserves to overloaded lives*. Tyndale House Publishers.

The American Heritage Dictionary. 3rd Edition. (1994). Houghton Mifflin Company.

Thomas, A. and Chess, S. (1977). *Temperament and Development*. New York. Bruner/Mazel.

Webster's II New Riverside Dictionary, Revised Edition (1996). Houghton Mifflin Company.

White, Ellen G. (2005). The Fiery Furnace. *Prophets and Kings. Vol. 2*. p. 513. Pacific Press Publishing Association.

White, Ellen G. (2005). The Touch of Faith. *The Desire of Ages*, Illustrated Edition, p.347. Pacific Press Publishing Association.

White, Ellen G. (2005). The First Evangelists. *The Desire of Ages*, Illustrated Edition, 354- 355. Pacific Press Publishing Association.

White, Ellen G. (2005). Lazarus, Come Forth. *The Desire of Ages*, Illustrated Edition, p. 535. Pacific Press Publishing Association.

Wilcox, W. B. (2008). Focused on their families: Religion, parenting, and child well-being. In K. K. Kline (Ed.), *Authoritative communities: The scientific case for nurturing the whole child* (pp. 227-244). The Search Institute series on developmentally attentive community and society. New York, NY: Springer.

Periodicals

Abramson, L.Y., Seligman, M.E.P., and Teasdale, J.D. (1978). Learned helplessness in humans: Critique and reformulation. *Journal of Abnormal Psychology, 87*, 49-74.

Anda, A. F., & Felitti, V. J. (2000). *The Adverse Childhood Experiences (ACE) Study*. Ongoing collaborative research between the Centers for Disease Control and Prevention, Atlanta, GA; and Kaiser Permanente, San Diego, CA.

Baumrind, D. (1971). Current patterns of parental authority. *Developmental Psychology, 4*, 1-103.

Bridges, L., & Moore, K. (2002). Religious involvement and children's well-being: What research tells us (and what it doesn't). *Child Trends Research Brief.* Washington, DC.

Calkins, S. D. (2002). Does aversive behavior during toddlerhood matter? The effects of difficult temperament on maternal perceptions and behavior. *Child Development, 67*, 523-540.

Chatters, L. M., Taylor, R. J., Bullard, K. M., & Jackson, J. S. (2008). Spirituality and subjective religiosity among African Americans, Caribbean Blacks, and non-Hispanic Whites. *Journal for the Scientific Study of Religion*, 725-737.

Corbin, T., Bloom, S., Wilson, A., Rich, L., and Rich J. A., (2010). Approaching the health and well-being of boys and men of color through trauma-informed practice. In *Changing places: How communities will improve the health of boys of color*. Edley Jr., C. & Ruiz de Velasco, J. (Eds.). Chief Justice Earl Warren Institute on Race, Ethnicity and Diversity at Berkeley School of Law. Berkeley and Los Angeles, CA. University of California Press.

Periodicals (cont.)

Ditton, Paula. (1999). U.S. Department of Justice. Office of Justice Programs. Bureau of Justice Statistics Special Report: *Mental Health and Treatment of Inmates and Probationers.* July, 1999, NCJ 174463.

Dworkin, J. B., & Larson, R. (2001). Age trends in the experience of family discord in single-mother families across adolescence. *Journal of Adolescence, 24,* 529-534.

Freidman and Creeden, (2005). "Children Who Witness Violence." *Children Who Witness Violence Project:* Cleveland, Ohio.

French, D. C., Eisenberg, N., Vaughan, J., Purwono, U., & Suryanti, T. A. (2008). Religious involvement and the social competence and adjustment of Indonesian Muslim adolescents. *Developmental Psychology, 44,* 597-611.

Grusec, J. E., and Kuczynski, L. (1980). Direction of effect in socialization: A comparison of the parent's versus the child's behavior as determinants of disciplinary technique. *Developmental Psychology, 16,* 1-9.

Hiroto, D.S., and Seligman, M.E.P. (1975). Generality of learned helplessness in man. *Journal of Personality and Social Psychology,* 31, 311-327.

Jahromi, L. B., Putnam, S. P., & Stiffer, C. A. (2004). Maternal regulation of infant reactivity from 2 to 6 months. *Developmental Psychology, 40,* 477-487.

Kelly, J. B., & Emery, R. E. (2003). Children's adjustment following divorce: Risk and resilience perspectives. *Family Relations, 52,* 352-362.

Kerestes, M., Youniss, J., & Metz, E. (2004). Longitudinal patterns of religious perspective and civic integration. *Applied Developmental Science, 8,* 39-46.

King, P. E., Furrow, J. L., & Roth, N. (2002). The influence of families and peers on adolescent religiousness. *Journal of Psychology and Christianity, 21,* 109-120.

Laursen, B., Coy, K. C., & Collins, W. A. (1998). Reconsidering changes in parent-child conflict across adolescence: A meta-analysis. *Child Development, 69,* 817-832.

Layton, E., Dollahite, D. C., & Hardy, S. A. (2011). Anchors of religious commitment in adolescents. *Journal of Adolescent Research, 26,* 381-413.

Maccoby, E. E., Martin, J. A. (1993). Socialization in the context of the family: Parent-child interaction. In E. M. Hetherington (Ed.). *Handbook of Child Psychology: Vol. 4, Socialization, personality, and social development* (4th ed. pp. 1-101). New York: Wiley.

Maxwell, C. D., Garner, J. H., & Fagan, J. A. (2002). The preventive effects of arrest on intimate partner violence: Research, policy and theory. *Criminology and Public Policy, 2,* 51-80.

Moore, K. A., Chalik, R., Scarpa, J., & Vandivere, S. (2002, August). Family Strengths: Often overlooked, but real. *Child Trends Research Brief,* 1-8.

Prins, S. J., & Draper, L. (2009). Improving outcomes for people with mental illnesses under community corrections supervision: A guide to research-informed policy and practice. *Council of state governments justice center*, New York, NY.

Prior, M., Kyrios, M., and Oberklaid, F. (1987). Temperament in Australian, American, Chinese, and Greek infants: Some issues and directions for future research. *Journal of Cross-Cultural Psychology, 17,* 455-474.

Rickman, M. D., and Davidson, R. J. (1995). Personality and behavior in parents of temperamentally inhibited and uninhibited children. *Development Psychology, 30,* 346-354.

Rothbart, M. K., Ahadi, S. A., & Evans, D. E. (2000). Temperament and personality: Origins and outcome. *Journal of Personality and Social Psychology, 78,* 122-135.

Seligman, M.E.P. (1972). Learned helplessness. *Annual Review of Medicine, 23,* 407-412.

Periodicals (cont.)

Seligman, M.E.P., and Maier, S.F. (1967). Failure to escape traumatic shock. *Journal of Experimental Psychology*, *74*, 1-9.

Shanahan, L., McHale, S. M., Osgood, D. W., & Crouter, A. C. (2007). Conflict frequency with mothers and fathers from middle childhood to late adolescence: Within- and between-families comparisons. *Developmental Psychology*, *43*, 539-550.

Steadman, H. J. Osher, F. C., Robbins, P. C., Case, B., & Samuels, S. (2009). Prevalence of serious mental illness among jail inmates. *Psychiatric Services*, *60*, 761-765.

Steinberg, L. D. (2001). We know some things: Parent-adolescent relationships on retrospect and prospect. *Journal of Research on Adolescence*, *11*, 1-19.

Stevens-Watkins, D., & Rostosky, S. (2010). Binge drinking in African American males from adolescence to young adulthood: The protective influence of religiosity, family connectedness, and close friends' substance use. *Substance Use & Misuse*, *45*, 1435-1451.

Tamis-Lamonda, C. S., Way, N., Hughes, D., Yoshikawa, H., Kalman, R. K., & Niwa, E. Y. (2008). Parent's goals for children: The dynamic coexistence of individualism and collectivism in cultures and individuals. *Social Development*, *17*, 183-209.

Warren, S. L., & Simmens, S. J. (2005). Predicting toddler anxiety/depressive symptoms: Effects of caregiver sensitivity of temperamentally vulnerable children. *Infant of Medical Health Journal*, *26*, 40-55.

Online References

Bridges, L., & Moore, K. (2002). Religious involvement and children's well-being: What research tells us (and what it doesn't). *Child Trends Research Brief.* Washington, DC: Author. Available: www.childtrends.org

Bureau of Justice Statistics, (2010). *Criminal Victimization, 2010.* Retrieved from http://bjs.ojp.usdoj.gov/index.cfm?ty=tp&tid31

Dictionary.com (2011)

Merriam-Webster's Online Dictionary (2008). Encyclopedia Britannica Company

National Alliance on Mental Illness (NAMI, 2008). *Major Depression: What Is Major Depression?* http://.www.nami.org/

The PEW Center On The States. (2008). *One in 100: Behind bars in America 2008.* http://www.pewtrusts.org/en/research-and-analysis/reports/2008/02/28/one-in-100-behind-bars-in-america-2008

Appendix B
Further Reading

Music

Wright, Eleanor. (1995). *Hallelujah! Home At Last: 14 Timeless Gospel Songs by Eleanor Wright*. Eleanor Wright Song Book Series: Volume One. Eleanor Wright Trust: 2920 Otterbein Avenue, Dayton, OH 45406: Ohio Full Court Press. U.S.A.

Self-help

Buettner, Dan. (2008). *The Blue Zone: Lessons For Living Longer From The People Who've Lived The Longest*. Washington, DC: National Geographic Society.

Canfield, Jack, Hansen, Mark Victor, and Lagana, Tom. (2000). *Chicken Soup for the Soul: 101 Stories to Open and Rekindle the Spirit of Hope, Healing and Forgiveness*. Deerfield Beach, FL: Health Communications, Inc.

Carter, Norma J. (2003). *Without Warning: Successfully Coping With Sudden Loss*. Duncanville, TX: Helping Hands Press.

Clason, George S. (1955). *The Richest Man In Babylon: The Success Secrets of the Ancients*. USA/Canada: Hawthorn/Dutton.

Collins, Dandridge, R. (2007). *The Trauma Zone: Trusting God For Emotional Healing*. Chicago, IL: Moody Publishers.

Couden, Barbara. (1999). *Understanding Intimate Violence*. Hagerstown, MD: Review and Herald Publishing Association.

Evans, David, G. (2004). *Healed Without Scars: Discovering the Path to Wholeness in Christ*. New Kensington, PA: Whitaker House.

Self-help (cont.)

Evans, Patricia. (1996). *The Verbally Abusive Relationship: How to recognize it and how to respond*. Expanded Second Edition. Holbrook, MA: Adams Media Corporation.

Everly, George S., Jr., and Mitchell, Jeffrey, T. (1999). *Innovations in Disaster and Trauma Psychology Volume Two: Critical Incident Stress Management-CISM: A new Era and Standard of Care In Crisis Intervention* (2nd ed.). Ellicott City, MD: Chevron Publishing Corporation.

Farrar, Steve & Mary. (2003). *Overcoming Overload: Seven Ways to Find Rest in Your Chaotic World*. Sisters, OR: Multnomah Publishers, Inc.

Forward, Susan, with Buck, Craig. (1989). *Toxic Parents: Overcoming Their Hurtful Legacy and Reclaiming Your Life*. By the author who wrote: *Men Who Hate Women & The Women Who Love Them*. New York, NY. Bantam Books.

Kubler-Ross, Elizabeth (1969). Paperback Edition (2003). *On Death and Dying: What the dying have to teach doctors, nurses, clergy, and their own families*. New York, NY: Scribner.

Kubler-Ross, Elizabeth, and Kessler, David. (2005). *On Grief and Grieving: Finding The Meaning of Grief Through The Five Stages of Loss*. New York, NY: Scribner.

Kunzman, Kristin, A. (1990). *The Healing Way: A Guide for Recovery from Childhood Sexual Abuse*. Center City, MN: Hazelton Educational Materials.

Murphy, John, J. (1996). *Reinvent Yourself: A Lesson In Personal Leadership*. Grand Rapids, MI: Venture Management Consultants, Inc.

Murphy, John, J. (1997). *Get A Real Life: A Lesson In Personal Empowerment*. Grand Rapids, MI: Venture Management Consultants, Inc.

Salmons, Sandra. (1995). *Depression: Questions you have …Answers you need*. Allentown, PA: People's Medical Society.

Seaward, Brian Luke. (1999). *Managing Stress: Principles and Strategies for Health and Wellbeing*. Web Enhanced Second Edition. Sudbury, MA: Jones and Barlett Publishers.

Stark, Evan, and Flitcraft, Anne. (1996). *Women At Risk: Domestic Violence and Women's Health*. Thousand Oaks, CA: SAGE Publications, Inc.

Whitfield, Charles L. (1995). *Memory and Abuse: Remembering and Healing the Effects of Trauma*. Deerfield Beach, FL: Health Communications, Inc.

Wilson, Reid, R. (1986). *Don't Panic: Taking Control of Anxiety Attacks*. Harper Perennial. New York, NY: Harper & Row Publishers, Inc.

Zarit, Steven H., Orr, Nancy K., and Zarit, Judy M. (1985). *The Hidden Victims of Alzheimer's Disease: Families Under Stress*. New York, NY: New York University Press.

Inspirational

Anthony, Gavin. (2007). *The Refiner's Fire: In All Things God Works For Good*. Review and Herald Publishing Association. Hagerstown, MD.

Black, Barry C. (2006). *From The Hood To The Hill: A Story of Overcoming*. Nashville, TN: Nelson Books.

Blanco, Jack, L. (2008). *Savior: Four Gospels. One Story. : A fresh look at Jesus Christ, His Ministry, and His Teachings*. Hagerstown, MD: Autumn House Publishing. Review and Herald Publishing Association.

Canfield, J., Hansen, M. V., and Lagana, T. (2000). *Chicken Soup for the Prisoner's Soul: 101 Stories to Open the Heart and Rekindle the Spirit of Hope, Healing and Forgiveness*. Deerfield, MI: Health Communications, Inc.

Colson, Charles. (1996). *Loving God: An Inspiring Message and A Challenge to All Christians*. Grand Rapids, MI: Zondervan Publishing House. A Division of HarperCollins Publishers.

Dobson, James. (1993). *When God Doesn't Make Sense*. Wheaton, IL. Tyndale House Publishers, Inc.

Inspirational (cont.)

Dobson, James. (1997). *In The Arms of God*. Wheaton, IL. Tyndale House Publishers, Inc.

Duewel, Wesley L. (1990). *Mighty Prevailing Prayer*. Grand Rapids, MI: Francis Asbury Press of Zondervan Publishing House.

Jakes, T.D. (2004). *He-Motions: Even Strong Men Struggle*. G.P. Putnam's Sons. New York.

Jakes, T. D. (2014). *Instinct: The Power to Unleash Your Inborn Drive*. New York, NY: FaithWords.

Johnsson, William, G. (2007). *Jesus: A heart Full of Grace*. A Daily Devotional. Hagerstown, MD: Review and Herald Publishing Association.

Kelly, Eric. (1998). *Pepper In The Salt Shaker: One Man's Spiritual Journey Through Corporate America*.

Knight, George R. (2002). *Walking With Paul Through The Book of Romans*. Daily Devotional for Adults. Hagerstown, MD: Review and Herald Publishing Association.

Lucado, Max. (1994). *When God Whispers Your Name*. Comfort Print Edition. Dallas, TX: Word Publishing

Murphy, J. J. (1997). *Get A Real Life: A lessen In Personal Empowerment*. Grand Rapids, MI: Venture Management Consultants, Inc.

Poitier, Sidney. (2000). *The Measure Of A Man: A Spiritual Autobiography*. HarperSanFrancisco. A Division of HarperCollins Publishing.

Venden, Morris L. (1989). *Love, Marriage, and Righteousness By Faith*. Boise, Idaho: Pacific Press Publishing.

White, Ellen, G. (2004). *To Be Like Jesus*. A Daily Devotional. Hagerstown, MD: Review and Herald Publishing Association.

White, Ellen, G. (1911). *The Acts Of The Apostles*. Volume 4. Conflict of The Ages Series. Pacific Press.

White, Ellen, G. (1958). *Selected Messages*. Book Two. Review and Herald Publishing Association. Washington, DC.

White, Ellen, G. (2005). *The Great Controversy*. Illustrated Edition. Conflict of The Ages Series. Pacific Press.

Wright, Walter L. (2006). *My Daddy Told Me So*. Fallbrook, CA: Hart Books.

Informational

Cole, Thomas R., and Winkler, Mary G. (1994). *The Oxford Book Of Aging: Reflections On The Journey Of Life*. Thomas R. Cole and Mary G. Winkler (Eds.). Oxford University Press.

Collins, J. (2001). *Good to Great: Why some Companies Make the Leap and Others Don't*. New York, NY: Harper Business. *An Imprint of* HarperCollins*Publishers*.

Dubler, J. (2013). *Down in the Chapel: Religious Life in an American Prison*. New York, NY: Farrar, Straus, and Giroux.

Hood, Jr., R. W., Hill, P. C., and Spilka, B. (2009). *The Psychology of Religion: An Empirical Approach,* 4th Edition. New York, NY: The Guilford Press.

Marsh, D. T. (1992). *Families and Mental Illness: New Directions in Professional Practice*. New York, NY: Praeger Publishers.

Newberg, A. & Waldman, M. R. (2006). *Why we believe what we believe: Uncovering our biological need for meaning, spirituality, and truth*. New York, NY: Free Press. A Division of Simon & Schuster, Inc.

Newberg, A. & Waldman, M. R. (2009). *How God changes your brain: Breakthrough findings from a leading neuroscientist*. New York, NY: Ballantine Books.

The Interpreter's Bible: A commentary in Twelve Volumes. Volume 5: *The Book of Ecclesiastes, The Song of Songs, The Book of Isaiah, and the Book of Jeremiah*. Abingdon Press.

White, W. L. (1998). *Slaying the dragon: The history of addiction treatment and recovery in America*. Bloomington, IL. Chestnut Health Systems/Lighthouse Institute.

Clinical

Crain, William. (1992). *Theories Of Development: Concepts and Applications (3ʳᵈ ed.)*. Prentice-Hall, Inc., Englewood Cliffs, NJ 07632.

Gurman, Alan S., and Kniskern, David P. (1991). *The Handbook Of Family Therapy, Volume 2*. Alan S. Gurman and David P. Kniskern (Eds.). Brunner/Mazel, Inc. New York, NY 10003.

Hardy, Kenneth V., and Laszloffy, Tracey A. (2005). *Teens Who Hurt: Clinical Interventions To Break The Cycle Of Adolescent Violence*. The Guilford Press. New York, NY 10012.

Kirsch, I., Lynn, S.J., Vigorito, M. & Miller, R.R. (2004). The role of cognition in classical and operant conditioning. *Journal of Clinical Psychology, 60,* 369–392.

Knapp, Samuel, and Vandercreek, Leon. (1994). *Anxiety Disorders: A Scientific Approach For Selecting The Most Effective Treatment*. Practitioner's Resource Series. Professional Resource Press. Sarasota, FL 34277.

Marsh, Diane T. (1992). *Families and Mental Illness: New Directions In Professional Practice*. PRAEGER. West Port, CT.

Martin, Gary, and Blair, Joseph. (1996). *Behavior Modification: What It Is And How To Do It*. Fifth Edition. Prentice Hall, Upper Saddle River, NJ 07458.

Rosenblatt, Paul C. (1994). *Metaphors Of Family Systems Theory: Toward New Constructions*. The Guilford Press. New York, NY 10012.

Seligman, M.E.P. (1990). *Learned Optimism*. New York: Knopf. (Reissue edition, 1998, Free Press, ISBN 0-671-01911-2

St. Clair, Michael. (1996). *Object Relations and Self-Psychology: An Introduction (2ⁿᵈ ed.)*. Brooks/Cole Publishing Company. Pacific Grove, CA 93950.

VandeCreek, L. & Jackson, T. L. (Eds.). (1999). *Innovations in clinical practice: A resource book* (Vol. 17). Sarasota, FL. Professional Resource Exchange, Inc.

Watzlawick, Paul, Weakland, John, and Fisch, Richard. (1974). *Change: Principles of Problem Formation and Problem Resolution*. Mental Research Institute, Palo Alto, CA. W.W. Norton & Company. New York, NY 10110.

Williams, Tom. (1987). *Post-Traumatic Stress Disorders: A handbook for Clinicians*. Tom Williams (Ed.). Published by Disabled American Veterans. National Headquarters. Cincinnati, OH 45214.

White, W. L. (1998). *Slaying the dragon: The history of addiction treatment and recovery in America*. Bloomington, IL. Chestnut Health Systems/Lighthouse Institute.

Appendix C

Songs of Inspiration
Referenced in Book Chapters

An Eleanor Wright Composition: *A Better Day*

An Eleanor Wright Composition: *Cover Me*

An Eleanor Wright Composition: *Faith Enough To Try*

An Eleanor Wright Composition: *"I Wouldn't Have It Any Other Way"*

Audrey Wright Dickerson: *Faith Is The Key*

BeBe Winans: *In the Midst of the Rain*

John W. Patterson: *It Took A Miracle*

Rhea F. Miller: *I'd Rather Have Jesus*

The Brooklyn Tabernacle Choir: *How Long Has It Been?*

Suggested Music To Inspire

An Eleanor Wright Composition: *Praise Him Over and Over*

Byron Cage: *Broken But I'm Healed*

Donald Lawrence: *Encourage Yourself*

Dorinda Clark Cole: *Take It Back*

Heather Headley & Smokie Norful: *Jesus Is Love*

Helen Baylor: *Look A Little Closer*

Hezekiah Walker: *Lift Him Up*

Hezekiah Walker/Marvin Sapp: *God Favored Me*

James Fortune: *I Trust You*

James Fortune: *Live Through It*

Suggested Music To Inspire (cont.)
James Ingram: *Mercy*

Jason Nelson: *I Am*
Jason Nelson: *Nothing Without You*

Kirk Franklin: *Imagine Me*
Kirk Whallum: *Falling In Love With Jesus*
Regina Bell: *I Call On Jesus*
Shekinah Glory: *"Jesus"*
Smokie Norful: *Justified*
Tamela Mann: *Take Me To The King*
Tamika Patton: *God Won't Let Me Fail*

The Brooklyn Tabernacle Choir: *Calvary Came Through Once Again*
The Brooklyn Tabernacle Choir: *Use Me*

The Pinnacle Project: *Simply Redeemed*
Tramaine Hawkins: *He's That Kind Of Friend*
Ty Tribett: *My Joy*
Vicki Yoh'e: *Deliverance Is Available*
Wess Morgan: *You Paid It All*

William McDowell: *Withholding Nothing*
William McDowell: *I Give Myself Away*

Yolanda Adams: *Never Give Up*
Yolanda Adams: *Hold On*
Yolanda Adams: *This Too Shall Pass*

Appendix D

Suggested Web Sites/Contacts
And Educational Information

1). http://www.ojp.usdoj.gov/bjs/pub/pdf/mhtip.pdf
Bureau of Justice Statistics Special Report: *Mental Health and Treatment of Inmates and Probationers*.

2). http://www.ojp.usdoj.gov/bjs/pub/pdf/mhppji.pdf
Bureau of Justice Statistics Special Report: *Mental Health Problems of Prison and Jail Inmates*.

3). http://gainscenter.samhsa.gov/pdfs/jail_diversion/Practical/AdviceOnJailDiversion.pdf
14 million annual arrests, 1.1 million have current symptoms of serious mental illness, and approximately three quarters have co-occurring substance abuse disorders. Practical Advice On Jail Diversion: Ten Years of Learning on Jail Diversion from the CMHS national GAINS Center (2007).

4). http://www.nami.org/
National Alliance on Mental Illness (NAMI). 1-800-950-NAMI; info@nami.org
Major Depression: What Is Major Depression? (2008).
Supporting Schools and Communities in Breaking the Prison Pipeline: A Guide to Emerging and Promising Crisis Intervention Programs for Youth. (2009).

5). www.prainc.com
Persons with serious mental illness in our community are 11 times more likely to be victims of violence than persons without serious mental illness.

Linda Teplin's Report on crime victimization. Policy Research Associates, Inc. 345 Delaware Avenue, Delmar, NY 12054. (518) 439-7415.

6). http://www.pediatrics.org/cgi/content/full/123/4/e716
Screening for Child and Adolescent Depression in Primary Care Settings: A Systematic Evidence Review for the US Preventive Services Task Force. Selvi B. Williams, Elizabeth A. O'Connor, Michelle Eder and Evelyn P. Whitlock. *Pediatrics* 2009;123; e716-e735. DOI: 10.1542/peds.2008-2415.

7). http://www.vetcenter.va.gov/
In 1979, the Veterans Administration began its Vet Center program, designed specifically to treat veterans and their families for trauma-related difficulties. Vet Centers are community-based counseling centers that provide a broad range of services to assist in readjusting to civilian life.

8). http://www.Crosswalk.com
"Today God is First." A free devotional newsletter from crosswalk.com, the world's largest Christian website.

9). http://www.alz.org/index.asp
Alzheimer's Association.

10). http://www.aecf.org/
The Annie E. Casey Foundation: *Helping vulnerable kids & families succeed.*

11). http://www.ncjj.org
National Center for Juvenile Justice: *Effective justice for children and families through research and technical assistance.*

12). www.shoppbs.org
PBS Home Video's:

a. *The Medicated Child*, DVD from the popular Frontline Series, confronts psychiatrists, researchers, and government regulators about the risks and benefits of prescription drugs for troubled children.

b. *Caring For Your Parents*, DVD, As the population ages, many adult children are grappling with an unprecedented social, cultural, economic, and personal revolution as they transition into the primary caregiver role for their aging parents. Caring for Your Parents is a moving film that draws much-needed attention to this universal reality, underscoring today's struggle through an intimate look at five American families.

13). Trauma-Informed Care Websites

http://www.healthcaretoolbox.org/index.php?gclid=CMTeppGL8r0CFfNxOgoduDoA0w

http://educate.crisisprevention.com/ResourcesGuideTraumaInformedCare_ppc.html?code=ITG079TI-CRG&src=Pay-Per-Click&gclid=CImS7c2N8r0CFY1xOgodT1QAvQ

http://www.articlesbase.com/mental-health-articles/post-traumatic-stress-disorder-a-framework-for-understanding-1903514.html

http://www.samhsa.gov/nctic/trauma.asp

http://www.nasmhpd.org/TA/nctic.aspx

https://www.thenationalcouncil.org/topics/trauma-informed-care/

http://www.safestartcenter.org/publications/trauma-informed-care-tip-sheets

http://boysandmenofcolor.org/wp-content/uploads/2012/09/Chapter-13-Trauma-Informed-Practice-Rich-et-al..pdf

http://www.mentalhealth.gov/blog/2014/04/creating-trauma-informed-congregations.html

http://minorityhealth.hhs.gov/templates/content.aspx?lvl=3&lvlID=9&ID=6474

14). Suicide Prevention Resources/Websites

National Suicide Prevention Lifeline: 1-800-TALK (8255) or Online at: www.suicidepreventionlifeline.org

American Association of Suicidality (AAS)
www.suicidality.org

Suicide Prevention Resources/Websites cont.

American Foundation for Suicide Prevention (AFSP)
www.afsp.org

Crisis Link: Prevention, Intervention, Support and Training
www.crisislink.org

GLBT Youth Suicide
www.eriegaynews.com

The Link's National Resource Center
www.thelink.org

LivingWorks Education Inc.
www.livingworks.net

Means Matter, Harvard School of Public Health
www.hsph.harvard.edu/means-matter

Metanoia
www.metanoia.org/suicide

National Council for Suicide Prevention (NCSP)
www.ncsponline.org

National P.O.L.I.C.E. Suicide Foundation
www.psf.org

National Organization of People of Color Against Suicide (NOPCAS)
www.nopcas.com

Suicide Awareness Voices of Education (SAVE)
www.save.org

Suicide Anonymous
www.suicideanonymous.net

Action Alliance for Suicide Prevention
www.actionallianceforsuicideprevention.org

Suicide Prevention Resource Center
www.sprc.org

Tears of a Cop
www.tearsofacop.com

15). Federal Government Sources:

Centers for Disease Control
http://www.cdc.gov/Violence
Prevention/pdf/Suicide-DataSheet-a.pdf

CDC-US Mortality Statistics
www.cdc.gov/ncipc/wisqars/

National Institute of Mental Health
http://nimh.nih.gov/health/topics/suicide-prevention/index.shtml

The Substance Abuse and Mental Health Services Administration

www.samhsa.org

16) National Strategy Documents

National Strategy for Suicide Prevention-National Action Alliance for
Suicide Prevention
www.surgeongeneral.gov/library/reports/national-strategy-suicide-pre-
vention/index.html
www.actionaallianceforsuicideprevention.org/NSSP
www.samhsa.gov/nssp

Charting the Future of Suicide Prevention: A 2010 Progress Review
of the National Strategy and Recommendations for the Decade
Ahead, 2010
Educational Development Center, Inc.

www.sprc.org/library/ChartingTheFuture Fullbook.pdf

Reducing Suicide: A National Imperative, 2002
Institute of Medicine
http://www.nap.edu/openbook.php?isbn=0309083214

Youth Suicide Prevention Sources
Active Minds on Campus
www.activeminds.org

Youth Suicide Prevention Sources cont.
Jason Foundation
www.jasonfoundation.com

The Jed Foundation
www.jedfoundation.org

School Based Youth Suicide Prevention Guide
http://theguide.fmhi.usf.edu

Signs of Suicide-Suicide Prevention Program for Secondary Schools (SOS)
www.mentalhealthscreening.org/highschool/index.aspx

Services for Teens at Risk Center (STAR)
www.wpic.pitt.edu/research/star/default.htm

TeenScreen: Adolescent Suicide and Mental Health Screening Programs
www.teenscreen.org

Youth Suicide Prevention Program
www.yspp.org

Yellow Ribbon Youth Suicide Prevention Program
www.yellowribbon.org

17). Epidemiological Studies

http://www.science.gov/topicpages/d/developing+countries+poverty.html

http://scholar.google.com/scholar?as_sdt=0,39&q=epidemiological+-data+for+disease,+poverty,+and+homelessness&hl=en&as_vis=1

18). Largest Branches of Christianity in the U.S.

   (self-identification, PEW Research Council, 2002)

In February and March 2002 the Pew Research Council conducted a survey of 2,002 adults. Questions about religious preference were included. People who identified their religious preference as Christian were asked about which branch of Christianity they belonged to.

The table below was published on page 49 of the Pew report at http://pewforum.org/publications/reports/poll2002.pdf:

Survey Response	%, June 1996	%, March 2001	%, March 2002
Protestant	53	53	52
Catholic	23	23	24
Mormon (Latter-day Saints)	2	2	2
Orthodox	1	1	*
Non-denominational	1	0	0
Something else (Specify)	1	*	2
Not practicing any religion	1	0	0
Don't know/Refused	2	3	2
TOTAL CHRISTIAN	84%	82%	82%

The percentages shown in this table reflect the number of members of each branch as a proportion of the total U.S. population, not just the Christian population. So the Catholic percentage of 24% for 2002 means that 24% of Americans identified themselves as Catholic in 2002.

This table matches data from Gallup, Barna, and other polling organizations, which all show that Protestants are clearly the largest branch of Christianity in the United States, followed by Catholics, who have about half as many members. Latter-day Saints (Mormons) are the 3rd largest branch, comprising about 2% of the U.S. population. Catholics, Latter-day Saints, and Orthodox Christians are all **branches** *as well as* **denominational families**, but the Protestant branch of

Christianity comprises multiple denominational families. More detailed denominational family statistics are shown <u>below</u>.

This table was published in a study titled <u>"Americans Struggle with Religion's Role at Home and Abroad"</u>, released on March 20, 2002.

The authors listed are:

Andrew Kohut, director of The Pew Research Center For The People & The Press

Melissa Rogers, executive director of The Pew Forum on Religion & Public Life
Methodology:

"The nationwide survey of 2,002 adults, conducted Feb. 25–March 10 by the Pew Research Center and the Pew Forum on Religion and Public Life..."

People who identified their religious preference as Christian were asked about which branch of Christianity they belonged to:

"Q.19 Are you Protestant, Catholic, Mormon, Orthodox — such as Greek or Russian Orthodox — or something else?" (page 49)

17). Largest Denominational Families in the U.S., 2001
(based on church attendance, ARIS/Barna)

Religious identification is only one component of religious statistics, and identification with a particular religious group may or may not be sociologically meaningful for a particular meaningful. As Kosmin notes in the ARIS report:

> For some, religious identification may well be a social marker as much as a marker designating a specific set of beliefs. For others, it may be a reflection of a community or family anchor point to one's sense of self. For others still, it may simply be the "gut response" evoked by the question, "What is your religion, if any?" without any wider emotional, social or philosophical ramifications. This

survey made no attempt to define for people what the meaning of any religious identification might be.

The following table combines self-identification statistics from the ARIS report (2001) with church attendance figures obtained from the Barna survey. The Barna survey was conducted from January 2000 through June 2001, and had a sample size of 6,038 adults. The survey asked people if they attended a church service, other than a special event such as a wedding or funeral, in the past 7 days. The proportion responding affirmatively can be thought of as the highly active segment of a particular denominational community.

ARIS: Total number of adults, U.S., 2001: 207,980,000

Denomination/ Denominational Family	# of Adults self-identification 2001	% of U.S. pop. self-identification 2001	% weekly church attendance this denom. 2001	% of U.S. pop. in attendance at this denom. during a given week
Catholic	50,873,000	24.5%	48%	11.74%
Baptist	33,830,000	16.3%	50%	8.13%
Methodist	14,150,000	6.8%	49%	3.33%
Lutheran	9,580,000	4.6%	43%	1.98%
Pentecostal/Charismatic/Foursquare	4,407,000	2.1%	66%	1.40%
Presbyterian	5,596,000	2.7%	49%	1.32%
Mormon/ Church of Jesus Christ of Latter-day Saints	2,697,000	1.3%	71%	0.92%
Non-denominational Christians	2,489,000	1.2%	61%	0.73%
Church of Christ	2,593,000	1.2%	58%	0.72%
Episcopal/Anglican	3,451,000	1.7%	30%	0.50%
Assemblies of God	1,106,000	0.5%	69%	0.37%
Congregational/ United Church of Christ	1,378,000	0.7%	* 30%	0.20%
Seventh-Day Adventist	724,000	0.3%	47%	0.16%

* *The Barna poll did not report attendance figures for the United Church of Christ/ Congregationalists. Figure used here is from the sociologically similar Episcoplians.*

All of these figures are collected from independent surveys with large sample sizes, and do not come from any religious organization. Thus, they constitute a set of numbers which are highly uniform in methodology, and are not subject to internal institutional variations in the way that membership and activity is counted or estimated.

The resulting figures in the last column are estimates of the total adult U.S. population attending church services of a given denominational group during a given week. So, while 24.5% of American adults identified themselves as Catholics in 2001, in any given week, 11.74% of all Americans attend Catholic church services. However, this does not necessarily suggest that only 11.74% of Americans are "active Catholics": religious groups generally consider a member "active" or "practicing" who practices less than weekly church attendance.

Different religious groups exhibit wide variation in the proportion of their adherents who are active members. But for the most part, this table's estimation of regularly attending adherents does not change the relative size of the denominational groups. When counting only active members, the changes in relative order among denominational groups are: Episcopalians drop below both Latter-day Saints and Church of Christ members, and there are more active Assemblies of God members than Congregationalists/United Church of Christ members.

Finally, note that the Barna survey data report the proportion of *self-identified* adherents who reported church attendance. This is not necessarily the same as the attendance rate as a proportion of official church membership. A religious body's membership estimate may be more or less than the number of people who actually identify themselves as members. For example, in 2001, 3.5 million American adults said they were Episcopalians. But in 2000 the Episcopal Church reported a total constituency of 2,317,794 people, including fully-committed members and inclusive adherents. This signifies a gap between those who are *affiliated* with the church (on membership rolls), versus those who self-identify with a particular denominational label but in most cases have no practical connection to the denomination and do not attend services.